Commercializing Blockchain

Commercializing Blockchain

Strategic Applications in the Real World

Antony Welfare

This edition first published 2019
© 2019 John Wiley & Sons Ltd.

Registered office
John Wiley & Sons Ltd, The Atrium, Southern Gate, Chichester, West Sussex,
PO19 8SQ, United Kingdom

For details of our global editorial offices, for customer services and for information
about how to apply for permission to reuse the copyright material in this book please
see our website at www.wiley.com.

Wiley publishes in a variety of print and electronic formats and by print-on-demand.
Some material included with standard print versions of this book may not be included
in e-books or in print-on-demand. If this book refers to media such as a CD or DVD
that is not included in the version you purchased, you may download this material
at http://booksupport.wiley.com. For more information about Wiley products, visit
www.wiley.com.

Designations used by companies to distinguish their products are often claimed as
trademarks. All brand names and product names used in this book are trade names,
service marks, trademarks or registered trademarks of their respective owners. The
publisher is not associated with any product or vendor mentioned in this book.

Limit of Liability/Disclaimer of Warranty: While the publisher and author have
used their best efforts in preparing this book, they make no representations or
warranties with respect to the accuracy or completeness of the contents of this book
and specifically disclaim any implied warranties of merchantability or fitness for a
particular purpose. It is sold on the understanding that the publisher is not engaged
in rendering professional services and neither the publisher nor the author shall be
liable for damages arising herefrom. If professional advice or other expert assistance is
required, the services of a competent professional should be sought.

Library of Congress Cataloging-in-Publication Data is Available:

ISBN 978-1-119-57801-7 (hardback)
ISBN 978-1-119-57802-4 (ePDF)
ISBN 978-1-119-57803-1 (epub)

Cover Design: Wiley
Cover Image: © Visual Generation / Shutterstock

Set in 10/12pt WarnockPro by SPi Global, Chennai

Printed in Great Britain by TJ International Ltd, Padstow, Cornwall, UK.

10 9 8 7 6 5 4 3 2

Contents

About the Author

The Retailer

I am a lifelong retailer, author of the #1 Bestseller *The Retail Handbook*, qualified accountant and a Blockchain leader, helping to develop, and understand, the new technologies transforming retail, CPG and supply chain businesses. Being born into a retail family, and working since a young age, has given me an insatiable desire to grow, develop, and nurture business and change within business.

The world is transforming at an ever faster pace and keeping track of the latest technologies inspires me to learn more, and help others understand the transformational impacts of these technologies. I started my research into Blockchain in 2016 and have learnt more than most about the technology and its impact on business and society.

I am a Blockchain advisor to the UK Government, a lecturer on the UCL Executive Blockchain programme, and judge and retail advisor for Blockchain Live. I run the Retail Week Technology blog for Oracle, and am a speaker on Blockchain at many events, including Tech: Retail Week, FT Future of Retail and Retail 4.0 (Berlin).

I focus on the retail and supply chain use cases for Blockchain, and other complementary technologies such as IoT, AI/ML, and RPA.

My experience in Blockchain has led me to inspire hundreds of people on the future of Blockchain, so that together we can learn how this technology will transform our lives. I have spoken at many events in the UK, Europe, South America, and Canada to all people interested in Blockchain and the transformational opportunities it gives.

Crypto Investment

My interest in Blockchain started in February 2016 when I asked a colleague 'What is Bitcoin? And why are retailers not using it?' Little did

I know, that one conversation would open my mind to the potential of Blockchain technology. I spent three months researching, discussing, and finding out how Blockchain worked, using books and online information, and attending meetups. During this research I came across Ethereum and started to research Ethereum in depth.

In August 2016, I bought my first 11 ETH for £8.88 each – £100 well spent. Once I was literally invested, I started to research daily. I kept my focus on Ethereum, as this is a true Blockchain and can support many types of Blockchain use case. I joined the Enterprise Ethereum Alliance and attended many of the Ethereum meetups – when there were less than 100 of us (now there are 1000s attending these meetups!).

Blockchain Leadership

As a leader in the Blockchain world, I spend most of my days working with organizations providing Blockchain technology solutions for organizations wanting to use Blockchain solutions. I meet many different people each day, and find out more about the future of Blockchain technology all the time.

My main role is to develop and deliver the Blockchain message to help people understand the future potential. This helps to bring more people into the ecosystem who can contribute to the development of the Blockchain solutions.

I keynote at many conferences and ensure that my focus is on the practical use cases of Blockchain technology. I enjoy presenting the vision of the future to people from all walks of life and experience. After all my keynotes, I am inundated with questions and eager people wanting to learn more (one of the main reasons for writing this book).

About the Contributors

We are at the beginning of the Blockchain technology revolution and as such, not one person can call themselves an expert in Blockchain technology, which, together with the speed of the movement in Blockchain technologies, means that I have introduced a number of 'Blockchainers' to contribute to this book.

They are all clearly referenced in their sections within the book, but I want to thank them all at the beginning – their expertise and input, will give you the reader, a deeper and more varied understanding of this revolutionary technology.

The majority of my contributors have given their view on the future of Blockchain in their own words – have a look at the final chapter to see what these global Blockchain experts (plus a few more) think the future of Blockchain holds – a very interesting read!

My contributors, in no particular order:

Damien Moore MP – Member of Parliament for Southport and Chairman of the All-Party Parliamentary Group (APPG) for Blockchain. Damien was born in Cumbria and spent most his childhood there. He moved to Preston in 2002 where he studied for a bachelor's in history at the University of Central Lancashire. He spent the majority of his career in the retail sector and was a retail manager for supermarket chain ASDA before becoming an MP. Since being elected to Parliament, Damien has been elected onto the Science & Technology Committee and the Petitions Committee – and is also involved in many All-Party Parliamentary Groups (APPGs). He is Chair of the APPGs for Tunisia and Blockchain.

Paolo Tasca – Paolo is a fintech economist specializing in P2P financial systems. He has served as an advisor on Blockchain technologies for different international organizations including the EU

Parliament and the United Nations. Paolo is founder and Executive Director of the Centre for Blockchain Technologies (UCL CBT) at University College London.

Nikhil Vadgama – Nikhil is the Deputy Director of the UCL Centre for Blockchain Technologies. He is also a founding member of the Retail Blockchain Consortium. He is actively involved in the commercialization of AI and Blockchain academic research in the finance, real estate, and education sectors in the UK and China. He also advises numerous early-stage Blockchain and AI companies. He has previously worked globally as an Investment Banker for HSBC. Nikhil holds an MBA from INSEAD, an MPhys from the University of Oxford and has passed all three levels of the CFA Programme.

Vikram Kimyani – Vikram is a Blockchain and cloud solutions architect who currently works for Oracle in their Financial Services team. He is married with two kids and lives in London with a cat affectionately known as 'scaredy cat'. He often speaks at conferences, meetups and to customers about Blockchain strategy and use cases within enterprises. He has an extensive IT background having worked for an investment bank where his team looked after one of the largest private cloud deployments in Europe.

Geri Cupi – Geri is currently CEO and co-founder of MonoChain, a Blockchain start-up which is developing provenance and tracking for the luxury second life market. He has been in the blockchain space since 2014 doing research for a Bitcoin ETF and Bitcoin use cases in other industries while he was working as a VC at Velo Partners. Geri is the co-founder and technical director of Retail Blockchain Consortium, where he looks after the DLT development and thought leadership for the consortium. Also, Geri is a research fellow at UCL Centre for Blockchain Technologies and a visiting lecturer at the University of Bath and the University of Edinburgh. Previously, Geri co-founded two retail e-commerce technologies: Jook, a social commerce company, and Social DNA, which was acquired by Levi's.

Chris Wing – Chris is a Solution Architect at Oracle Corporation. He has a degree in Computer Science from Kent University and is a software developer at heart. Currently his interests include the application and development of Machine Learning for Document Analysis; Blockchain technologies and its use cases; and Computer

Vision and OCR. Chris has appeared at multiple events talking about a variety of topics, including DevOps for modern business, Blockchain and its use cases and IoT & AI in the modern world.

Areiel Wolanow – Areiel is the managing director of Finserv Experts, an independent consultancy providing delivery and advisory leadership services in technology-enabled business transformation for banking, insurance, and financial markets worldwide. Areiel has led Blockchain implementations for global financial enterprises, such as HSBC and Lloyd's of London. He has advised central banks and financial regulators in Asia, Europe, and the Middle East on Blockchain adoption, and is currently an expert advisor for the UK Parliament's working group on Blockchain. He is passionate about financial inclusion and has spoken at the G20 about the potential of DLT and other emerging technologies to revolutionize how banking and insurance are made available in parts of the world that would derive the most benefit from them.

Marta Piekarska – Marta serves as the director of ecosystem at Hyperledger. Prior to Hyperledger, she worked as a security architect at Blockstream. Marta obtained her BSc in Electrical and Computer Engineering from Warsaw University of Technology and a double master's in Computer Science and Informatics at Technical University of Berlin and Warsaw University of Technology. Her undergrad thesis was on voice encryption on android platform and grad work on GPU-aided payload delivery on Linux Kernel. Marta recently received PhD. in user-informed design of privacy tools, while working for one of the hottest Silicon Valley start-ups, Blockstream, as their security architect. As a post-doc, she also teaches and works at the Technical University of Berlin.

Carlos Vivas Augier – Carlos is a Nicaraguan computer science engineer and global head of enterprise education at ConsenSys. He co-founded two start-ups, one was purchased and, the other acquired by one of its shareholders. He leads the Academy Program of Opinno, a tech consultancy firm, and the Spanish editors of MIT Technology Review and Harvard Business Review. He's been involved in the Blockchain space since late 2014. He has worked as a Blockchain advisor for tier 1 and large corporations from Finance, Energy, Health and Retail industries, he was awarded 2nd place in a national-level blockchain hackathon and he co-authored 2 Blockchain books with top experts from the space.

Michael Forhez – Michael is global managing director for the Consumer Markets Industry Solutions Group at Oracle. He brings over 25 years of diversified sales, marketing, and management consulting experience to his current role. Michael is frequently called upon to write and speak on various subjects related to the consumer products and retail sectors. He serves as an evangelist within the consumer markets and has committed his career to engaging with various stakeholders to better understand and reflect their collective requirements.

Peter Bambridge – Peter has over 30 years of experience providing consulting services and software solutions to the retail and consumer goods industries. As part of Oracle's Global Consumer Markets team, Peter focuses on emerging technologies such as Blockchain, AI, and IoT and how they can be utilized in the industry. Peter creates and maintains industry solutions that are focused on addressing specific industry needs. Previously Peter was an independent industry analyst and consultant to the retail, fashion, and consumer packaged goods industry providing recommendations and services addressing product life cycle management, sales and marketing, supply chain, and IT strategies. Prior to that, Peter worked in business development, sales, and consulting roles across a number of companies providing solutions to retail and consumer goods customers, which allowed him to acquire strong competencies in diverse areas such as supply chain, product life cycle management, ERP, planning and forecasting, with a deep expertise in the unique requirements of the retail and consumer goods sector. Peter has a BSc in Nuclear Engineering from Queen Mary University of London.

Eric Wallace – The views, thoughts, and contributions in this book do not represent the views of the United States Air Force or the United States. Eric Wallace has spent the last 3 years independently researching and developing frameworks and architectures for distributed ledger technology solutions for both enterprise and government use cases.

Emma McClarkin MEP After first being elected to the European Parliament representing the East Midlands in 2009, Emma joined the European Parliament's Committee on International Trade (INTA) in early 2012. By 2014, Emma was appointed as the ECR Group Coordinator for the committee, meaning that she is the lead MEP in the Group on Trade matters. This includes the EU-US trade deal, the Trade in Services Agreement, and the EU–China Investment Agreement.

Emma has been at the forefront of opening up trade deals and modernizing some of those already in place, such as the trade pillar of the Global Agreement with Mexico and the free trade agreement with Australia. Emma also represents the ECR on the Parliament's WTO Steering Committee and both the INTA steering groups on Brexit and the US.

Emma works extensively on policy relating to emerging technologies and the Digital Single Market. As part of her work on INTA, she was the first MEP to publish an Own Initiative report that considers the use of Blockchain in a specific policy area. Emma is also a Substitute Member of the Parliament's Internal Market and Consumer Protection Committee and Culture and Education Committee. As part of these portfolios, Emma has worked on cybersecurity, Copyright in the Digital Single Market and most recently the EU regulation to prevent the dissemination of terrorist content online.

As part of her expertise in Blockchain policymaking, Emma has spoken at and worked with several organizations and industry stakeholders including the European Centre for International Political Economy, Allied for Startups, and the All-Party Parliamentary Group on Blockchain in the House of Commons.

Foreword

Before my election to Parliament in 2017, I must confess that my knowledge of Blockchain technology was underdeveloped. Of course, I knew of cryptocurrencies – who didn't? Stories of people trading Bitcoin and making huge fortunes and losses were and continue to be widely reported. I certainly had little appreciation of the enormous importance of the Blockchain technology behind cryptocurrencies and how it has the potential to radically change our society. It may seem surprising, therefore, to find myself as the chairman of an exciting and active APPG in the heart of UK politics.

The reason behind my decision to set up the APPG was simple – I wanted to make government more efficient and believed that Blockchain was an opportunity to achieve this. A chance conversation with a colleague who was waxing lyrical about Blockchain technology got me intrigued, and I knew I had to act, thus the APPG for Blockchain was established.

In seeking to make a worthy contribution I wanted to establish a group that reached out to experts. Facilitated by the Big Innovation Centre, our first meeting received an overwhelming attendance. It was at this meeting that I met the author of this book, Antony Welfare, who became a board advisor to the APPG.

Antony's enthusiasm for the possibilities of Blockchain technology on many areas from the economy, industry, and society is profound. It is this enthusiasm and characteristically easy-to-understand style that makes this book such an invaluable resource.

In a world where there is much contention around data and who controls it, this book clearly asserts how this can work in favour of the consumer. Key to this are the constant themes of openness and transparency, and the persuasive argument that if we want to see the benefits of this technology then we must embrace change.

A leader in retail with a wide range of experience, Antony takes the reader on a journey. This is made all the more vivid by his use of his fictional retailer the 'Antony Stores Group' to illustrate the use cases. The 'how' and 'why' we would use Blockchain help the reader to visualize the real potential of this technology.

This in-depth, yet easy to understand, book is a must for those that want to gain a greater insight into the practical, yet transformative, potential of Blockchain.

Damien Moore MP

Damien Moore MP – Member of Parliament for Southport and Chairman of the All-Party Parliamentary Group (APPG) for Blockchain.

Foreword

Once the widespread potential of Blockchain was understood, people began to see their life through the lens of this technology. With Blockchain you can solve this problem, with Blockchain you can solve that...Blockchain as the panacea to all our problems. This was – and I would say that in some cases it is still – the attitude of innovators and early adaptors when asked what they think about Blockchain. This euphoria was reflected in the price of Bitcoin, touching US$20,000 in December 2017, with US$7.4 billion raised by start-ups though token sales in 2017 alone.

Then, someone began to realize that perhaps moving 'from theory to practice' in Blockchain still has a long way to go. Indeed, Bitcoin – which was expected by the 'maximalists' to supplant VISA or Mastercard – is capable of supporting only around seven transactions per second. Visa's network can handle about 24,000 transactions a second. Hopes are high, but so too are the obstacles. Scalability, limited consumer adoption, regulatory uncertainty, and a lack of standards are just a few of the many challenges that are hindering the mass adoption of digital currencies and Blockchain.[1]

According to the technology life cycle, we have just exited the Embryonic phase, characterized by hype and overexcitement, and we are now into the era of Ferment, with its technology variations, rivalry and competition, and technical uncertainty in which user preferences

---

1 Tasca, P., & Widmann, S. (2017). The challenges faced by blockchain technologies– Part 1. *Journal of Digital Banking*, 2(2), 132–147; Tasca, P., & Widmann, S. (2018). The challenges faced by blockchain technologies–Part 2. *Journal of Digital Banking*, 2(3), 259–281; Tasca, P., & Tessone, C. (2018) Taxonomy of Blockchain Technologies. Principles of Identification and Classification. *Ledger Journal*.

are not clear. Indeed, if you asked me how many Blockchains have so far been implemented and do actually exist I would have some difficulty in providing the exact figure. New Blockchains enter the market every day. We can say that there are roughly fifty different consensus mechanisms (the engine of the blockchain) and about two thousand unique tokens and digital currencies. And there are still other, proprietary Blockchains which are tokenless and often private.

Each new Blockchain promises better throughput, higher levels of security, more privacy. In this complex space it is very difficult to differentiate accurately and to assess the quality of each technological component. What is generally needed is a Blockchain matrix or analytical framework.[2]

According to the Gartner Hype Cycle model we are 'sliding into the trough of disillusionment' where companies become impatient as they realize that the new technology is not a panacea for all their problems. Blockchain technology is characterized as having poor performance, slow industry adoption, and lacking a clear value proposition. As industry experts and the media emphasize these challenges rather than the opportunities of the technology, we enter into a long period in which companies fail to deliver on projects and investors become more prudent and risk adverse.

The period of enlightenment and productive adoption of Blockchain – in which early adopters gain experience with the new technology, best practices emerge and its real-world value becomes accepted by industry – is still ahead of us. But we are gaining ground every day.

Additional steps are needed if we are to reach the critical point of mass adoption, as happened in the past with other innovations. In principle, a sound regulatory framework and the creation of common standards would boost trust in Blockchain technology and digital tokens, and stimulate investment. In addition, rejecting the hypothesis that one chain will rule them all – indeed, different communities of Blockchain users deserve different governing laws and different Blockchain protocols provide an answer to those different needs – interoperability will also need to be addressed to enable Blockchains to exchange information with each other.

For these reasons a book that introduces well thought-out examples of strategic applications of Blockchain in the real world is timely and well placed to assist entrepreneurs, investors, and regulators to move quickly from the phase of disillusionment to the richly rewarding phase of productivity and adoption. *Commercializing Blockchain* aims to raise awareness of the promises and perils of Blockchain technologies by

   i) taking a snapshot of the current state-of-the-art in order to draw a line between past and future applications;

  ii) helping businesses and individuals to understand the real impact of Blockchain and how it could disrupt entire markets and industrial processes;

 iii) guiding its readers to a full understanding of how to use Blockchain technologies; and

 iv) imagining how society will adapt itself to Blockchain and what it might look like 20 years from now.

In a space that moves as quickly as Blockchain, it is useful to pause and reflect on how the evolution of this technology has brought us to the present day – what has worked, what has not – to better map out where Blockchain is going next. *Commercializing Blockchain* is a key part of that vital discussion and will be equally useful to veterans of the space and to those only just beginning to discover this technology.

Paolo Tasca

---

2 Tasca, P., & Widmann, S. (2017).

Preface

Welcome to *Commercializing Blockchain: Strategic Applications in the Real World*. I became part of the Blockchain world in 2016 and I have been obsessed with this exciting new world ever since.

Imagine a world where the data that we produce on a daily, if not hourly, basis is 'owned' by us – it is our data and we choose what it is used for and where it is transferred....

Imagine a world where you can 'scan' my shirt and it will tell you the cotton plant it started from, the cotton mill where the cotton was spun, the shirt factory where it was sewn together, and the journey it took to my wardrobe....

Imagine a world where you 'scan' a bottle of champagne, and it shows a beautiful video of where the grapes were picked, how they were harvested, how the champagne was fermented, and how the bottle was rested over its lifetime....

Imagine buying your forever home and being able to fully track all the previous owners, the changes made and the records of all alterations made during its hundred year life....

Imagine no more – these are all real possibilities for Blockchain technology to fundamentally transform our lives.

This ground-breaking technology will allow us to own more of our data, see more transparently than ever before and trust more in our governments and businesses.

We are at the beginning of the next revolution, where Blockchain technology will lead the world into new and exciting opportunities, with the key values baked into the heart of the Blockchain technology: *Trust and Transparency.*

We will be able to 'own our own data' and see where our data is being used transparently. We will have visibility on our digital footprint and ensure that the truth is seen and facts are never deleted.

I am a passionate 'Blockchainer' and I understand how Blockchain technology will transform our lives over the next 20 years. We are only at the beginning of the revolution – maybe at 0.8 or 0.9 at the moment, but we will move quickly to 1.0 and beyond.

The technology is ready, the people and process are the stumbling blocks and these are where the world needs to focus – changes are difficult for humans and we need to be open to this new technology, which will give us more trust and transparency in the world around us.

In this book, I focus on how I believe Blockchain technology will revolutionize all our lives through moving forward our tired and complex systems, to quicker and more efficient systems, simultaneously allowing us to establish a level of trust and transparency that has been lost in the current world.

There is an exciting world ahead powered by Blockchain technology and your journey begins here with my book.

Please enjoy the ride (and my book) and please feel free to interact with me in the digital world @AntonyWelfare and Commercializingblockchain.com.

Many thanks and best wishes to you all.

Antony Welfare
April 2019
Commercializingblockchain.com

Introduction

Commercializing Blockchain

Welcome to *Commercializing Blockchain*, which has been written to steer you through the exciting and transformational new world built on Blockchain and other groundbreaking technologies.

My interest in Blockchain started in February 2016 when I asked a colleague, 'What is Bitcoin? And why are retailers not using it?' Little did I know that this one conversation would open my mind to the revolutionary potential of Blockchain technology.

I spent three months researching, discussing, and finding out how Blockchain worked, using books, online research, and attending meetups. During this research I came across Ethereum and started to research Ethereum in depth. (Ethereum is a Blockchain on which many different use cases of Blockchain have been built and is one of the biggest Blockchain solutions in the market at the moment.)

The book is split into 14 chapters covering all parts of Blockchain technology from a business and use case perspective. I am not a technical developer; I am a business leader who understands the potential of Blockchain technology and how it can transform governments, businesses, enterprises, and communities.

The book is not meant to be a technical guide to Blockchain, its purpose is to help you understand the uses of the technology, especially in enterprise and business. My background as an accountant and strategist leans the book towards practical advice, information, and ideas – I am a straightforward author giving you my extensive experience and thoughts around this exciting new technology.

I have also brought you some of the best thought leaders from the Blockchain world, who have written parts of the book, to give you their opinions, expertise, and explanations of some of the concepts in depth.

Commercializing Blockchain: Strategic Applications in the Real World,
First Edition. Antony Welfare.
© 2019 John Wiley & Sons Ltd. Published 2019 by John Wiley & Sons Ltd.

Their support is vital to give you a great understanding of how Blockchain technologies will revolutionize governments, communities, and business.

Antony Stores Group (ASG) Retail Business Illustration

Throughout the book we will be using our own fictional retail business called '**Antony Stores Group**' or '**ASG**'. This is a large retail business experiencing many of the issues retailers and brands face in the current world.

Using ASG, we will illustrate the uses of Blockchain technology in a highly complex retailer. See more details about ASG in the next section.

Real-World Enterprise Level Use Cases – Financial Services, Retail, Supply Chain, and CPG

The final section of *Commercializing Blockchain* will take you through a few live use cases which are happening in late 2018 and early 2019. These are areas where Blockchain technology is making the biggest impact today and where we are experiencing many different projects, proofs of concept, trials, and implementations.

These use cases will of course be out of date by the time you read this, but they are real use cases, happening or have happened. This is important to review as this will show you where to look for the start of your journey on the Blockchain revolution.

Who Will Benefit from Reading Commercializing Blockchain?

The book is written as a practical guide to Blockchain. Anybody who wants to understand what Blockchain is, and how it will transform the world, will enjoy the book and learn from this.

If you are a commercial business, you will gain from my extensive network of people and resources looking at Blockchain on a daily basis – few people in the world have an extensive and comprehensive Blockchain network like mine.

Antony Stores Group (ASG) Illustration

ASG Background

To help you understand the ideas, concepts, and examples, I will refer to ASG, a retailer established in the UK in 1923. ASG is a global, complex retail business, with multiple suppliers, systems, and channels of operation.

ASG represents the wide range of issues current retailers, CPG and supply chain companies are dealing with and where Blockchain technology can improve significantly.

I have had the pleasure to work with global retailers and brands my entire life and have used this experience to create this fictional retailer. ASG is therefore a great example of the complexities for many current retailers across the world.

History of ASG

Founded on 23 March 1923, ASG started out as a provisions store in Sidcup, Kent, UK. Originally named after the original owner H. H. Chapman (my great-grandfather) and selling a wide range of provisions from its double-fronted shop on the high street.

During the twentieth century, it opened over 250 stores across the UK. By the turn of the millennium, the business was thriving, and acquired a high street clothing retailer in 2001. This immediately gave the group 200 new clothing stores to add to the grocery store estate.

In 2002, the chain rebranded to 'Antony Stores Group', and the business looked to integrate the two brands into one and started to build synergies between both retailers, especially with the backend systems and supply chains.

In my previous book, *The Retail Handbook*, you can find the history of the shop and how it operated in the 1900s.

Stores were merged and relocated to have food and clothing in the one store. Fresh food was removed from the range, and home products were added. ASG became a retailer of clothing, ambient food, and homewares.

In 2003, ASG launched its online channel, to adapt to the competition and expand its footprint digitally.

During the next 10 years, ASG expanded into Europe, opening over 400 stores in 10 European countries, expanding the UK stores to 400, and launching the 'ASG Card' for loyalty across the group.

By 2013, ASG was taking over 10% of sales online and started to look at reducing its UK store portfolio, in line with the growth of online shopping. The group turnover broke the £10bn mark during this year, as online continued to grow thanks to the group's Omnichannel strategy.

By 2018, ASG comprised:

- £14bn turnover
- 75,000 employees
- 250 UK stores

- 300 European stores
- 25% of sales from Online across Europe
- 10,000 SKUs (3000 Food, 2000 Home, 5000 Clothing)
- 2100 direct suppliers (500 Food, 600 Home, 1000 Clothing)
- 170 warehouses across Europe (100 Food, 30 Home, 40 Clothing).

Let's look at the current challenges for ASG, and during the rest of the book we will reference these, to show how Blockchain technology will revolutionize retailers and supply chains.

ASG Challenges and Pain Points

As we have seen, ASG has grown from a one-store business to a complex, large-scale retailer based on organic growth and acquisitions. This makes the company a significantly complex organization, which would benefit greatly from Blockchain technology, owing to its:

- Multiple countries of operation
- Multiple product ranges spanning clothing, home, and food
- Various channels of operations (stores, online, mobile, marketplaces, collection points, call centre, etc.)
- Large, complex, and outdated IT systems from legacy systems to own built systems
- Old systems with the operations/back-end systems over 10 years old
- Challenges for the business to be a truly mobile first retailer, due to the scale and complex business
- ASG Card (The loyalty scheme) is old and not fit for the current customer expectations
- Gift cards are still very manual, processed overnight and suffer from significant fraud levels
- Returns process – the rise of online sales, has led to a significant rise in returns, which is managed inefficiently and is a big profit destroyer
- Financial reporting, taxes, intercompany, and management information are all complex and need constant manual reconciliation
- With a complex supply chain, and over 1000 direct suppliers, the visibility is very limited
- Inventory visibility is poor, due to the vast range of warehouses, stores, and collection points
- High stock holding levels are in place, due to the poor visibility and demand forecasting

- Lead times for fast fashion clothing are significantly behind the competition
- Own brand clothing is suffering from counterfeiting
- Customers are becoming more interested in the provenance of the products and expect detailed product history
- Its high-end own brand products are being sold through second life markets, but lack tracking and authenticity
- Food traceability is complex and takes too long
- Operating in 11 different currencies, it is costing a significant amount in transaction fees and delays in settlements across borders.

1

Introduction to Blockchain Technology

Welcome to the world of Blockchain technology, which I fundamentally believe will change our businesses and lives forever.

> Blockchain technology is by far the biggest revolution since the birth of the internet. Blockchain technology will affect the entire world – citizens, businesses and governments will transform, thanks to Blockchain.

Let us start by understanding what Blockchain technology is and where it 'fits' into the current world.

Blockchain technology is a type of 'distributed ledger technology' which looks to **share data** and **transactions** across a number of different **places**. Unlike traditional **databases**, distributed **ledgers** have no central data store or administration functionality. A ledger is a record of data, which can be any data you wish to store and share. This ledger is **tamper-proof** and the data is **encrypted** for security.

Blockchain Technology Definition

Simple definition in nine words:
'Trusted and efficient way of sharing data and transactions'
And a longer definition:
'Blockchain technology can be viewed as a distributed ledger of information, which maintains a continuously growing list of records, called blocks, secured from tampering and changes.

Commercializing Blockchain: Strategic Applications in the Real World,
First Edition. Antony Welfare.
© 2019 John Wiley & Sons Ltd. Published 2019 by John Wiley & Sons Ltd.

Each block contains a timestamp and a link to a previous block. This means that blockchains are inherently resistant to modification of the data – once recorded, the data in a block cannot be altered retroactively.'

What Are the Reasons Why We Have Blockchain Technology?

My view is that Blockchain technology is the progression of three developments made in the last 20 years: The internet, centralization, and the 'trustless' world.

The Internet and Blockchain

Since the inception of the internet, we have progressed from Internet 1.0, which was the initial start of the technology and its adoption, to Internet 2.0, which is where we currently live.

Internet 2.0 is all about transactions and data – think about how you use the internet today – shopping, listening to music, banking, watching films, and social media – all of these activities are transaction based.

We all use the internet throughout our lives and it has become critical to our daily lives and our businesses. This has led to the second development: centralization and Blockchain.

As the internet grew through the 2.0 world, the largest global companies have been born: Apple, Facebook, Google, Microsoft, Amazon, Uber, etc. These companies now control our lives on the internet – everything we do one of these companies 'owns'; we do not 'own' our data and transactions on the internet, these companies do.

This centralization of a few global technology giants has given them complete power and influence over governments and our lives. They decide what governments do and they decide what we do.

This power of the giants, together with mainly failed political systems across the world, has led to the third development described below.

The 'Trustless' World

We now live in a world where we lack trust in large companies and governments. In Western governments, there has been a trend towards nationalism and 'localism', causing global trade wars, global immigration issues, and governments who cannot operate effectively in the new world.

Ask a millennial if they trust the government and they are likely to say, maybe, no, or (even worse) I don't care. The trust that governments once had is slowly decreasing and a new political system is needed across the globe.

Large companies' trust levels are even worse:

- Do younger people trust banks? If they did why would the Monzo, Revolut, and Starling banks be growing so fast?
- Do younger people use Facebook? If they did, Mark Zuckerberg would not be facing government enquires for illegally selling its users' data.
- Is Google bringing back search results for you? Or has it been paid more to surface a different product to you?
- Is Uber cheaper, faster, and more comfortable than the centralized black cab world in London?

I will not continue as I am sure you understand my point (I am not trying to be political or opinionated here; I am surfacing facts and experiences that I have seen).

Let me quote a millennial I spoke to in 2018 as to why he was interested in Blockchain and cryptocurrency investments:

> Banks give low interest so I wanted to invest a part of it (although cryptocurrency can be risky it really looks promising for the future).
>
> The technology itself. I do think blockchain has so many advantages that I think a lot of companies will be interested to invest in and will use it for the future.
>
> Power of the banks. Although banks claim crypto is a bubble, I don't trust them a lot. They have a lot of power and regularly they use it in the wrong way. Within cryptocurrency I believe people can control where and how much they can invest so you know what happens with your money.

This is obviously only one person's view, but I thought it summarized the issues with banks and centralization very well.

To summarize this section, in my opinion, Blockchain is developing from these three factors:

- The internet
- Centralization
- The 'trustless' world.

Blockchain: The Internet of Value

One way to look at Blockchain technology is 'the Internet of Value'. The current internet focuses on transactions and data transfer. This is quickly progressing from 'data' into 'value' – our data is becoming ever more valuable.

Big data is a phrase used to describe the vast amounts of data that there is in the world. We interact with digital devices throughout the day, and these interactions are stored in data lakes, pools, and oceans. This data is often 'owned' by a large organization and can then be used to help offer better services, help find cures for medical conditions and be used to sell more products that you may want.

This data can also be used for marketing and advertising products to you, informing you of issues that may come up in the future and selling you products you do not need – data has become a blessing and a curse.

With Blockchain technology, you have the ability to 'own your own data' and use that to create value and transfer and transact value. Once you have control of your own data, you can decide what happens to this data and where it is used.

Data has become 'value' and that value is to you as an enterprise, person, or government. Using Smart contracts and other Blockchain technologies, this value can then be shared, reallocated, sold, bought, and generally used in a way that is much more flexible than today.

Importantly, with Blockchain technology, the Internet of Value is transparent and trusted – we will be able to own our own data (value) and do with it what we wish.

A very exciting and interesting new world of opportunities will emerge from the Internet of Value and the possibilities this opens for governments, business, and communities.

Blockchain has Five Important Characteristics

Let's now get into the basics of what is Blockchain – the best way to look at Blockchain technology is to look at the five most important characteristics:

1. Blockchain for truth and trust
2. Blockchain for transparency

3. Blockchain for security
4. Blockchain for quality and certainty
5. Blockchain for efficiency.

Let's explore these further:

1. Blockchain for Truth and Trust

One of the fundamental attributes of Blockchain technology is the immutability of the data – once the data is entered into the Blockchain (and verified) the data is there for eternity and cannot ever be changed, altered, or destroyed. Coupled with the decentralized nature of the Blockchain – where each party has the exact same copy of the data, this means that there is 'ONE VIEW OF THE TRUTH'.

We are in a world that lacks trust in many ways – something that has crept in over the last 20 years, is now a major issue for governments and institutions.

Blockchain has taken a role in the 'post-truth' era to help solve issues around trusted parties – with Blockchain transactions and interactions being shared and immutable, so any issues down the line can be tracked and traced.

Blockchain records in time that a transaction took place – which can never be changed.

Now, we have to remember that Blockchain is a technology, and technology relies on its design and, most importantly, inputs. Blockchain will not solve the issue of mistakes and poor data – the data that is entered into the Blockchain could be incorrect, but the fact that it cannot be changed means this mistake can be found easily and the source of the incorrect information can be traced quickly.

2. Blockchain for Transparency

We live in a world of hidden data, processes, and technologies. Data on our lives is collected 24 hours a day – where we shop, where we eat, where we drive, where we party, where we work, where we enjoy life – and all this data is collected by many different parties, who use it in different ways and for different reasons – some of which we know and some of which we do not know.

If we apply Blockchain technology, we will have a transparent view of the data. Anybody who has access (on a public Blockchain this would be anyone, and on a private or hybrid Blockchain this would be who is authorized to access the data) can see what data is kept and what this data is used for.

The principle of open and shared data is key here. The data collected is clearly collected for a reason and that reason is known to the parties who then agree (or disagree) to the data being collected.

In order to ensure the data is collected correctly, the 'owner' of the data can check the detail on the Blockchain and all this will be transparent to those authorized to view. Any incorrect data, or data used incorrectly, will easily be seen and can then be changed (with a new set of data as the old data cannot be deleted).

This new world where 'we own' our data, is very appealing. At the moment, the tech giants are using our data (often with our forced consent) to improve their profits and business. With Blockchain technology, we can change to a world where 'our data' is only used for the purposes we agree to, and we benefit from this data.

For example, I may want a retailer to record my personal details and my transactional details, to offer me a better deal or a promotion. This benefits me and the retailers, and is not a one-sided deal.

Ownership of our data is critical as more and more data on us is produced – we are data machines, every action we take is producing data and companies are using this for their benefit. This can continue, if we agree, but we need to be able to see what data they have on us and what they are using this for.

The General Data Protection Regulation (GDPR) in Europe, and Freedom of Information acts, have given more control to users, but these are still in the early stages, and the data is still not very transparent.

Blockchain can help make data transparent which makes it easier for us to control and understand.

3. Blockchain for Security

The data held on a Blockchain is immutable and timestamped. This is critical for the success of Blockchain technology. Being able to ensure that there is one true data point, which cannot be altered or deleted, gives more transparency and certainty to our data world.

Securing this data using cryptography is a key part of Blockchain technology, and this helps ensure the data is only used for the purpose agreed and is safe from theft and data attacks.

As with all technology, Blockchain technology is not the total fix for securing data, but it is a great step forward in the world of data security.

4. Blockchain for Quality and Certainty

The data on a Blockchain can be entered from any source (i.e. manually, from an Internet of Things (IoT) device, from another database, or through an API, etc.). This data should be validated before it enters the Blockchain (see Chapter 2 for consensus and automation of this).

If the data is validated before it enters the Blockchain, it will be of higher quality than if it is not. Likewise, if the data is entered from a secured database or secured IoT device, it will also have a higher level of certainty and quality.

The old adage of 'crap in, crap out' still holds true, but with Blockchain technology you have the opportunity to enter data which is of better quality. The Blockchain technology also allows bad data to be found, tracked, and traced quickly, which helps fix any issue with poor quality data much quicker than before.

5. Blockchain for Efficiency

One of the great benefits of Blockchain technology is the removal of 'middle men' or intermediaries. When I say the removal, I do not mean the total removal, but a significant reduction of their use and a change of where they become of benefit to the ecosystem For example, in the marketplace chapter, I make the argument that middle men are needed to make the marketplace a success.

That aside, the technology will allow the replacement of intermediaries, who add time and cost to processes. This will add to better control and efficiency of the ecosystem around the Blockchain technology.

Removing part or all of the intermediaries, using Blockchain technology, relies on the correct set up and running of the Blockchain technology solution. Consensus and the mechanisms around this are key to success and are covered in depth in the next chapter. Without a good consensus and governance process, the intermediaries will be needed and the complexity you wanted to remove will be added back.

The second part of the efficiency benefits of Blockchain technology concerns 'Smart contracts' or programming language using Blockchain technology. I am no expert on Smart contracts, but I do know that their use is fundamental to an efficient Blockchain solution.

Discussed later, the basic premise of a Smart contract is to automate some of the Blockchain transactions, according to agreed contracts or principles. The basic process: 'If this happens, then do this'.

The automation of low-level, high-volume transactions is critical to the efficiency of the Blockchain technology. In a later chapter, I discuss the world of intercompany transactions – which is based on high-volume, low-value transactions – if these can be automated, this would save significant time and resources for any large enterprise or government.

Blockchain Regulation and Global Trade

A very hot topic, and a very important topic is regarding the regulation of Blockchain technology. There are many discussions, debates, and research into this area and I am by no means an expert on regulation and trade rules.

My chosen way to approach this subject is to discuss the global trade aspects of Blockchain technology, and how governments can use regulation to help develop the use of Blockchain technology for making global trade more effective and efficient.

Staying true to the purpose of the book – real solutions – is why I have used the discussion around global trade regulation as the area to cover. If we can get the regulation for global trade working, we will easily be able to solve regulation in other areas.

I cover the significant benefits of Blockchain technology for the global supply chain in depth in this book, and here I want to introduce a global expert on trade, a person with a clear understanding of how the European government can embrace Blockchain technology and help regulate the technology where needed.

I have asked a very qualified contributor to add some details and thought leadership here. Emma McClarkin is a Member of the European Parliament and in 2018 submitted a MOTION FOR A EUROPEAN PARLIAMENT RESOLUTION – Blockchain: a forward-looking trade policy (2018/2085(INI)).

The purpose of this report is to highlight the current sub-optimal issues in supply chains, EU trade policy and customs procedures, to identify the plausible benefits derived from widespread blockchain implementation, and to recommend achievable and gradual policy steps to the European Commission and Member States to enable this technology to function.

I have asked Emma and her team to share with us her thoughts and research around the global trade benefits using Blockchain technology. Emma and the team will cover the following areas:

- Current issues with global trade
- Current solutions for global trade issues
- How Blockchain can revolutionize global trade
- What needs to happen to make this work
- What the future will look like with this implemented.

Blockchain and Global Trade
Emma McClarkin, MEP

1. Current Barriers within Global Trade

In my many years working in the European Parliament as a member of the International Trade committee, I have witnessed first-hand the barriers to efficiency and innovation in global trade. Businesses, governments and trade organizations alike have told me of the obstacles to trade that they face, from access to specific markets or regions, to managing streams of customs paperwork and data. These barriers are persistent and multifaceted; however, I believe there is a good reason to feel positive about the future of the global trading system. The reason? Blockchain.

There has never been a more exciting moment to look at radical solutions to barriers within global trade. The emergence of technologies from artificial intelligence to the Internet of Things has sparked a torrent of innovation set to break down barriers to trade on an unprecedented scale. However, when scrutinizing the potential of these technologies to dismantling barriers within the global trading system in the European Parliament, Blockchain stands out as a fundamental game changer.

The sheer pace of innovation in Blockchain solutions by large corporations such as IBM, to Blockchain start-ups and national governments, demonstrates that there is much more to blockchain than media-generated hype. As such, I believe it is crucial that policymakers stay open to the potential uses of blockchain to address barriers to global trade. Whilst it is important to stay mindful of the challenges that blockchain presents, it is crucial to set a flexible forward-looking strategy for the future of global trade that allows Blockchain-based solutions to flourish.

Often policymakers regulate to address weaknesses or create a legal framework for businesses to invest. It is a core part of our role to ensure businesses have the environment to invest and grow. The use of such technology as Blockchain can become a key tool to assist, or even transform, the regulatory approach. It is up to us to seize the opportunity to understand its potential.

In this section, I will briefly summarize some of the global trade barriers including transactional costs associated with intermediaries and paperwork, trade facilitation and customs procedures, and preferential market access, setting the scene for a discussion on the revolutionary potential for Blockchain solutions in global trade.

Transactional Costs Associated with Intermediaries and Paperwork
International transactions rely heavily on the role of intermediaries and physical paperwork. Different actors and entities check, process, authorize, add, and edit products and goods on supply chains. Operating across multiple jurisdictions and working environments, this protracted process can add significant time, resources and cost that burden operators seeking to produce goods and access markets.

There are several different types of international trade documentation that are issued and processed. These are commercial documentation, trade financing documents, logistics and transportation, and customs and other border documents. All of these different documents require extensive coordination across different organizations, agencies and operators, with inherent administration costs and time consumption. As such, these processes are susceptible to mistakes and fraud, which can damage the reputation of producers as well as create further delays and additional costs. Moreover, operators are often required to submit the same information to various competent authorities, which imposes an unnecessary workload to both public authorities and businesses.

In 2015, the World Trade Organization (WTO) published a study that concluded that trade-associated costs could be tantamount to a 134% ad valorem tariff in high-income countries and a 219% tariff in developing countries. Such costs include physical paperwork and duplication of administrative procedures by interacting with sometimes over a dozen different customs and government agencies. Whilst the importance of complying with different regulations on health, food, safety, and consumer protection cannot be overstated, there is a clear need to simplify and streamline customs and border procedures to reduce spiralling costs.

Reducing bureaucratic barriers to trade is one of my core objectives as a policymaker. Technology can simplify the need for duplications, unnecessary interactions to provide overlapping documentation, and administrative paperwork. We need to be open-minded about how old systems can be assisted and reformed by emerging technologies to find practical, workable solutions.

Trade Facilitation and Customs Procedures
Trade facilitation has received increasing attention owing to the potential to assist businesses that have to navigate a myriad of procedures, rules, and operations at the border. Costly and inefficient border procedures present a significant burden on operators. Businesses applying for customs clearance may be required to first obtain different licenses, permits, certificates, and other authorizations from a competent authority, which is then submitted to customs control and these supporting documents are checked to determine the placement of goods under a customs procedure. Customs authorities are then required to check the certificates and licences issued by other competent authorities to certify goods comply with standards and regulations.

This is just a brief overview of the process businesses have to navigate and in itself demonstrates why technology has been incorporated as a tool to assist trade facilitation. I believe we can go further than this and the World Customs Organization's pioneering research into the potential of emerging technologies in customs and trade facilitation signposts the way.

Exchange of Information
Limited and inconsistent information throughout the supply chain is commonplace and hinders the flow of goods. Different stakeholders such as certifiers, laboratories, producers, regulators, and consumers carry out inputting and processing on a supply chain. With such frequent exchanges between parties, there can be issues with data quality, delays in the submission of data, and mistakes in data. Indeed, the

necessary information is not always fully accessible between those who require it. This creates further delays and duplications that can result in goods not reaching their destinations in time and adds cost to manufacturers and producers.

In such cases of inadequate exchange of information, the traceability and accountability of goods are more susceptible to fraud vulnerabilities relating to security and safety of supply chain. Customs authorities are therefore forced to make greater interventions to investigate and test products against their compliance with various procedures and regulations.

Seamless exchanges of information between different parties across supply chains, customs officials and regulators will improve trust in the provenance of products and increase business compliance. We must explore ways in which Blockchain can facilitate instantaneous and secure information being shared with specific entities.

Increasing the Use of Preferential Trade Access
The primary function of a country's trade policy tools is to further enhance the preferential market access of its producers and widen the choice of consumers. One such tool is the negotiation and conclusion of Free Trade Agreements (FTAs). However, there is growing concern over the underutilization of the trade preferences guaranteed by these FTAs. Conditions attached to greater levels of reciprocal market access can be complex and burdensome. Under non-preferential access, a textile manufacturer in country A may incur a tariff when exporting goods to country B. An FTA may facilitate the lowering of these tariffs or remove them altogether. In most cases, to make use of this reduced tariff, the exporter will need to demonstrate compliance with the country's rules of origin. This is where an exporter needs to demonstrate the nationality of a good to ensure the product is what it says it is. For instance, 40% of a particular garment may need to be produced in country A in order to qualify for the preferential tariff in country B. Exporters are often reluctant to produce the necessary paperwork and certification to demonstrate the composition of the good its exporting as this total cost can often be higher than the tariff they would incur outside the preferential access.

Explanations for this centre around two issues. One is the difficulties in understanding the rules for obtaining preferential origin. Another is the cumbersome procedures for obtaining documents needed to benefit from preferential treatment. Such issues are a particular disincentive to small and medium-sized enterprises (SMEs), for whom the challenge of navigating these complex rules is far greater than larger companies who are able to absorb any necessary cost.

Technology can lessen and remove the disincentive complex rules created for businesses to utilize the hard-won access granted by FTAs. The production of electronic certificates and online processing systems is just the first step to incorporate other exciting and emerging technologies.

Illicit Goods, Trade-Based Money Laundering (TBML), and Lack of Transparency

Operators can struggle to isolate and identify an instance where a contaminated, faulty, or tampered-with product has entered and been distributed on a supply chain. Large-scale recalls on health, safety or consumer protection grounds can be incredibly costly and take a prolonged period of time, during which more faulty products are being purchased and consumed. For instance, if particular models of a car had a fault, it will take time and resources to investigate the genesis of the fault. If the fault was caused at one particular assembly plant, a recall would be restricted to cars that passed through that plant. Still, such undertakings involve significant expense and delay to businesses.

Legitimate trade is often used to mask illicit criminal activity. This trade-based money laundering (TBML) often comprises schemes that seek to over-complicate the documentation and processing of legitimate trade. Overvaluation or undervaluation of goods on invoices, and peculiarities in the transit routes are common indicators of illicit trade. Customs organizations require greater exchange of information with producers and other entities to detect, investigate, and remove illicit goods from circulation.

Consumers increasingly wish to know the provenance of goods and the conditions of extraction, production, assembly and delivery –from understanding whether food and agriculture have been procured from sustainable sources to whether textiles have been assembled in ethical conditions. Businesses compete to ensure they can provide greater information on the products they sell, but doing so can involve great expense to track, store information, and label accordingly.

By incorporating blockchain and other technologies into the range of tools customs officials have at their disposal, they can highlight, investigate and intervene to remove possibly illicit or fraudulent products, thereby safeguarding the interests of consumers and businesses.

2. Current Technological Solutions for Global Trade Issues

Since the advent of the internet, new technologies that better enable businesses to invest and export are developed on a daily basis. Advances in technology have had the twin effect of reducing the natural barrier of distance and simplifying the complex web of rules and regulations.

I will briefly discuss a few different technologies that are particularly prominent in the field of international trade. This varies from the perspective of both customs and regulators to that of businesses.

Measures such as paperless trade are being explored and piloted by a range of governmental organizations. For instance, the United Nations Centre for Trade Facilitation and Electronic Business (UN/CEFACT) developed recommendations to incorporate electronic information flows to simplify, standardize and harmonize procedures. However, where paperless and electronic trade procedures measures have been introduced, there are issues regarding the inadequate implementation. In some economies, they are little beyond the pilot and concept stage of implementation.

Sophisticated simplification platforms have also been researched and piloted on a large scale to address some of the complexities within customs rules and procedures. Most prominent of these are 'single window systems'. These systems for customs organizations enable businesses to electronically submit applications for certificates, licenses, permits, customs declarations, and payment of tariffs and other fees at one single point. Reducing the multiple channels of interactions with different officials, regulators and inspectors to one single entry point significantly cuts the paperwork and inefficiencies associated with duplication.

Different technologies are increasingly being piloted and incorporated into global supply chains. Data analytics, track-and-trace technology, and/or Internet of Things (IoT) devices, Radio Frequency Identification (RFID) technology and artificial intelligence to name but a few. These technologies can identify the past and current locations of inventory items along a supply chain in order to reduce the burden on manufacturers and producers to produce a detailed audit trail. Owing to their well-tested potential to reduce costs, these technologies are located in several different industries, such as retail, logistics, food, and drink.

The different technologies discussed here should not be viewed as necessarily an alternative or rival to blockchain. Instead, a holistic analysis is required which considers how blockchain can interact with these different technologies, where are the shortfalls with each system and how could another technology remedy this. In order to obtain the larger picture of how these technologies can work, it is vital to understand precisely what blockchain means for international trade.

3.   How Blockchain Can Revolutionize Global Trade

I have witnessed first-hand how blockchain can be harnessed to break down the barriers to efficiency in global trade and streamline persistently paperwork-intensive customs procedures. However, can blockchain fully revolutionize international trade? This question has dominated conversations with my colleagues in the European Parliament, alongside the myriad headlines claiming that blockchain can transform all manner of policy problems.

Whilst blockchain is not a silver bullet, its key features of immutability, proof of origin and verification certainly have the potential to transform how we conduct global trade. And it is ready to be deployed today.

Blockchain can reduce the cost of transactions between parties by removing the need for physical paperwork, as well as the administrative hurdles imposed by third party intermediaries.

The revolutionary potential of blockchain stems from the enhanced trust that blockchain instils in transactions between parties. This in turn improves transparency, and strengthens the certainty of provenance of goods.

Among the multitude of benefits and applications of blockchain, I will discuss its potential to revolutionize two key areas within global trade, streamlining documentation and securing data flows.

Streamlining Documentation

The current paperwork-intensive nature of global trade transactions means that documents can be prone to errors, losses, and fraud. Blockchain has the potential to revolutionize global trade processes by reducing this dependency on large volumes of paperwork and manual verification of documents.

However, blockchain is not a single solution and we are a long way from digitizing global trade processes from start to finish. Even as blockchain solutions start to become integrated into trade transactions, it is inevitable that some forms of documentation and paperwork will still be required. Nonetheless, the streamlining effects of blockchain have the potential to facilitate further transactions on supply chains through reducing paperwork, thereby increasing global trade. When it comes to commercial transactions, I have noted from engagement with stakeholders that businesses may be averse to storing sensitive data on the blockchain. It is due to this reason that my report for the European Parliament's International Trade committee, 'Blockchain: A forward-looking trade policy', solely considered the use of private and permissioned blockchain for streamlining international trade procedures.

The notion of going paperless in global trade may not yet be fully realizable; however, the potential for blockchain to make customs more data-driven is real. For example, by participating in a blockchain network, customs organizations will be able to collect the data required for a good to pass through a supply chain in a more accurate and timely manner. Information recording the status, location, buyer and seller of a good could be collected and processed as data instead of a series of paper documents.

Distributed ledgers also allow all parties in a transaction to see the same information recording the status of consignments at the same time. This not only improves the ease of communication between parties in a transaction, but it also fundamentally provides mutual trust.

In order to ensure that blockchain can successfully drive down our dependency on documentation, both private companies and governments will need to work together to foster an open and transparent regulatory environment that remains flexible yet prepared to understand changes in technology. This is essential to allow for future innovation and developments in blockchain uses.

Securing Data Flows

Another important area in which blockchain has the potential to revolutionize global trade is through securing data flows.

Cross-border data flows are an integral function to global trade transactions, in addition to the blockchain architecture. By defining levels of access and validation procedures for users, blockchain has the potential to validate transactions across global trade transactions, from start to finish.

There is an undeniable connection between blockchain and cross-border data flows for global trade. A network based on blockchain can provide trust between different platforms by integrating previously disparate data from multiple sources. For example, data recording the provenance of a good and validating its progress along a supply chain may currently be stored in multiple sources. Blockchain can bring this data together in an immutable record.

Moreover, blockchain has the potential to facilitate and even strengthen the security of data flows to prevent the use of fraudulent documentation and counterfeit goods in global trade supply chains. For example, documents that require frequent amendments and verifications along multiple stages of a supply chain could benefit from greater certainty. This is because blockchain automatically registers documents and stores data chronologically without amending previous entries on the chain.

However, there is a notable challenge posed by the relationship between blockchain and the implementation of the EU's flagship privacy legislation – the General Data Protection Regulation (GDPR). By its fundamental nature as a database technology that allows for the decentralization of data, blockchain appears to be at odds with some of the requirements imposed by the GDPR.

However, the EU's Blockchain Observatory and Forum has stated that whilst there may be an impression that blockchain and the GDPR are incompatible, 'this is far from the truth'.

I believe that blockchain can actually provide solutions to the 'data protection by design' provisions of the GDPR through their shared fundamental common principles of ensuring secured and self-governed data.

In addition, the GDPR can have a more limited effect on commercial transactions, due to the absence of personal data stored on private and permissioned blockchains. There are intensive and currently inconclusive debates regarding the extent to which anonymized personal data stored on a blockchain can be compliant with the GDPR. However, the EU Blockchain Observatory and Forum has considered that the use of hashing to generate 'unique digital signatures of data' stored off the chain as a potential solution.

Given this evolving challenge, it is essential that necessary safeguards and regulatory oversight are implemented to consider cases in which GDPR applies to the storage of data on the blockchain. As part of this, blockchain architecture must be designed in compliance with the right to be forgotten and verified users of blockchain and blockchain-based applications should have access to the data directly related to transactions in which they are involved at all times, in accordance with rules of access.

Blockchain represents a new paradigm of data storage and processing which is capable of decentralizing all aspects of global trade, from human interactions along supply chains to trade finance. The rise in blockchain-based trade processes presents both opportunities and challenges for securing data flows, as data is immutable once entered in to the blockchain and shared with participating users.

It is important to recognize that blockchain by no means automatically supports data sovereignty, and therefore specific care must be taken to design blockchain architecture that achieves this. In this respect, blockchain and blockchain applications must integrate mechanisms into their design that ensure data can be fully anonymized. Private companies, national governments and international institutions need to continue to work to identify best practices for integrating these mechanisms as the deployment of blockchain solutions becomes ever more prolific.

When considering the transformative potential of blockchain for global trade, there are important implications for cross-border data flows. This is especially true of areas such as the fight against money laundering, tax evasion and the financing of terrorist activities. Through my work in the European Parliament's International Trade committee, I have maintained that the implementation of blockchain needs to be anticipated by delineating the information that will be stored on and off the chain – with an emphasis to personal data being stored off-chain. This is essential to ensure the positive potential of blockchain in global trade can be properly realized.

4. What Needs to Happen to Make this Work?

There are clearly a multitude of benefits and potential uses of blockchain for global trade. However, how can we actually make it work?

Several pilot projects and implemented use cases have demonstrated the widespread potential for blockchain in the global trade arena. There are at least 202 government blockchain initiatives in 45 countries around the world, with economies in the Asia-Pacific, Americas, and Middle East particularly investing in blockchain for trade.

In this context, it is more important than ever that best practices are shared in a policy and regulatory environment that is created to both foster an understanding of blockchain and encourage innovations in technology.

I will discuss three considerations that are essential to make blockchain work for global trade. These include regulatory considerations, international standards, and fostering greater understanding of blockchain to boost both commercial and public investment.

Regulatory Considerations
As Emmanuelle Ganne of the World Trade Organization states, 'going paperless requires more than the technology and technical interoperability. It requires a conducive regulatory framework'. The correct frameworks for recognizing digitized documents and transactions are essential for ensuring frictionless trade.

Given that countries have differing degrees of legal provisions to recognize tools, such as e-documentation and e-signatures, we are far from having a global trading system that allows for fully paperless trade.

Blockchain-based cross-border trade will require common definitions and regulatory frameworks; however, this does not have to mean the creation of burdensome legislation that will stifle innovation. Quite the opposite. Policymakers should be taking this opportunity to consider how regulations can be designed flexibly, to stand the test of time and welcome developing technologies. Commercial organizations must feed in to the design of these frameworks, placing priorities for business at the heart of regulation.

The UN/CEFACT points out national regulators will play a 'special role' as they provide a point of convergence for data. Since one of the key benefits of blockchain is the potential to integrate data from multiple sources, it will be essential for regulators to build mechanisms that can recognize and facilitate convergence.

Similar to commercial businesses, national authorities are unlikely to share access to sensitive information with participants outside of their jurisdiction. As a result, UN/CEFACT have highlighted that new ways to verify and share data with other countries in an appropriate manner will need to be developed.

The potentially heightened security created by storing data on a decentralized, immutable ledger could enhance current global trading practices by providing trust. However, flexible regulatory frameworks that can change with developments over time are necessary to facilitate this. After all, the impact on trust, security and consumer confidence from blockchain deployment in the future could be unprecedented.

International Standards
Another consideration for how we can make blockchain work for global trade is the development of coherent international standards.

In this area, the International Standards Organization (ISO) and UN/CEFACT are already making great strides towards developing technical standards that will allow blockchain to flourish across the world.

For example, the ISO is currently working to develop 11 international standards for blockchain, ranging from terminology to taxonomy and ontology, guidelines for governance to privacy and personally identifiable information protection considerations.

Furthermore, UN/CEFACT is considering the opportunities presented by blockchain for trade facilitation and improving e-business, identifying gaps in its existing standards for new specifications that focus specifically on blockchain. To achieve this, UN/CEFACT have proposed the development of a conceptual model of the international supply chain that demonstrates the role of emerging technologies, including blockchain, within a broader map of stakeholders, services and standards. Initiatives such as this are integral to building an international environment that shares understanding of how blockchain can best enhance global trade.

We need these internationally recognized standards to ensure that blockchain deployment can work across international supply chains and in global trading agreements. This is why my report, 'Blockchain: a forward-looking trade policy', called on the European Union and its member states to lead in the process of standardization.

Yet this is not solely a task for international institutions and national governments – commercial businesses must take the reins and actively contribute to advisory and working groups where appropriate to feed in their experience and perspectives.

Building Shared Understanding

Stakeholders from across commercial business, civil society and government must work to build a shared understanding of blockchain and its implications for global trade. This is crucial for encouraging investment in blockchain deployment through building confidence in the technology itself.

For example, the Government of Gibraltar launched a trade association in 2018 that aims to facilitate communication between policymakers and the private sector on driving approaches to blockchain. Through promoting high standards for professional conduct in blockchain and educational programmes to advance a fundamental understanding of the technology, this initiative looks set to build much needed confidence for the technology.

Moreover, through its Going Digital project, the Organisation for Economic Co-operation and Development (OECD) has actively reached out to national governments to raise awareness and increase understanding of digital transformation. Drawing on the need for cooperation and collaboration on a domestic level, the project highlights that digital transformation is truly transversal. In this vein, it is essential that the streamlining and trust-building opportunities provided by blockchain are harnessed in outreach to developing countries and transitioning economies.

Stakeholder engagement is at the heart of blockchain deployment for global trade. From citizens to commercial business, NGOs to national governments, the clearest way to make blockchain deployment work is to start from a holistic perspective. By sharing best practices and concerns about security, data protection and deployment, international frameworks can be designed with users in mind.

Through an open dialogue, a better understanding of the benefits of blockchain can be developed amongst stakeholders for global trade, thereby boosting confidence to invest in this technology.

5. A Blockchain-Based Future for Global Trade?

Although we are still a long way from a purely blockchain-based global trading system, the future for this technology does look brighter than the hype generated by the Bitcoin buzz.

A multitude of use cases now exist, from those pioneered by IBM, including the creation of TradeLens with Maersk and collaborations with Walmart, to the deployment of the world's first blockchain for cross-border trade in Singapore. These use cases demonstrate the wide-ranging potential of blockchain to streamline customs procedures and cut paperwork.

Ultimately, blockchain solutions to global trade problems should play a part in policy considerations. However, the international regulatory environment must remain flexible for now, in order to allow innovation to flourish. Nonetheless, commercial business and governments alike must be prepared to approach policy challenges related to blockchain head-on, and collaborate with stakeholders to find holistic solutions that do not constrain technological development.

There are, of course, those who will have concerns that through cutting paperwork and streamlining existing procedures, the implementation of blockchain-based solutions could risk jobs in global trade in the future. Yes, blockchain solutions have the potential to improve cost efficiency. However, the advent of blockchain in global trade also presents the opportunity to grow a new industry for research and engineering in its own right.

Indeed, blockchain must be researched and analysed in conjunction with other emerging and existing technologies. It is imperative that blockchain is not used as the sole solution or alternative means of working in every instance, as in some cases existing technology may be a more rational investment.

The potential impact of blockchain solutions in the global trading system on trust, security and consumer confidence is massive. This is a race to innovate, not a race to regulate. As such, whilst it is important to be mindful of the challenges that blockchain presents, business and policymakers alike must remain open to the radical potential of this technology and ready to step in where necessary to implement innovative solutions to finally break down barriers in global trade. Blockchain is the key to unlock huge potential and increased global trade creating prosperity for all.

Other Important Blockchain Benefits

Blockchain Theory for Good

The first part of my Blockchain research was highly focused around the world of decentralization and the sharing world or economy. This side of the Blockchain technology is potentially of great interest to me, but not for this book or for enterprise Blockchain.

Let me explain my views. A completely decentralized and shared world is becoming a discussion area in many circles, from academics to government to millennials to business. The vision of a world where everybody is equal and we all 'own' our share of the world which is all equal, could happen, and Blockchain technology would be a great supporter or enabler of this type of future.

My view is not so decentralized. We are all born into a centralized system – we get some sort of centralized ID when we are born. We attend a centralized education system; what it teaches is irrelevant, as most of the world has a centralized education system. We enter the world of work, often employed by a centralized organization, where we are given an employee number. We go to the health services and are given centralized records and numbers. I will not continue, but you get my point – we are 100% centralized, whether we accept this or not.

If you accept that this is our life and has been for hundreds of years, then I question how we can move to a decentralized world so quickly? We are not capable as humans to change that quickly, and most humans do not or cannot change – the majority of people like the status quo.

So if we accept that we are centralized and the majority do not want change, why would we have a decentralized world? It just seems impossible in the next few generations. I have no doubt that in 100 or 200 years, there could be a decentralized world, but there could also be aliens running the world or robots in charge!

In my first few months, especially around the Ethereum community, I explored this concept and how Blockchain can help to achieve this. I soon learnt that this, whilst noble, was a journey that would take centuries, and so I stuck to the world of real uses for Blockchain over the next 50 years, which will make decentralization a distant possibility, but a fundamental principle of Blockchain technology.

I look at this part of Blockchain technology as a 'belief system' and the vision of the 'shared and decentralized world' is a long way in the future. But we can take significant steps towards this vision by using Blockchain and other emerging technologies to become less reliant on centralized powers, and understand what these powers do and do not control.

Watching the price of Bitcoin during 2017 to 2019, it is obvious to me that the vision of a global decentralized currency has ruffled many feathers. The 'control powers' have made it very very clear that they will not let Bitcoin take over the payments and tax systems and government controlled systems. This is clearly, from the price crash and the control of the prices, to help drive miners out of business.

Was this a concerted effort by the powers that be, or was it just the natural markets playing out what markets are set up to do? If you look at regulated (aka centralized) markets they are governed and manipulated by the control structures; if you look at the unregulated world of Bitcoin and crypto exchanges, they are at the free will of any manipulation, by any party.

I am not suggesting that Bitcoin is the best example of Blockchain technology (in fact I do not think it is, and explain this later in Chapter 8), but I think it's a great example where the centralized authorities have made it crystal clear they do not like the decentralized currency.

As Blockchain technology matures, and more excellent use cases are implemented, the control structures will intervene – they always do. My hope is that they intervene pragmatically and do not stop the innovation that is happening in this world.

Without people thinking differently, the world will not change, and let's face it, the world in 2019 is having a very tough time. Change is not easy, and most people do not embrace change, but my end message on this is to 'step out of your comfort zone and learn about the transformation impact of Blockchain technology on your life and your business'.

Blockchain and Diversity

One area in which Blockchain technology is a massively important topic is around the diversity of the new world and the eco system. Within the Blockchain community, there is no old school stereotypical majorities and ownership. The fact that this is a new and innovative technology, which appeals to innovators, academics, entrepreneurs as well as the people who want a decentralized, less controlled world, has led to an exciting and beautiful mix of people.

> I see a complete mix of people around the Blockchain technology world who cross boundaries, borders, religion, sex, age, beliefs, sexual orientation, status, wealth, intellect, hobbies, disabilities, etc. The people who are looking into this technology see no boundaries and have a global mindset – this is important.

The ability to see the foundations of a technology which allows more control to each person, improves trust (in a world of fake news) and allows more direct relationships (fewer intermediaries) has brought together everyone from every sphere of life.

I love this part of the Blockchain world. I see fresh ways to look at the world:

- More trust
- Lots more sharing
- More collaboration
- Less judgement
- New and developing ideas.

There seems to me to be an 'in it together' mentality where we can develop this together and we are all equal in our contributions. Nobody, at this stage anyway, knows any more than any other person – Blockchain technology is still too new. If anyone tells you otherwise they are lying – it takes 10 years to become an expert and the reality of Blockchain technology is only around 5 to 7 years.

The mentality of 'in it together', is helping to develop some amazing communities, consortiums, and groups. I have been to countless meetups, held countless keynotes and met with countless users of Blockchain technology, and each time I find a new piece of information and learn something new about my world now and the world in the future.

The birth of this new technology, which is global and free, has meant that the old networks are now defunct – you do not need a certain name, a certain salary, drive a certain car or live in a certain country to add to this world – you can add to the development of Blockchain technology from anywhere with an internet connection.

This is exciting – this means you can be truly global and truly work with people from any background – I do this daily and I can only see this getting wider and more inclusive as we progress.

Technology is not just about making money and building business, it is also an enabler to a brighter, more inclusive and more culturally diverse world – embrace it and don't fight the change.

Blockchain for All Types of Organization

The great part of this being new technology and decentralized in nature, enables any organization of any size to get involved. The fact that the technology is relatively cheap to test and build (most of the main Blockchain technologies are open source and shared) means that we can all try and build Blockchain solutions. Of course, the larger business can exploit the tests on a much bigger scale, but individual people and start-ups can also use the technology.

Every day, I interact with Blockchain people, and these are from all areas of business, government, and academia. This wide pool of expertise has allowed many new parties to work together in ways that would not have happened in the past.

For example, the large corporates are hosting meetups, to allow the individuals and smaller companies the opportunity to work with them on solutions; the UK Government has established the All-Party Parliamentary Group on Blockchain (where I am a board advisor) which is made up of many different experts, companies, and government organizations; and the Blockchain-related conferences are filled with large and small organizations, all working together to build the Blockchain technology use cases and ecosystem.

This wide opportunity will allow different business models, organizations, groups, and structures to appear.

Blockchain for New Business Models

We are at the beginning of a new paradigm for life and business. In science and philosophy, a paradigm is a distinct set of concepts or thought patterns, including theories, research methods, postulates, and standards for what constitutes legitimate contributions to a field.

As you progress through the book, you will see that there are already a vast number of new concepts and thoughts which are shaping the world with Blockchain technology. I have covered the high level areas in this chapter, and will explore many more as we progress through the book.

What the new paradigm offers, is a new set of global ecosystem opportunities. These are still at an early stage, but you can see that this will lead to new ways of working together, new organizations, new markets, new ways to govern, new ways to manage your health records, etc.

This is the exciting part of Blockchain technology, where you can look to totally new ideas and work with others to build these ideas into real solutions and use cases for life and business.

Example: The DAO – Decentralized Autonomous Organization

A DAO is a new concept that relates to how a new company could be formed with no central authority and just a set of rules, coded into the Blockchain to make the business happen.

Let us take an autonomous self-drive car, which is driving around the streets dropping off its latest rider. After dropping the rider off, the car uses its profits for a trip to drive to a charging station to recharge its batteries. Except for the initial programming, the car does not need outside help to determine how to operate and fulfil its role as a driverless car.

A 'thought experiment' by former Bitcoin contributor Mike Hearn describes how Bitcoin could help power leaderless organizations 30-plus years into the future.

What Hearn described is one future use case for a decentralized autonomous organization, or a DAO, an idea that swirled through the community not long after Bitcoin was released in 2009. The thought is that if Bitcoin can do away with financial middlemen, then maybe companies and other organizations can one day operate without hierarchical management.

So, DAO's aim to program in code (Smart contracts), certain rules that a company would use from the beginning.

These smart contracts can be programmed to carry out a variety of tasks, such as doling out funds after a certain date or when a certain percentage of voters agree to fund a project.

Some followers say it can work for an organization where any sort of decision needs to be made, not just those related to money. Essentially, they see it as a way to cryptographically guarantee democracy, where stakeholders can vote on adding new rules, changing the rules, or ousting a member, to name a few examples.

My personal opinion is similar to my views on decentralization as a whole. There are obvious benefits to these types of organizations, but we are far too early in the maturity of Blockchain technology, and the maturity of our own selves when it comes to centralization.

Nevertheless, this is a great theory which some people within the ecosystem are actively testing, and I am sure there will be some great use cases around this over time.

New Blockchain Companies

Blockchain technology is bringing about many new opportunities and with new opportunities there will always be new business models and new companies.

Many of these companies are not even thought out yet, but there are many new use cases, which are leading to changes in the current world and opening opportunities for the new world.

Within the use cases, you will see new opportunities and some of these will grow to new companies. I also discuss at length how I believe the marketplace model will be transformed with Blockchain technology.

Blockchain Is Not a Verb!

And my final part of this introduction is around my favourite quote which is based on years of meetings and discussions around the world of Blockchain technology:

Blockchain is not a verb – you cannot Blockchain it

I have spent many meetings where people discuss Blockchain as a verb. . . 'Well we could Blockchain this' and 'We can Blockchain that'. You cannot 'Blockchain' anything!

We can implement Blockchain technology to help improve a process, or develop a new idea, but we cannot 'Blockchain it'.

This is a little tongue in cheek, but I do find that many people still have no idea what Blockchain technology is, and even more have no idea of the potential of Blockchain technology.

As you read through this book, I hope it will educate you further on the transformational possibilities of this new technology, and this will give you the thirst to learn more. The more people understanding the technology, the more widely adopted the technology will become and the more benefits of this technology will be seen, and sooner.

Let us now look at the different types of Blockchain technology to help develop our learning right away.

2

Types of Blockchain

There are many different types of distributed ledger technologies (DLTs) and many of these are classed as Blockchain networks. We will concentrate on the Blockchain networks and discuss the differences between the main three categories:

- Public
- Permissioned
- Hybrid.

The different types of Blockchain networks have different roles and will achieve different tasks. I believe that we need to work in a hybrid world where the Blockchain networks are interoperable and work together. Over the next few years, we will see many more Blockchain networks and DLTs – all of these need to work together as the unique characteristics of each network, complementing each other and enabling a significant ecosystem of many different solutions.

I have asked Chris Wing to talk about the different types and here is his excellent section on the different types of Blockchain networks.

Different Types of Networks

Chris Wing

a. Public Networks

Public Blockchain networks are networks that are public-facing and require no permission to access; anyone is allowed to join, read and write to a public network. Anyone in the world can send transactions through

---

Commercializing Blockchain: Strategic Applications in the Real World,
First Edition. Antony Welfare.
© 2019 John Wiley & Sons Ltd. Published 2019 by John Wiley & Sons Ltd.

the network and see them on the distributed ledger as long as the transaction is considered to be valid by the rest of the network. Although anyone can commit blocks to the ledger, data within the blocks and the identity of the individual making the transaction remains anonymous.

An example of a public Blockchain network would be the Bitcoin network. In its simplest form, Bitcoin is an electronic payments mechanism based on mathematical proof. Bitcoin uses a consensus mechanism called Proof-of-Work. The idea of Bitcoin is to provide a means of exchange without the need to rely on a central body to facilitate the transactions.

The influence of Bitcoin is ever-growing, giving individuals the ability to pay for real-world commodities, such as housing, technology and even beer. Within the world of currency and exchange, Bitcoin differs from traditional digitally traded fiat currency in several important ways.

Let's first explore what a fiat currency is and then we will explore in what aspects Bitcoin differs from these fiat currencies.

What are fiat currencies?
A fiat currency is by definition a worthless object, such as paper or cotton, which is given a monetary value by a state or government to be used in the exchange of goods or services within that jurisdiction.

Due to the fact that fiat money is not linked to physical reserves (such as gold, oil, water), it does have a high risk of becoming worthless due to hyperinflation. An example of a fiat currency going through hyperinflation would be the Zimbabwean dollar between 2008 and 2009. At the height of inflation, $1 (USD) would have been worth Z$2,621,984,228.

How are fiat currencies different from cryptocurrencies?
There are a number of key differences between cryptocurrencies and fiat currencies, aside from the obvious that one is real and the other is virtual; other differences include the supply of cryptocurrencies and how the currencies are stored.

1. Supply   The most notable difference between cryptocurrencies and fiat currencies is the actual supply of the currency itself, i.e. how the currency gets its value. Fiat money can be considered to have an unlimited supply, meaning government or authoritative bodies cannot limit or cap the amount of currency in circulation. Cryptocurrencies, on the other hand, have a hard stop at which they are capped; meaning once the limit of circulation is reached (for Bitcoin this cap is 21 million coins), no more coins or currency will be introduced into circulation.

2. Storage   Due to the nature of cryptocurrencies being a virtual currency, the manner in which they are stored or held is inherently non-tangible too. Cryptocurrencies are stored in virtual wallets, which is essentially a piece of software that holds an individual's private key corresponding to the account they hold on the cryptocurrency's network. Although these wallets claim to be secure, some have been hacked, resulting in people losing large amounts of money. Fiat money, on the other hand, is most commonly held within a bank vault to physically secure the currency within. Fiat money can also be held and transferred digitally, via the use of online platforms such as mobile banking, a service provided by all major banks.

b. Permissioned Networks

Permissioned Blockchain is a type of Blockchain network that requires users to have a special set of permissions or access rights before they can start reading, writing or even accessing the network. These networks control what subset of their users can be validators of blocks of transactions, or limit who can participate within the network's consensus mechanism. Another key attribute to permissioned networks is that in some cases the participants of the network may have the ability to limit and restrict who else can create smart contracts (if available) and/or commit transactions to the network.

An example of a permissioned Blockchain network would be Hyperledger Fabric. Hyperledger Fabric is a collaborative cross-industry solution which aims to provide 'plug-and-play' components that are aimed for use within enterprise scale applications.

Hyperledger Fabric requires all network participants to have a known identity; all network participants will also have roles which fall into one of three categories, these are:

- Endorser
- Committer
- Consenter.

The logic for processing a new transaction is as follows. An endorser peer receives a transaction proposal, which is then endorsed by one or a number of endorsers (the number of endorsers required depends on the predefined endorsement policy). Once an acceptable number of endorsements have been made, a batch of block transactions are sent to the committer peers, which then proceed to validate the endorsement policies and make sure they were adhered to. Finally, once both of these checks are completed and verified, the transactions are committed to the network's ledger.

Due to Hyperledger Fabric's (a Blockchain framework) network architecture, only endorsers and committers have access to the transaction, meaning the security of data on the network is improved as there are a fewer number of people who have access to key data points.

c. Hybrid Networks

In this section, we will explore two meanings of the term 'hybrid Blockchain network'. The first meaning is a network which comprises components from both public and permissioned Blockchain; the second will contain an explanation on Interledger, or, inter-network communication.

1. Public + Permissioned = Hybrid
Hybrid Blockchain networks are essentially a combination of both public and permissioned networks. They combine aspects of both (privacy of permissioned and openness of public) network types to form an entirely new network structure.

A hybrid network will typically consist of two components, a publicly accessible Blockchain and a privately accessible network (accessible by invitation only). Hybrid networks ensure that every transaction remains private but is still verifiable by an immutable record on a Blockchain that is public-facing.

Although the public aspect of a hybrid network allows anyone who joins the network to have the equal rights to view, modify, and append their consent to a transaction, individual identities still remain anonymous. This can cause an issue with enterprise organizations (for example financial institutions, or industries under heavy regulation) as they will always have strict KYC (Know Your Customer) policies put in place.

This can be tackled with the permissioned aspect of hybrid networks. Although permissioned networks are decentralized, secure, transparent and immutable much like its public network counterpart, permissioned networks restrict the right to view, modify and append transactions to only a few selected members of the network. This means that, for any given member, if an individual does not want their transaction information publicly visible without their permission, they can restrict the rights to view, modify, or come to a consensus with other members on the network.

What is the business case for Hybrid Blockchain? One of the biggest markets for hybrid Blockchain networks would be cross-border currency exchange and settlements. Currently, the infrastructure in place relies heavily on governments, large businesses, and banking groups to handle data and transactions could potentially lead to more internal processes and longer wait times for transactions to be completed. These governing bodies currently in place could greatly benefit from the efficiency and transparency Blockchain offers.

The reason Blockchain technology has not yet been adapted into this area is because multiple governed centralized organizations are required to be interacted with in order to perform a cross-border transfer or settlement. These organizations are governed in completely different ways and as such, no single Blockchain solution could accommodate this.

In summary, hybrid Blockchain networks can be used to build enterprise grade solutions that combine the power of both public and permissioned networks, using open-source technology across different industries to create powerful solutions to real-world use cases.

2. Interledger, cross-ledger communication
This section covers the ideas and technology behind Interledger, a platform that allows inter-ledger communication between different networks.

Imagine you and your friend are both on the same public Blockchain network, and you want to send money to your friend as you owe them for something. This is a simple task to complete: you get the details relating to their 'wallet', enter how much of the digital currency you wish to send and create the transaction.

Details of the transaction will be contained within a block; this block is then distributed to everyone on the network in order to verify it is valid and not fraudulent. Once general consensus is met, the block is then approved and committed to the existing ledger. Your friend then receives the amount you sent them and the transaction is publicly viewable within the network.

As mentioned before, this is a simple task to achieve. Now let's imagine, however, Person A is on Network A and Person B is on Network B. Both of these networks operate in a completely different way, use different consensus mechanisms and one is public and the other is permissioned. This now makes the act of sending money from one party to another a whole lot harder.

This is where the idea of inter-ledger communication comes into play. Inter-ledger communication of Blockchain networks gets its inspiration from the architecture of the Internet itself. The Internet is not just one network, rather multiple networks of networks, all connected together and communicating with each other using various protocols (in the Internet's case, TCP/IP). The Internet is analogous here as each person using it has a different ISP (Internet Service Provider); however, they are all still able to communicate with everyone else using the Internet.

When thinking about inter-ledger communication, the different Blockchain networks can be thought of as the different ISPs, and the nodes (people) on each Blockchain network can be thought of as people accessing the Internet.

This brings us to Interledger. Interledger is not a Blockchain technology, token, or service, but rather a set of standardizations and protocols to allow intercommunication between financial systems. As the example above, Interledger is largely inspired by the architecture of the Internet.

The suite of protocols provided by Interledger can be used within any network type – public, private and permissioned.

When two parties want to send money between one another, the party sending the money is called the sender and the party receiving the money is called the receiver. If the sender and receiver are not on the same Blockchain network or using the same digital currency, a number of connector parties must be placed in between to make the transaction happen. Connectors are used within the Interledger architecture to forward money from sender to receiver.

These connectors provide the services of forwarding packets of information (transaction information) and moving money, they also take on risk as they do so. As a reward for this, connectors are allowed to charge a transaction fee. It is these connectors that have the task of converting cryptocurrencies from one form to another; for example if Person A (P-A) wanted to send Bitcoin (BTC) and Person B (P-B) wanted to receive Ethereum (ETH), it's the job of the connector to make this conversion.

Packets of information relating to the amount of BTC being sent from P-A are sent to Connector 1 (C-1), C-1 then applies the current exchange rate of BTC to ETH and then sends a new set of packets relating to the value of ETH (minus any transaction/broker fee that may be applied) to P-B where they receive the funds.

Interledger sends information in packets, very similar to how the Internet Protocol (IP) works. Interledger uses three different types of packets, these are:

- Prepare
- Fulfil
- Reject.

Prepare packets are first created by the sender. This packet contains information about the transaction the sender is proposing. Connectors then forward this packet on until it reaches the receiver at the other end of the transaction queue. Receivers then either send back a Fulfil or Reject packet back to the sender (forwarded down the transaction chain once again by the Connectors) based on if the transaction is validated or not.

Prepare packets represent a commitment to pay the receiver if and only if the Connectors can prove that the receiver was paid.

Fulfil packets include the information that validates the claim that the receiver was paid. The proof here comes in the form of a hash (a function that converts data) that the receiver generates upon receiving the Prepare packet; this then gets sent back to the sender in the form of a Fulfil packet. If a Prepare packet gets lost or misrouted on its journey to the receiver, the sender will never get a Fulfil packet and thus money will never leave their account.

A Reject packet is sent from the receiver to the sender if the Prepare packet the receiver receives was not wanted in the first place, or does not meet the checks in place. It's important to note here that Connectors may also send Reject packets to the sender if the Prepare packet expires before a Fulfil packet is sent back to the sender.

Differences to a Database

Many people talk about Blockchain and databases interchangeably, and that is not correct. In order to explain, I have asked Vikram Kimyani, who is a Blockchain technical expert, to explain the differences.

Differences to a Database
Vikram Kimyani

There are quite a lot of explanations which will start off by saying that Blockchain is like a shared database, but not delve into the particulars. Some other descriptions will more accurately reflect that it is a shared ledger.

There is a subtle difference between a database and a ledger and it is useful to know what it is because this helps inform us of suitable use cases for Blockchain.

A database is a service where the value of some piece of data is stored somewhere and whenever there is an update to this value it is done in situ. It's also possible to remove information about data in a database and there are various strategies how this is handled and done.

A ledger works differently because it behaves like a document that has entries added to it. Entries are not modified if a value changes; rather, a new entry is created whenever something is updated. If you want to delete an entry, you stop recording related entries and corrections should be done by ADDING corrected entries.

Example:

Let's walk through an example of how this works in practice between the two stores of data. Let's say Andrea has a balance of 400 and that Bob has a balance of 200. In a database these values are simply created and recorded in some sort of table and if Andrea pays Bob 50 then both entries are updated in place. If no special measures are taken then there is no history of the original balances and it is a simple matter of looking up the balance to know Andrea has 350 and Bob now has 250.

In a ledger Andrea would have an entry for her initial balance of 400 and likewise Bob would have one for 200. If Andrea pays Bob then an entry is added to say that Andrea has paid Bob 50. In order to work out Andrea's balance you have to do something called 'walking the ledger', you start with the first entry and walk down the ledger until the last entry concerning Andrea. In our example you would note she had a 400 starting balance and then paid Bob 50 out of it and is therefore left with 350. You also have the full history of the transactions without needing to do anything special as it's a property of ledgers.

Why are we talking about these differences?

We are doing this because the audit or history properties of a ledger are what make it useful for some of the real-world use cases we are seeing. When you couple this with some of the other properties such as making it evident if a ledger is modified, sharing the ledger with all parties and having consensus upfront then there was quite a bit of excitement in the financial services industry about using the technology behind Bitcoin and they were one of the first industries to take Blockchain technology seriously.

Consensus and Blockchain

A fundamental part of building the Blockchain technology is the approach to consensus – this is where you need to understand that with Blockchain databases, you verify transactions WHEN they are entered into the Blockchain, whereas with a normal database, you reconcile and audit the transaction AFTER the transaction is entered into the database.

This is one of the fundamental concepts of Blockchain technology – the data is verified on entry and therefore all records of that data are final and cannot be changed.

I have asked Chris Wing, who is an emerging tech architect to take us through the different types of consensus and he starts with taking us back to the age of the Roman empire.

Consensus and Blockchain
Chris Wing

Section 1 – Byzantine Generals' Problem

To explain the Byzantine Generals' problem, we must first take a trip back to the Middle Ages. Imagine you are a spectator on a Roman battlefield, witnessing the Byzantine army preparing to attack a castle in the middle of a field.

The army has the castle surrounded, with a battalion stationed on either side, each a mile from its edge so as not to be seen by the enemy. Each battalion is in the command of a General who fully controls their every move.

A successful attack can only happen if all battalions attack the castle at the same time, swarming from all sides will surely overrun the enemy. However, if each battalion attacks individually, they will all be defeated. The Generals could, in theory, send messengers to one another to coordinate the attack, but there is a chance these messengers will be intercepted and killed by the enemy. This could also result in imposter messengers with fake messages, leading to each battalion doing something different and being defeated by the enemy. Additionally, one of the Generals could in fact be an imposter agent and purposefully send fake information to other battalions, once again resulting in all battalions doing something different (i.e. attacking at different times or retreating) and causing defeat across the Byzantine army.

And thus here the problem lies; how can the Generals organize a coordinated attack (or retreat) on the castle in a reliable and trustworthy manner? In other words, how can the Generals come to a general consensus on what action to perform?

This problem can be translated into digital communication in the situation where unknown parties are exchanging information with one another on a network and the reliability of each source is unknown to the rest of the participants on the network.

Byzantine Generals' Solution
Now we know the problem itself and how it comes about, how can we solve this to prevent it from happening in the real world?

The answer here is Blockchain technology. Within Blockchain, Generals can be thought of as nodes, messages being passed between Generals can be thought of as transactions, and the castle they are attacking can be thought of as a 'man in the middle' trying to alter the message information.

The solution Blockchain brings is a decentralized approach to handling transactions between nodes in a system. Messages on the network are digitally signed by the sender via cryptographic algorithms.

Section 2 – Different Consensus Mechanisms

a. What Is Consensus and Why Do We Use It?

As defined by the Oxford English Dictionary, Consensus is 'A general agreement', meaning it is an agreement between all parties involved within a transaction or process on the fact that something is to be determined as true.

Within Blockchain, different algorithms have been developed to achieve just this, agreement between parties that the value of a specific set of data can be considered valid. The purpose of these algorithms is to achieve a high level of reliability within a network that contains multiple unreliable peers.

'Doesn't this sound like voting?' I hear some of you asking; consensus mechanisms and voting on an outcome are vastly different. Voting on the one hand, while voting settings the majority rule without considering the emotional feeling of the people involved, general consensus ensures that the outcome of the decision is mutually beneficial for all party members involved.

These algorithms are called 'Consensus Mechanisms', and we are going to take a deeper look into six of them now.

b. Proof of Work (POW)

At a glance: Proof of work is essentially a requirement to define an expensive computational calculation; this can also be called mining. A reward is given to the first miner to solve a computational problem, or in other words, solving the blocks hash to get it added to the ledger. Miners on a network compete for these rewards by trying to out compute one another in order to find the solutions to these mathematical problems.

Proof of work is the original consensus mechanism used within Bitcoin. POW is a piece of data which is difficult to produce because it is mathematically costly and time consuming; however it is very easy to verify.

Within POW, miners compete against each other to complete transactions on the network to get rewarded. Within these networks, users send each other digital tokens; a list of these transactions are then gathered into blocks and stored within the ledger.

Producing a POW can be a random process with a low probability, meaning a lot of trial and error is required on average before a transaction within the network can be validated.

An example of a POW algorithm would be the Hashcash system used in Bitcoin. Below we will explore in more detail how the Hashcash algorithm works.

Hashcash   Hashcash is a POW system used to limit email spam and malicious attacks (such as denial of service) within networks, as well as the consensus mechanism within the Bitcoin network. This algorithm was first proposed in 1997 by Adam Back, a British cryptographer from London.

Before going into the technical details of how Hashcash works, it's important to note here that the specific algorithm and how it works is altered slightly to fit its purpose for Bitcoin. First we will explain the underlying principles of how the algorithm works, and then we will go into more specific details on how it has been adapted to be used within Bitcoin.

Base algorithm   For the algorithm to work, Hashcash requires a selectable amount of work to compute, but the proof can be verified efficiently. For use within emails (where Hashcash was originally intended), a textual encoding of a Hashcash stamp is added to the header of the email to prove the sender has expended an acceptable amount of central processing unit (CPU) time calculating the stamp prior to sending the email. Essentially, if it can be proved that the sender has taken a lot of time to send the email, it is likely they are not spammers and therefore the email can be thought of as trustworthy. It is also relatively easy for the receiver to verify the validity of the sender's stamp at minimal computation cost.

An example of a Hashcash header would look like this:

```
X-Hashcash:

1:20:1303030600:christopher.wing@oracle.com::McMybZlhxKXu57jd:ckvi
```

The header itself contains a number of values used within the Hashstamp. These include:

- ver: Hashcash format version, 1 or 0
- bits: Number of 'partial pre-image' bits in the hashcode

- date: The time that the message was sent, in the format of YYDDMM [hhmm[ss]]
- resource: The resource data string being sent, could be IP address or in the above case, an email address.
- ext: Extension (optional)
- rand: String of random characters, base-64 encoded
- counter: Binary counter, base-64 encoded.

c. Proof of Stake (POS)

At a glance: Within proof of stake, the probability of mining a new block is determined by the total amount of cryptocurrency the miner holds. So for example, a miner that holds 1% of the network's wealth may only ever mine 1% of the 'proof of stake blocks'.

Proof of stake is another cryptographic algorithm which aims to achieve distributed consensus within a Blockchain network. Within POS-based cryptocurrencies, the creator of the next block is chosen via various combinations of random selection and wealth (the value of the stake). In contrast to this, POW (mentioned earlier) utilizes mining to solve mathematically and computationally intensive puzzles to validate transaction and add new blocks to the ledger.

POS was first developed as an alternative to the POW mechanism, tasked with tackling the inherited issues that came with it – most notably that POW is computationally expensive.

When a transaction is initiated, the data which is put inside a block is then duplicated across multiple computers or nodes on the network. It's important to note here that the maximum size of one block within a POS network is 1 megabyte (MB).

Within POS, nodes are used as an administrative body to verify the legitimacy of the transactional data within each block. Computational puzzles need to be solved by nodes within the network to do this verification step; this is known as the proof of work problem. A coin is then awarded to the first node to decrypt each block. Once a block of transactions has been verified, it is added to the Blockchain.

POS attempts to solve one of the issues that the POW algorithm has; POW requires heavy amounts of computational power to be productive at mining in the network, which comes at real-world costs, such as monetary and environmental strains. POS solves these issues because the basis of the algorithm is not determined on the computational 'grunt' that each user (node) within the network brings, but more so the value of their investment in the network.

d. Delegated Proof of Stake (DPOS)

At a glance: Delegated POS relies on a subset of users within the network to be trusted advisors and verify transactions between everyone else. Advisors are selected by the network and are voted on based on reputation and trust within the community.

DPOS works in a similar but distinctively different way from regular POS. DPOS employs a 'witness' system to rely on a select bunch of individuals to verify transactions within the network. Only the witnesses in the network are paid (similar to transaction fees), and usually the top 20 witnesses are paid more. These witnesses are selected through a voting process performed by the whole network; usually only 100 witnesses are selected for the role.

When voting for new witnesses, the voting strength of each individual in the network is determined by the number of tokens they hold. So an individual with more tokens to their name will have a stronger weighted vote compared to someone else with fewer tokens.

As each network using DPOS grows in size, it becomes harder to remain as one of the network's witnesses as there is larger competition amongst users.

The power in DPOS systems resides in the fact that users within the network have the ability to retract their votes on select witnesses and re-purpose them elsewhere (i.e. to other potential witnesses) if they feel the witness in question is not doing a good enough job of securing the network and verifying transactions. This adds pressure to active witnesses to ensure they are consistently adding value to the network, ensuring the network is secure and only verifying legitimate transactions.

A DPOS system works because it enables users within the network to flush out unwanted and useless witnesses. This type of network, however, is fundamentally reliant on its users, meaning all users need to be active within the voting community, informed on what makes a good witness and how to increase the overall well-being of the network.

e. *Proof of Elapsed Time (PoET)*

At a glance: Proof of elapsed time is an alternative consensus mechanism which operates in an entirely different way. It requires users of a network to subscribe to using secure software environments which allows them to prove they are waiting for a 'truly random' time period. The user who waits for the shortest time gets to verify the new block and commit to the ledger.

Proof of elapsed time is a different consensus mechanism often used in private and permissioned Blockchain networks.

PoET requires each node within the network to wait for a randomly allocated amount of time, after which a node 'wins' and is allocated the new block. The 'winning' node is the node that completes its period of waiting first, so essentially within PoET networks the node to commit a new block to the ledger is allocated at random.

There are two important factors within the PoET network to consider when discussing its order of operations:

1. The nodes within the network genuinely select a wait time at random and do not fix the odds by purposefully selecting a short time.
2. The nodes with the shortest wait time (and therefore the 'winner') has indeed waited for the correct allocation of time.

The PoET consensus mechanism was developed by Intel and relies on a specialized CPU chip and instruction set called Software Guard Extension (SGX) to operate. SGX allows applications on that machine to run code that is considered trusted within something called a Protected Runtime Environment. Within PoET, the trusted code is the code that determines how long an individual will wait for, and ensuring that the 'winner' did indeed wait for the full time they were supposed to. This helps to keep the random selection between nodes in the network fair.

SGX This is a specialized piece of hardware that allows user-level code to allocate private regions of memory (also called enclaves) that are protected from other processes running on the system with higher privileges.

Aside from PoET, other use cases of the SGX chip include:

- Secure web browsing
- Secure remote computation
- Digital rights management.

Code that is deemed trusted by the SGX Chip must run in a private runtime environment, which is private to the rest of the system it is running on. In this context, private means the rest of the system cannot inspect the memory space of the trusted code.

By forcing a node within the network to run code in a private runtime environment, it enables a greater level of trust between the remaining nodes, as it removes the ability for malicious users to 'fix the odds' and make it so they are always assigned a shorter time to wait and therefore always win the new block.

f. Proof of Importance (POI)

At a glance: Proof of importance (POI) is a consensus mechanism which uses a node's importance within the network to determine who should be validating new blocks. Importance of a node is determined by various factors, and the overall score of the node determines their mining efficiency .

POI is a consensus mechanism used within the NEM (New Economic Movement) cryptocurrency.

This consensus mechanism is used to determine which nodes within the network are eligible to commit new blocks to the Blockchain. This process is known within NEM as 'harvesting'. In exchange for 'harvesting' a new block, a node is able to collect a transaction fee within that block. Nodes with a higher importance relative to others will have a higher percentage chance of being picked to commit a new block to the Blockchain. The initial criteria a node must meet before even being considered to be a 'harvester', is to hold at least 10,000 vested XEM (a cryptocurrency).

POI and POS work in similar ways in that, when deciding on what node should be chosen to commit a new block to the Blockchain that value of their holdings it has taken into consideration; however, POI has one subtle difference.

As explained in the 'Proof of Stake' section, POS limits a node's mining range by their current stake in the cryptocurrency's network. For example, if a node only owns 10% of a cryptocurrency then they are limited to mining 10% of each new block. This consensus model incentivizes nodes to save their coins to gain a larger percentage split of each new mined block.

Unlike POS, however, POI takes into account each node's overall support – or importance – to the network. This assignment of importance is calculated using graph theory to work out each node's rating within the system. The NEM Network does this by using three key pieces of information on each node:

- Vesting
- Transaction partners
- Number and size of transactions within the past 30 days.

Vesting:

- For each node within the network, a minimum of 10,000 vested coins are required before harvesting.
- A node with a larger amount of vested coins results in a higher POI Score.
- A node must have had these vested coins in their account for X number of days before they are counted towards improving your POI Score.
- 10% of currently unvested amount is vested each day to prevent coin hoarding between users.

Transaction Partners:

- POI works by rewarding users who make transactions to other users on the NEM Network.
- Nodes within the system cannot 'game the network' by trading back and forth between mutually owned accounts. This is because the POI algorithm only recognizes total net transfers over time.
- Number and Size of Transactions within last 30 days.
- Every transaction above a minimum size counts to the node's POI Score.
- The more frequently a node makes transactions, and the larger each transaction is, the greater their POI Score will be impacted.

Delegated Harvesting   The NEM Network is the first of its kind to offer a feature called 'delegated Harvesting'. Essentially this is an efficient way to pool together account power (here referencing individual node POI Scores rather than compute power) to increase the chance of harvesting a new block. For delegated harvesting, users will connect to a remote node and use that account's computing power to compute blocks on its behalf. Because each node has its own POI Score which dictates its chances of harvesting a block, pooling nodes together and adding POI Scores together can be beneficial and help increase a node's chance of harvesting a block.

Some of the key features of Delegated Harvesting include:

- A person's computer doesn't have to be running 24/7 to harvest new blocks.
- An account's private key is never exposed while harvesting, so there is no risk attached to it.
- Transaction fees can be collected for both multi-signature and messaging when harvesting new blocks.

Section 3 – Tragedy of the Commons

a. What Is It? Tragedy of the Commons relates to a scenario within Game Theory that concerns itself with market failure. The scenario occurs when a common good is produced in lower quantities than the public requires, or when a good is consumed in greater quantities than desired.

An example for this scenario would be pollution; it is within the public's best interest not to pollute, as collectively we are damaging the environment, but it is in our interest to do so as burning fossil fuels produces cheap energy – and individually each person does not contribute much to the environment damage.

b. How Does It Relate to Bitcoin? Tragedy of the Commons relates to Bitcoin in a hypothetical manner when the block reward for mining a new block drops to almost nothing. Due to the way the Bitcoin network is designed, miners get rewarded with Bitcoin (essentially a transaction fee) for verifying a new hash before it is committed to the ledger.

It is possible that in the future users will pay less and less for their transaction fees, causing the honest miners within the network to be under-incentivized for a lower fee, meaning there will be fewer and fewer miners to utilize – and thus the Tragedy of the Commons is realized.

This could potentially lead to various types of 51% attacks on a frequent basis, resulting in Bitcoin not functioning properly and a large lack of trust being placed within the system.

Due the nature of Bitcoin having a fixed max circulation (~21 million coins) a point in the future will be reached where no new blocks can be mined, and thus the incentive for miners to participate in the network will dramatically reduce.

c. Enterprise Blockchain – Cannot Be Affected by Enterprise Tragedy of Commons Enterprise Blockchains differ from standard Blockchain networks, such as Bitcoin and Ether, because they are engineered to suit a business focus and, as such, do not include cryptocurrencies. Some of the areas enterprises focus on are:

- Finding and preventing fraud
- Reducing cost/time of transactions
- Procurement systems.

For more information on real-world use cases, see Chapter 14 on the application of Blockchain use cases.

Enterprise Blockchain does not suffer from Tragedy of Commons because of the fact there is no cryptocurrency present, so there is no currency to consume and thus no supply and demand chain associated with it. The whole idea of Enterprise Blockchain is to improve efficiency and costs within an Enterprise, not to bring value and demand to a virtual currency. An example of an enterprise Blockchain network would be Hyperledger Fabric, a project which is part of the Linux Foundation.

ASG Consensus Example

 Let's think about this practically, when you record the stock receivables for ASG. When the finished goods arrive into the ASG warehouse:

With Enterprise Blockchain	Without Blockchain
The stock is entered into the Blockchain and immediately updates the whole network with the exact levels of stock.	The stock is entered into the database and immediately updates the database with the exact levels of stock.
This means that there needs to be a verification process to ensure the item quantity and quality is correct.	The data is not checked or verified and held on one database.
This could be where one ASG employee checks the garments and quantity and enters onto the Blockchain transaction pending, and the second ASG employee checks the garments and quantity and enters onto the Blockchain transaction confirmed.	At the end of the period, a stock count is taken and this finds that there are 100 items short of the original data entry. Due to the nature of the database, the person entering the data is not shown and there is no way to check the stock accuracy when it was entered.
If a stock count finds an issue later, you will know who entered the information onto the Blockchain and who verified this – speeding up an investigation.	In this case ASG would likely have to write off the value of 100 items.

Consensus is very different in an enterprise or permissioned Blockchain versus a public Blockchain.

The ASG example shows the enterprise consensus where the data has to be verified before committing to the permanent Blockchain record.

Current Blockchain and DLT Ecosystems

There are a number of Blockchain technology solutions currently being used. I will concentrate on the current four where I see the most benefit for enterprise Blockchain technology.

I will cover the Bitcoin Blockchain in Chapter 8 and will focus here on:

1. Ethereum
2. Hyperledger.

There are many more Blockchain ecosystems out there, but I have chosen to focus on these two in this book.

I have asked experts in each of the two Blockchain technologies to answer five questions about their respective Blockchain technologies:

1. What is [your Blockchain technology]?
2. What does [your Blockchain technology] aim to solve?
3. What are the main use cases running currently?
4. Why should enterprise clients use [your Blockchain technology]?
5. In your view, what will [your Blockchain technology] look like in 5 years?

In the following sections you will see their answers, views, and expertise.

Ethereum

Carlos Vivas Augier

Carlos is a Nicaraguan computer science engineer and the Global Head of Enterprise Education at ConsenSys. He co-founded two start-ups, one that was purchased and the other that was acquired by one of its shareholders. He led the Academy Program of Opinno, a tech consultancy firm, and the Spanish editors of MIT Technology Review and Harvard Business Review. He's been involved in the Blockchain space since late 2014. He has worked as a Blockchain advisor for tier-1 and large corporations in Finance, Energy, Health, and Retail industries, he was awarded 2nd place in a national-level blockchain hackathon and he coauthored two Blockchain books with top experts from the space.

1) What Is Ethereum?

Ethereum can be explained from both a technical and business perspective. Technically speaking, Ethereum is a decentralized platform for running a new kind of application known as a smart contract. A smart contract is code running on and taking advantage of Blockchain technology. The name can be misleading as it gives the impression that it is just for applications related to legal contracts. The term 'smart' references its capacity to make decisions from received inputs and its predefined conditions. The term 'contract' references its capacity to enforce rules and conditions between its users. It is easier to think of smart contract as just code running on a Blockchain; therefore, they are also immutable, secure, traceable, resilient, and trustworthy.

Before the Ethereum Blockchain existed, we did not have software that allowed us to run code or applications that leveraged the innovations and benefits introduced by Blockchain technology. The Bitcoin Blockchain enabled a peer-to-peer payment system, including some native scripts for escrow and multisig-wallets. Despite Bitcoin's usefulness, its features are limited when we consider the thousands of applications we use daily and that could be improved by Blockchain technology. Hence, Ethereum emerged as the platform to reimagine all the applications we use every day online and on our smartphones, and instead rebuilding them on top of Blockchain to take advantage of its core features such as immutability, traceability, security, resilience, and decentralization.

Though Ethereum is a technical breakthrough, its most significant impact is and will be for business. Just as TCP/IP (the protocol today's Internet runs on) gave birth to today's top players like Google, Uber, Airbnb, Facebook, and Amazon, Ethereum will enable the next version of today´s digital and shared economy. For example, we will be able to have all the services Facebook, Whatsapp, Uber, and Amazon offer to their users without any of these companies centralizing all the wealth and controlling all the data. Imagine that the fees companies like Airbnb or Uber charge their users (about 15%) reduced below 2%, and the rest of the value was split between provider and customer – leading to higher revenue and significant savings, respectively – for the exact same service. I personally believe that large corporations will benefit from Ethereum by introducing efficiencies and incremental innovations. The disruption of, impact on, and transformation of several incumbent industries, however, will stem from Blockchain start-ups and the 250,000+ developers of the Ethereum community.

2) What Does Ethereum Aim to Solve?
This question probably has several answers, depending on who you ask. If I had to summarize it in a simple statement, I would say Ethereum solves today's issue of 'trust', i.e. that we are forced to transact through intermediaries like banks in order to go about our daily lives. Ethereum aims to solve this by enabling a trusted environment for a peer-to-peer society. Today, we – individuals and companies – rely (or have to rely) on a third party for trust. Merchants trust payment processors, and individuals trust companies with their data (e.g. medical, identity, files, financial), companies trust external auditors and attorneys, and we

trust regulators to moderate the system, just to list a few examples. This trust model is very expensive and inefficient, and has proven itself unreliable on more than one occasion. Ethereum is enabling a new model for trust by not forcing us to trust others and keeping everyone accountable.

To illustrate, today, if I want to trace a product from its origin to check any specific characteristic (e.g. organic, fair trade, clean energy, green energy), I have to trust the information that the vendor provides me with. If I don't trust the vendor, I would have to track down the product's history myself and hardly anyone would invest this much time (I know I wouldn't). Therefore, I either trust the system or I run into a dead end. Ethereum allows me to check the product's history in a matter of seconds, trusting the data because the product's history is verified directly by each of the parties involved in it and the vendor has no capacity to manipulate it.

3) What Are the Main Use Cases Currently Operating?
Publicly, we are just seeing the tip of the iceberg in enterprise and mainstream adoption of Ethereum. Companies from a variety of industries have developed Ethereum-based products; however, most of them are still being tested in pilots or awaiting regulation to create legal clarity for Blockchain-based solutions. We must take into account that Blockchain technology has just emerged and the ecosystem needs to evolve and mature to support the creation of a larger number of use cases. We need to have supporting regulation, reliable infrastructure, generally accepted standards and norms, skilled Blockchain professionals, and user-friendlier tools before we see more use cases and mainstream applications. These drives have been one of the main lines of actions of key players from the Blockchain ecosystem and, despite great achievements, more efforts are still needed. However, it is just a matter of time. According to the World Economic Forum, '10% of global gross domestic product [will be] stored on Blockchain technology' by 2025.

Ethereum's most important applications will come from data applications, not cryptocurrency or tokens, despite ICOs being one of the most common applications currently running on Ethereum. Some examples of entities using Ethereum are:

- South Africa Reserve Bank (SARB) leveraging Ethereum technology to enable a wholesale payment system (Project Khokha).

- Kaleido providing enterprises with cloud-based infrastructure to quickly test and launch Ethereum-based solutions.
- BBVA bank issued a $150 million syndicated loan to Porsche Holding Salzburg (Europe's largest automotive distributor).
- Meridio enabling users to create and invest in shares of individual properties.
- The Austrian government is auctioning $1.3 billion worth of government bonds to be authenticated with Ethereum.
- Viant streamlines business processes, allowing companies and consumers to track digital assets on Ethereum.
- Atlas Insurance backs an insurance service using data stored in Ethereum, etc.

There are +1,125 live decentralized applications available on State of the DApps website.

4) Why Should Enterprise Clients Use Ethereum?
In addition to features such as immutability, security, traceability, privacy, permissioning, scalability, and decentralized applications that DLT technologies like Hyperledger Fabric or Corda offer, the reason I am a strong believer of Ethereum for enterprise clients is probably its feature companies value the least: a public Blockchain. This core component of Ethereum technology provides enterprise clients benefits that, as today, no other Blockchain or DLT technology provides.

Ethereum 2.0 natively enables interoperation between private and consortium Blockchains (permissioned Blockchain) and the public Blockchain (Ethereum Blockchain). Imagine a likely scenario where a bank is part of two different permissioned Blockchains, the financial Blockchain of North America and the financial Blockchain of East Asia. Sooner or later, the bank will have to move assets from one of these Blockchains to the other. Without the Ethereum Blockchain acting as a proxy between the two permissioned Blockchains, the bank is likely to have to pay, be dependent and trust some vendor's API (application programming interface) to move the assets. In addition, Ethereum Blockchain provides a space for all members of a permissioned Blockchain to snapshot the data in an immutable storage that no one can tamper with, especially members of a permissioned Blockchain with potential interest in manipulating their data. Moreover, the Ethereum Blockchain open source community is perhaps the largest Blockchain R&D laboratory in the world. Hence, all current and future Ethereum-based solutions will benefit from all the research and innovation developed by the Ethereum community. These are just some of the key elements of the value proposition of Ethereum to enterprise clients.

5) What Will Ethereum Look like in Five Years?
Ethereum will be the most technologically advanced Blockchain and the platform running some of the most important enterprise client and services of the digital and share economy. Today's limitations regarding regulation, privacy, storage and transactions per second will be over and forgotten (as we have forgotten about dial-up 128 kbps modems). Ethereum technology will intersect with other emerging technologies, like artificial intelligence, Internet of Things, and quantum computing, as the trusted environment and datasource for completely new and improved applications for changing the paradigm and disrupting the status quo.

A new generation of user-friendly tools natively integrated with Blockchain technology will be available for users, developers, and enterprises to develop entirely new business models on top of Ethereum Blockchain. The speculation and volatility around crypto will be over and Ether will become a global crypto-asset used worldwide for accessing mainstream financial, health, energy, legal, retail, education, governmental, travelling, and real estate services.

Hyperledger
Marta Piekarska

1) What Is Hyperledger?
Hyperledger is an open source collaboration of enterprises, open source community and developers that aims to promote the open source frameworks and Blockchain technology for business. We are hosted by The Linux Foundation that was set up 18 years ago to promote open source in every major industry. The Linux Foundation was started to give the backend for the PR, marketing, and legal infrastructure to help enterprises develop open-source frameworks while protecting their intellectual property. About three years ago, we started the Hyperledger collaboration, which is doing similar things with Blockchain for business technologies. Thus, we develop open-source Blockchain technologies and frameworks and bring that under the open-source umbrella.

2) What Does Hyperledger Aim to Solve?
Hyperledger aims to bring industry partners and open-source community together to create business Blockchain frameworks. The goal is to promote enterprise grade, open-source business Blockchain technologies, including distributed ledgers, smart contract engines, client libraries, graphical interfaces, utility libraries, and sample applications.

Hyperledger provides the underlying open-source software, on top of which anyone can set up apps to meet business needs. Built under technical governance and open collaboration, individual developers, service and solution providers, government associations, corporate members and end users are all invited to participate in the development and promotion of these game-changing technologies.

If Hyperledger could help, not only to forge common ground between different software development efforts, but also encourage a gradual detachment between standards, implementations, and global governance (whether that's around currencies or other use cases), then we will also accelerate adoption of Blockchain technologies widely and further reduce needlessly duplicated engineering and hardening efforts.

3) What Are the Main Use Cases Running Currently?
Within Hyperledger, we see the opportunity to develop a plethora of frameworks, rather than aiming for one framework. We think that the opportunity lies in giving people the ability to choose what they want to develop, rather than to tell them. We see ourselves like Sherpas that allow people to walk up that mountain and guide them through the process, rather than telling them how to do it. That is why the frameworks that are developed take the form of a Hyperledger ecosystem. Currently we have five different frameworks and six tools in the Hyperledger ecosystem. And probably there will be more to come.

Hyperledger Fabric is the most mature framework that we have in our portfolio. It is written in Go. It has its own smart contract language called Chaincode. Intended as a foundation for developing applications or solutions with a modular architecture, Hyperledger Fabric allows components, such as consensus and membership services, to be plug-and-play, which has graduated to version 1.2 in 2018.

Then we have Hyperledger Sawtooth which was initially donated by Intel and was one of the two – along with Hyperledger Fabric – initial frameworks. Hyperledger Sawtooth is written in Python. It allows for great flexibility and scalability. It is great for the Internet of Things (IoT) and supply chain use cases, even though it is also used in financial use cases. It uses a very interesting consensus mechanism called PoET, Proof of elapsed time, which targets large distributed validator populations with minimal resource consumption. Both Hyperledger Sawtooth and Fabric support pluggable consensus and solidity smart contracts.

There is Hyperledger Iroha, which is focused on mobile devices and IoT. It is very tightly memory controlled, written in C++. It is lightweight; you can actually run SPV proofs on mobile devices. Iroha comes from our Asian partners, a start-up Soramitsu. The consensus mechanism that is used in Iroha is called Sumeragi. While slightly less mature than our Hyperledger Sawtooth and Hyperledger Fabric, it is also a very interesting framework that I would highly recommend exploring.

Next, Hyperledger Burrow which is more of a library than a full-blown framework. Hyperledger Burrow is a framework that allows us to use the EVM – the Ethereum Virtual Machine – with all of our other frameworks. This is the implementation of Ethereum Solidity smart contracts under the Apache licence.

Finally, we have Hyperledger Indy, which is our answer to the identity problem. It has been donated to us by Evernym and Sovrin Foundation. It bases on the concept of storing private data off-chain and identity with the application to identity on the chain. Many governments today use it in production, though the framework has not yet graduated to 1.0.

We have six different tools that are major parts of Hyperledger. Tools usually start as part of a single framework and then they are abstracted to work with others. They usually start as useful developer tools and then become part of the Hyperledger offering.

There are no special regular global ratings so far to judge what are the best or worst use cases today. The trend is obvious. If Blockchain was initially perceived as a specific technical solution, today it has features of a basic solution for many industries and is viewed as a comprehensive technology. We have discovered endless possibilities of its application.

Of course, Blockchain is not a panacea. Nevertheless, it has unique characteristics for the business environment that were previously difficult to achieve, including accessibility, controllability, invariability of data, and improved trust infrastructure. Blockchain becomes an increasingly attractive tool for corporate governance, implementation of state structure functions, and, most interestingly – their decentralization and transfer to market participants. For instance, Smart Dubai is an initiative of the government of the Emirate of Dubai, which was created to accelerate and facilitate the interaction between citizens and the state by 2020 through Blockchain technologies.

Blockchain technology used to be hype, but now it is an opportunity to change the way we look at day-to-day business. Blockchain technology changes the way we interact in business context. It allows for an improved auditability, traceability, reliability of data. I don't see introduction of Blockchain technology as a revolution, but (when implemented properly) a massive opportunity for enterprises to reduce cost and trust they need to put in data coming from unreliable sources.

Some of the current use cases can be found at www.hyperledger .org/resources.

4) Why Should Enterprise Clients Use Hyperledger?
Under Hyperledger's umbrella are frameworks and tools that take different approaches to creating Blockchain solutions for business. The most important characteristic of Hyperledger is that we are not pay to play. Anyone can join, anyone can experiment and decide to join or leave at any point. We focus on permissioned enterprise-based Blockchain. And we welcome everyone to collaborate and to join.

There are many benefits to this modular approach:

- Allows for truly flexible modification of any of the components
- Common functional modules
- Defined user interfaces which improve the user experience
- Developers can re-use the common building blocks for ease of development.

Given the open-source nature of Hyperledger, enterprises have a guarantee that the code will not disappear with lack of support of a single vendor. It would have to be the whole community which decides that the project doesn't make sense for it to be removed.

Relying on one company to develop any single piece of code – Blockchain or not – is unsustainable in the long run. This is especially true when it comes to Blockchain technology. Think of the online games you played as a child that no longer get updated because the company went bankrupt. With open source someone else will be invested in this piece of code and will pick it up. So the code lifetime is longer than the lifespan of a single entity – this is especially important for the immutability of a Blockchain.

Often Blockchains within the Hyperledger project are permissioned Blockchains. The key is in the nature of Blockchain, which can be seen as a spectrum. If you look at how the Blockchain is structured, there are the permissionless public Blockchains, which is what the bitcoin or Ethereum Blockchain is.

On the very other end of the spectrum, there is the permissioned, private Blockchain. Those can be, for instance, medical records Blockchains. Blockchains where – in that case - you have a doctor and a patient, and they are the only ones to read from the Blockchain and write to that Blockchain.

And then there is a middle part of that spectrum: permissioned, public Blockchain, where only certain people can write to the Blockchain, but anyone can read from it. This could be your university certification Blockchain, where university professors could issue the university degree to a Blockchain, but anyone can read and make inquiries about whether this person graduated from that university.

You also have a Blockchain where anyone can submit information to the Blockchain but only certain people could read from that Blockchain. For instance, a voting system, where anyone can submit poll, but only certain people can verify those votes. That's permissionless, private Blockchain.

This is all in terms of technology, now, why do enterprises join Hyperledger as members? Because the project provides them with networking, PR, and marketing opportunities. Everything that is technical is open source and anyone can use it. But the hard work of connecting entities, which is crucial in today's Blockchain world, is the heavy lifting that Hyperledger does.

5) What Will Hyperledger Look like in Five Years?
Ultimately, there will be many public chains and millions of private chain distributed ledger systems designed for specific marketplaces. They will interoperate over standards and ideally each use a common base of technology, much like how the Linux community uses the common Kernel operating system. Potentially, each will have a different consensus mechanism, preferred smart contract language, and other unique characteristics.

In this environment, the most valuable role that Hyperledger can play is to serve as a trusted source of innovative, quality-driven open-source software development community, creating modular, open-source components and platforms. The optimal focus of Hyperledger is to advance industry goals of distributed ledger and smart contracts.

Hyperledger is forging a brand to be seen widely as the accepted default, 'safe' deployment platform for enterprise teams, and as a great home for active collaboration around new technologies.

Current Blockchain and DLT Ecosystem Summary

I have used two Blockchain technology ecosystems in this book, and there are hundreds of Blockchain technologies currently being tested and used. The focus on these two is to stay true to the theme of the book 'Strategic Applications in the Real world'. These Blockchain technologies are being used today with enterprise-level clients, and have some real applications that we have discussed.

This chapter is not investment advice and is not stating any preference for a certain type of Blockchain technology ecosystem.

3

Enterprise Blockchain

In this book, I will spend most of the time looking at Enterprise Blockchain technology. This is because the real adoption of Blockchain technology will be through large business and government organizations – organizations which process millions of transactions will be the biggest beneficiaries of Blockchain technology.

Enterprise Blockchain technology can also be known as private and permissioned Blockchain – these two further names give away some of the reasons why we have enterprise Blockchain

Enterprise Blockchain and Trust

Enterprise Blockchain is needed for the same reason as public Blockchain – the world of trust has changed and we live in a 'trustless' world (see earlier chapter for more on trust and Blockchain technology).

Enterprise organizations are complex and global – they span many divisions, teams, and entities internally AND they span many different external partners and organizations.

An enterprise network spans a significant number of different 'parties', the majority of which do not trust each other. Even inter-company is a trustless world – even though you are part of the same group company, you are still governed and incentivized by different people and leaders.

Outside the internal network, trust is extremely low – even though these organizations are your partners, you still do not fully trust them.

Commercializing Blockchain: Strategic Applications in the Real World,
First Edition. Antony Welfare.
© 2019 John Wiley & Sons Ltd. Published 2019 by John Wiley & Sons Ltd.

Characteristics of Enterprise Blockchain

There are a number of key characteristics of an enterprise Blockchain organization:

1. Global – organizations which span different countries and often span the entire globe.
2. Scalable – these organizations require solutions which scale to their needs which often involve millions of transactions.
3. Secure – these organizations often deal with large volumes of private data related to people and property.
4. Speed – these organizations work at speed, and they often need to process their transactions at speed and with accuracy.

Enterprise organizations, with these characteristics, need to use an enterprise Blockchain for the above-listed reasons.

Why Use Enterprise Blockchain?

You may wonder why you need to use enterprise Blockchain, and many reasons are covered in other chapters as to the general benefits of Blockchain. For enterprise organizations, the challenges are bigger and more complex – the need for a different type of Blockchain is important.

The world is changing fast, and digital transactions and technology are advancing quickly. This is causing unprecedented levels of competition – from existing organizations and new organizations who can grow and scale fast in the new world.

Adopting enterprise Blockchain technology will allow an organization to compete with the new entrants to their world and help keep them ahead of their competitors.

The following are main pain points your organization is experiencing and where enterprise Blockchain will make a difference.

- Enabling trust in business to business transactions, both internally and externally.
- Reducing or avoiding the cost of intermediaries, which can add significant costs in a highly competitive world.
- Avoiding the risks of intermediaries, which can slow down process or worse, allow data breaches or other risks to occur.

- Reducing the manual, human error-prone information exchange and processes across enterprise systems, both internally and externally.
- Reducing the high cost and delays of offline reconciliations, which slow down analysis and decision-making.
- Removing the poor auditability of records due to cross system discrepancies and reconciliation issues.
- Reducing the high risk and cost of fraud in cross company transactions.
- Eliminating the lack of real-time information visibility within a trading ecosystem.

Where to Use Enterprise Blockchain Technology

Blockchain technology is not a solution for every issue in your organization, so a great place to start is by asking yourself these questions – if you respond yes to most of these questions, then you need to look at implementing Blockchain technology in those areas affected:

- Is my business process mainly multi-department and cross organizations?
- Are there cross system discrepancies which slow down decision-making?
- Is there less than full trust among transacting entities?
- Do my processes involve intermediaries – charging fees and adding risk or delay?
- Do my processes require periodic offline reconciliations?
- Is there a need to improve traceability or audit trail?
- Do we need real time visibility of the current state of multi-party transaction?
- Can I improve a multi-party business process by automating certain steps in it?

There are many more questions to ask, but if you start with these, you will begin to establish which processes and business areas would benefit most from Blockchain technology.

The Next 20-Year Transformation

Over the last few years, we have had many transformations – BPO, digital transformation, Six sigma, etc. – and all of these have transformed the competitive landscape. We are now entering the next stage of transformation.

I would argue that we are at the start of the next 20-year transformation cycle – Blockchain technology will allow organizations to completely transform their entire business.

> I am not saying Blockchain technology will transform every business process, I am saying that the adoption of Blockchain technology will transform many parts of your organization, and this will transform your entire organization.

If the benefits of Blockchain technology can be harnessed effectively, businesses will be able to transform their current back end systems and gain significant efficiencies and benefits.

The complexities of large enterprises have grown exponentially, as they have developed new systems to keep up with the pace of change in the customers' world.

> This has led to many large, complex, and unwieldy systems, which now slow down the enterprise and act as an 'anchor to growth'.

The entire complexity of enterprise systems can be simplified, and in some cases automated, with Blockchain technology. This will allow the enterprise to concentrate on its customers, and ensure that they are continually meeting or exceeding the customer expectations.

Total Business Transformation Led by Blockchain Technology

Blockchain technology will transform many parts of an enterprise, and these changes will help to create a culture of change throughout the entire business. The changes will affect all areas of your business, and this will help to transform the culture and the people working within your organization.

One of the fundamental Blockchain concepts regards the sharing of data and transactions – currently, in most organizations sharing data is often complex, inaccurate, and time consuming. Data is often not shared for these reasons, and yet if we had the accurate data needed for our jobs, we would no doubt be able to perform much better in our roles.

If Blockchain technology helps the sharing of accurate data, I would suggest that your organization would be able to make better, quicker, and smarter decisions – decisions in all areas of the business which will have a positive effect on the business performance.

Improved Working Together

The sharing of more accurate and timely data will make people's roles easier, and allow them more time to analyse and question the data. We often have little time to review the data before we make a decision – and this often leads to complications in other parts of the organization.

If we had the time to look at the accurate data, we would have more time to work with our colleagues and find solutions and conclusions together – and remember: two (or more) brains are better than one!

We could also look at AI and ML (artificial intelligence and machine learning) which would be more accurate and useful if it was using accurate data in the first place.

Basics of an Enterprise Blockchain

An enterprise Blockchain is a permissioned Blockchain, where all parties in the Blockchain ecosystem agree to be part of the network and agree to the consensus rules.

To establish an enterprise Blockchain, the parties will agree the following areas:

1. The purpose of the Blockchain.

2. The data and transactions that will be implemented on the Blockchain.
3. The parties involved.
4. What the administration function will look like.
5. The consensus rules.
6. The dispute reconciliation process.
7. The channels to be set up (a channel is a private set of transactions between two parties within a Blockchain, which only they can see).
8. Technical areas, such as speed, verification, approval, and data usage.

I am not a technical expert so this is where my basics section will end, but there are some great technical blogs and books out there, where you can learn the intricate details of building an enterprise Blockchain.

Blockchain and ERP: The Future of the 'Back Office' – ERP 2.0

My background is finance within retail, and I am a qualified accountant, which means I have spent the majority of my career using two systems:

1. ERP – Enterprise resource planning tools
2. Excel – Spreadsheets.

An ERP system is best known as the 'back end' of the systems – this is the enterprise-wide system which accounts for all the transactions, finance, and other data. ERP is normally connected to the supply chain systems, which looks after all the physical products within the supply chain of the enterprise.

Alongside ERP, most enterprises also have an HR system in order to look after the employees within the business and CX systems (customer experience or front-end systems), such as ecommerce websites and mobile apps.

Together these back-end systems and CX make up the core of the business operating systems. These systems are often large, unwieldy, complex, and old – often over 20 years old in large global enterprises.

Can Blockchain Technology Supercharge ERP?

The problem with existing ERP systems is that they often perform transactions that are inefficient, expensive, and vulnerable. The transactions are also very costly to maintain and audit, and difficult to track.

Blockchain can help enterprise users gain advantage from the old systems. Core to their business, these systems need to be updated regularly and need to be flexible to adapt to the fast-changing customer world.

The current versions of ERP are based in the cloud, which gives a number of advantages, the main two being: (1) the 'always-on' technology, and (2) it is always the latest version of the ERP, and more importantly, the latest updates to take into account changes in business, regulation, and the general business environment.

Once a business is upgraded to the cloud with the back-end systems, there is then a great potential to superpower this by adding the emerging technologies, including Blockchain technology.

What Can Blockchain Add to ERP?

There are a number of areas where Blockchain can add value to ERP systems – remember that Blockchain is great for complex, cross-party transactions – the heart of ERP is complex with cross-party data and transactions.

Blockchain technology can extend the boundaries of the enterprise – with Blockchain technology you can take information, that would have previously been stored in the ERP silos of just one company, and it is available in a trusted system of records across different entities. When you apply this new capability to reinventing your ERP systems, the possibilities are practically endless.

Using ERP systems with Blockchain technology can provide greater visibility into a wide range of processes, including order capture, shipping, supply chains, equipment maintenance, and dispute resolution systems.

Transactions recorded via Blockchain technology are designed to be secure, trusted, immutable, and completely transparent to all parties within the enterprise network.

These are key to help you streamline the expensive, inefficient processes currently found in the ERP systems, with a new approach which can:

- Save time for all parties involved
- Lower costs throughout your network
- Significantly reduce risk
- Help build trust with your business partners
- Streamline future transactions.

ERP often works seamlessly with the supply chain and I talk about many of the great use cases within the supply chain later. There are also many use cases within finance services which will also be based on supercharging the ERP system.

Blockchain and Planning

One business function that every entity must (or should) carry out on a regular basis is around budgeting and forecasting. Any enterprise needs to manage a large amount of resources (i.e. people, assets, transactions, partners, etc.) and this takes a vast amount of planning and 'future gazing'.

The current process of forecasting and budgeting usually comprises of a planning system or a set of complex spreadsheets. These use forecasting metrics and levers to assess what the future may look like. This will give you the plans for the future requirements for the entity.

Once the enterprise is working, there is a need to analyse the results of the business and adjust the budgets and plans for the future. One major problem here is that the data which feeds the actuals, forecasts, and budgets is taken from many different systems and sources, and not all of these will be correct and accurate.

Blockchain and Analysis

The data taken from Blockchain has been verified and validated as it was entered into the Blockchain. This means that, statistically, it will be of better quality than data which has been entered into a database without any validation.

Analysis of data takes vast amounts of time and energy, not just computing power and big data, but for the humans (and even robots) who need to understand the data to look at trends, patterns, and next best actions. If you use low quality data for this, the results and findings will be of poor quality. This causes a vast amount of wasted time and resource.

In one of my previous roles, I was commercial finance director of an £8bn turnover retailer. My role was to forecast the buying requirements for the group of around £4bn across tens of thousands of product lines. The process was managed via a team of 20 analysts and a very large and complex set of spreadsheets. We used many input variables and made many assumptions to develop the forecasts and budgets for the retailer.

The problems we encountered:

1. Many different data sources and lack of validity on this data.
2. Many different assumptions and no validation of these.
3. Various people were involved, with different version numbers.
4. Data was sent at different times, and was a 'view' of the raw data at that time.
5. Reconciliation and validation of data was almost impossible due to the scale.

How Blockchain Technology Can Transform Forecasting and Planning

In my view, Blockchain technology can transform the process of forecasting and planning from where we are today.

We currently have many excellent planning and forecasting tools, which have now replaced the Excel spreadsheets which I once lived my life using. These systems take the 'spreadsheet' philosophy and automate the processes, listed above, which were problematic.

There is, however, the opportunity to use Blockchain technology to take these forecasting systems to the next level. Adopting the principles of Blockchain technology in forecasting and reposting would mean the following changes and benefits:

1. A shared ledger of the forecasts would ensure the same version of the forecast is seen by all parties all the time. Even with the excellent planning tools now, there can still be issue with version control.
2. Validation of the data as it enters the Blockchain will ensure that the analysis is completed with accurate and timely data – ensuring that the forecasts and analysis from this data held on Blockchain is more accurate and as current as possible.

Using Blockchain technology on top of the current forecasting and planning tools will give that extra level of accuracy and enable the entity to be even more efficient with their planning and analysis.

Use Case: Blockchain and Intercompany

An interesting use case relating to all enterprise entities occurs around intercompany transactions. For those who are not familiar with this, these are the transactions which take place between the different legal entities, divisions, groups, and countries within a government, or between enterprise organizations.

These transactions are estimated at 65% of the total global transactions. This is a scale beyond comprehension if you think that there are around 700 billion,[1] then you are talking about a vast number of transactions which are, in reality, internal to one group.

These transactions are sometimes referred to as 'wooden dollar' because they should not affect the overall profit or cash position of an entity. They are used for many things, such as:

- Transfer pricing – 'selling' goods and services internally to the group entity.
- Cost transfer – sharing costs from one entity to another within the group.
- Asset transfer – moving assets around the group.
- 'Cash' – settling outstanding bills internally with 'real cash'.

The issue with these transactions is that they currently need to be reconciled and each side needs to agree the amount; this is where Blockchain technology is critical. As I have discussed, trust is the main benefit of Blockchain technology and trust does not exist between all entities within a group.

This lack of trust leads to significant inefficiencies and time spent reconciling and 'arguing' about the amount of the intercompany balances.

This lack on one view of the truth leads to external issues:

1. Liquidity issues – if you have a number of intercompany balances and they are not settled daily, there will be 'real cash' sitting in parts of the group that may or may not be where you want it. For example, you may have a positive cash balance in your German entity,

---

1 See www.paymentscardsandmobile.com/global-non-cash-transaction-volumes/.

but due to intercompany issues, there is no settlement to the USA entity – this means the USA entity now needs to borrow cash instead of using the cash in the other entity.

2. Foreign exchange management – most intercompany issues span different currency regions, and as such, means that intercompany delays and issues stifle the ability to manage your FX risk well. For example, the German euro account could be better used in the US dollar account but the money is stuck in the wrong currency, which can lead to real losses for the group.

3. Tax and regulatory reporting issues – most countries have similar, but different, rules around accounting and reporting of financial performance. You could easily find a situation where you have a balance in one entity not agreed with another, but one entity must report a final figure for the regulatory deadline. With tax, this could mean paying too much or too little tax and not being able to maximize your tax liability efficiently across the group.

4. Mergers and acquisitions – when it comes to buying and selling entities, there is often a neglected intercompany balance sheet which could uncover surprises to both the seller and the buyer. If the intercompany accounts are not managed well, when one entity from the group is sold, there may be balances within that entity which should be in another entity – meaning that you could give away more or less of the business than you think.

Blockchain technology is a critical solution to the intercompany issue as it will automate the entire intercompany process, eradicating the need for intercompany reconciliations, and ensuring that any balances and issues are surfaced quickly and dealt with efficiently

The following are key benefits where Blockchain technology can solve the issues around intercompany processes:

1. Eliminate reconciliations and manual errors – if you completely automate the intercompany process, via agreed rules/consensus and automation of transactions, you will remove the need to reconcile the balances. You will instead move to an exception management process whereby exceptions are highlighted automatically and dealt with quickly.

2. Headcount efficiency – there are many people working on reconciling these transactions and these could total hundreds of people. These roles will be removed using Blockchain technology and the remaining teams can focus on agreeing the intercompany processes, implementing them, and dealing with exceptions and errors.

3. Liquidity management – once you have a clear view of your balances, especially cash, you will be able to manage the day-to-day cash needs of your enterprise quickly and transparently. You can move cash quickly to where it is needed, and ensure that your borrowing and expenses are minimized via transparent planning using the data held on the Blockchain.

4. Foreign exchange risk is minimized – nobody likes paying fees for exchanging currency, so a well-planned FX strategy is a must. This can only be managed if you have a transparent view of all your cash, across all your entities.

5. Foreign exchange risk is removed using cryptocurrencies – one real use case for cryptocurrencies is for international payments. If the group decided to use one currency across their business, they will remove the FX risk and transact on a very low cost basis vs. changing different currencies across the group.

6. Tax regulations – tax is a globally complex area. There are many tax laws which are different across countries, entities, and industries. Managing your tax to be the most efficient needs a transparent view of all the entities in the group and a single, and accurate, view of all the data and balances. The tax experts can then maximize the tax in a legal and efficient way.

7. Local regulations – these vary for each country, entity, and industry. There are many different rules and regulations that each entity within the group must adhere to. Having a transparent view of the entire business will enable the group to ensure that each entity is able, and armed with the right data, to deliver the requirements of their regulations as and when they are required.

8. Acquisitions and mergers – global enterprise groups are often buying and selling entities within their group. Intercompany balances do not help this process and can cause issue around valuations and regulations when they are trying to buy or sell an entity. Blockchain technology can help provide a transparent and accurate view of the single entities' balances, which can then be confidently understood and trusted in the transaction.

There is much more complexity around the intercompany world, but this gives you a great flavour of how implementing Blockchain technology solutions here will significantly benefit the enterprise, the governments, the regulators, the tax collectors, and ultimately ensure the customers and staff of the enterprise can trust that the enterprise is run in an efficient and trustworthy manner.

Due to the significant potential of Intercompany and Blockchain across all organizations, I asked an expert to tell me more about this and his experience of Intercompany on Blockchain. Vikram Kimyani tells us how he sees Intercompany on Blockchain:

Intercompany on Blockchain
Vikram Kimyani

Before we discuss this use case it's good to get a reminder of what a ledger is as it's important for this use case. Ledgers began life as a way to record quantities of an asset around 5000 years ago in Mesopotamia; they are the first form of writing known to man. Put another way, accounts were invented before writing! As time went on ledgers got more detailed and were used mostly for accounting purposes as they were a useful record of a particular account. However, central or single ledgers are prone to errors or corruption and this was a problem for trying to keep track of incoming and outgoing assets. This led to another innovation we know as double-entry bookkeeping, where the principle is such that a transaction must be recorded twice, once as a debit and once as a credit. In order to make sure there aren't errors, the sum of credits must equal the sum of debits. Over the years this system of double-entry accounting has stuck with us.

Now consider most large global organizations are not actually one company; they are often made up of a group company and various companies in different jurisdictions so that they can satisfy various local laws or ones that operate different brands or have been acquired over time. The same system is now spread across two entities within the same group and it must be checked and validated. As an example, say I am LargeBank group and I need to prepare my accounts for the shareholders. I will need to account for all my assets and liabilities and let's say LargeBank India has made lots of loans. Those loans will need to be recorded as a liability against that Indian entity in my group account and the chances are we are using different procedures, software, or systems. LargeBank India would need to send over their entries to the group and LargeBank group would need to share its view of the subsidiary's account. If they both match then we have nothing further to do and we are reconciled, if they don't then emails and phone calls will ensue to get to the bottom of the matter.

Problems start to arise when the two entities start to diverge and that's when both entities need to start exchanging information and verifying transactions. This can happen for various reasons such as renaming assets, incorrectly assigning items to the wrong entity, simply by using two systems or simple entry errors. This time, however, you will have the possibility of penalties for incorrect financial reporting. Month-end or quarterly-end reporting is a very frantic time for most large companies as they undertake their accounting exercise. They typically have dedicated teams just to reconcile all of this information, make sure it matches what has been recorded, carry out investigations and make corrections where needed.

The properties of a blockchain lend themselves well to the way accounting is done and can be considered as a potential triple-entry type of system. Each entity needs to maintain control over its data but must be able to share this either with the group or entity on the other side of the transaction. All transactions must be trusted but the entities do not necessarily trust each other to not make mistakes. This need to control, and the lack of trust between multiple parties within a single corporate structure, make this an ideal use case for a blockchain and because we are talking about needing control over the privacy of the data then we need at least a permissioned and closed blockchain for this.

As most financial reporting needs to go to some other party, we can also permission them to join into the network. Now as entries get created we will be able to match them as they come in and not even commit the ones that are problematic because we would not have consensus. That means we can trust all the entries that have made it onto the blockchain and anything that hasn't are the ones we will need to look at further. By taking advantage of these properties then the compliance and reconciliation teams can be smaller or redeployed to other activities that are more useful to the business. Auditing becomes easier as there is now an immutable record of transactions and potentially reporting to national bodies is no longer required as they have access to the information in real time to run their own reports.

ASG Intercompany on Blockchain Example

 Let's look at how Blockchain technology could improve the intercompany transactions of ASG.

As we know, ASG operates in 11 different countries and has a number of different entities in each country. This has led to a number of issues around the intercompany accounting:

1. Unreconciled transactions – each entity has a different view of the intercompany transactions which is often left unreconciled.
2. Transfer pricing agreements are often implemented poorly and some transactions are not currently handled.
3. The tax reporting deadlines in the different countries means that ASG often has outstanding balances reported externally, when they are not reconciled internally.

Let's look at intercompany process with Blockchain technology:

1. All ledgers are connected as nodes to the Blockchain network.
2. The intercompany transaction must be validated and verified by both entities before the transaction is confirmed on the Blockchain network.
3. The transactions cannot then be changed or altered in any way.
4. Settlement of these balances is then run by the treasury and tax functions, who can see all the outstanding balances via their Blockchain network node.
5. Settlements are carried out using smart contract on the Blockchain network initiated by treasury and shared instantly on the Blockchain network so that all entities see the current balances at all times.

The benefits of using Blockchain technology for ASG:

1. Significantly reduced finance teams – a large number of people were employed in each entity to reconcile intercompany accounts; these roles are now not needed.
2. Improved working capital, as treasury can now see all balances at all times and move the currencies where they are needed quickly and easily.
3. The tax liability has been reduced – the tax team have full oversight of the balances and can ensure that the transfer pricing policies and rules are implemented correctly.
4. Improved working together as the entities have no inert company issues, they can focus on working together and improving the customer experience for ASG.

Enterprise Blockchain Summary

In summary, enterprise Blockchain technology is the current process whereby large, complex organizations will use Blockchain technology to transform their business.

The key characteristics of an enterprise Blockchain are:

- Private or permissioned shared database.
- There is agreed consensus of data verification.
- There is control of capacity and cost.
- There is no cryptocurrency.
- Collective administration is implemented.
- Blockchain is used as tool not ideology.

Implementing enterprise Blockchain will take time and many areas will benefit from this. Most importantly, the culture and operations of the enterprise will transform and this will improve the enterprise performance metrics.

4

What Does Blockchain Solve?

In this chapter we will explore the areas where Blockchain technology can solve some of the current issues organizations are facing. When I say 'solve', I am giving you the practical advice to help solve the issues; obviously, the actual solving of these issues will depend on many factors, including your organization and how you actually implement these solutions.

We have already looked at the concepts around the key Blockchain benefits and now I want to look at *how* Blockchain technology will solve the top four issues for organizations.

Trust

We operate in a very complex world where trust has reduced and often evaporated when dealing with business, governments, communities, and processes. I would argue that trust has never really existed in most cases.

For example, for a retailer, there is the challenge to trust the suppliers and the partners in the supply chain. The supply chain is key to the success of a retailer, but there is always an underlying mistrust in the data and the transactions. This leads to a significant level of wasted time and resources on proving who has the current data and who is correct.

Another great example is intercompany – within any global organization, there will always be discrepancies in data between the entities, firstly due to the old legacy systems, and secondly, due to the differing structures and competing priorities of each entity.

All this lack of trust means that organizations spend significant amounts of time and resources on auditing and reconciling data – this is carried out after the transaction has been shared and reported. More importantly, the

Commercializing Blockchain: Strategic Applications in the Real World,
First Edition. Antony Welfare.
© 2019 John Wiley & Sons Ltd. Published 2019 by John Wiley & Sons Ltd.

data is reconciled and audited after decisions have been made – this means that organizations are making decisions based on incorrect data.

If we agree that trust does not exist (whether it did in the first place or not is irrelevant), then we should start to implement Blockchain technology at speed; the main solution of Blockchain is to improve trust between parties who do not trust each other.

In a Blockchain world, data and transactions will be governed by the consensus rules and the data will enter the system, significantly more accurate than previously. If it is incorrect, it will be found to be incorrect quickly and corrections can be made.

Transparency and Openness

Imagine a world where your main conversations with your partners, suppliers, customers, and organizations are open and transparent. A world where you can trust the data you have been given and can talk openly about the effect of this information.

The shared nature of Blockchain technology allows connected parties to share their data safely and securely. All parties will agree to what data is shared and with whom, this is then made available to all parties in real time. Decisions and discussions are made using this open and shared data.

Using shared open data must improve an organization's efficiency and no doubt performance. You will be able to use more relevant, accurate, and reliable information to prepare your analysis. This analysis will often lead to business decisions, which will have been made on better data.

Being open and transparent with your data not only saves time, but also helps the conversations and negotiations flow better; you will all trust the data in the first place and can concentrate on negotiating, rather than questioning the data and the source of the data.

Immutability

Once the data is entered on to the Blockchain, the data cannot be altered, deleted, or changed in any way. This is a fundamental concept and a great benefit to help improve trust and partnerships.

This does not mean that the data that is held on the Blockchain is correct, it means that the data has been entered into the Blockchain via the agreed consensus mechanisms, which inherently should make the data more likely to be correct.

If the data is incorrect, the great benefit of Blockchain technology is that you can quickly trace where the data was incorrect, and the details of the transaction. You can then quickly rectify the data once you have investigated what went wrong and why.

Transactions Automation – Smart Contracts

A large part of the Blockchain technology infrastructure is the automation of certain transactions and tasks – often called smart contracts. In basic terms, these are the same as computer programming language, where people write simple code in an executable language.

Contracts are the most important form of transactions which we would use a smart contract for. There are many opportunities and challenges for the legal side of smart contracts, which is a current hot topic in all Blockchain circles.

One way to look at smart contracts is to call it 'automating transactions'. If we view a smart contract as automation, we can see that there are many tasks in our organizations which could be improved using automated transactions.

Let's take an example of a common transaction where we have a set of transactions to expire at a certain time each month (e.g. prepayments and accruals). These transactions are often reversed at the start of each month and then set up again at the end of each month. We could write a smart contract to automatically reverse the transaction and check the data on the end of the next month to automatically post again (if the transaction meets agreed criteria).

The contracts world can be greatly improved using smart contracts on Blockchain, but it will require changes in legislation and adoption by legal institutions and authorities, if you require legal recognition of the transaction.

'Why Blockchain Will Be Transformative': Looking at the History of Contracts through to Present Day Usage

During one of my many discussions on Blockchain technology that I have each day, I met a fantastic Blockchainer called Areiel Wolanow, who was working with a large insurance broker in the City of London.

During the discussion, Areiel told me about the history of contracts, where the written word came from and the history of accounting. He has been researching the history for a number of years and his conversation fascinated me. As we continued the discussion, Areiel agreed to share his research, expertise, and history with you, and here are his thoughts on 'Why Blockchain matters'. I am very grateful to Areiel for his contribution.

Why Blockchain Matters – A Historical Perspective

By Areiel Wolanow

Managing Director, Finserv Experts. Global thought leader in DLT, machine learning, and financial inclusion

Part 1: Blockchain and the Hype Curve

Shortly after the end of the dot-com boom, Gartner[1] came out with a piece of research that mapped out how large, transformative innovations tend to be adopted over time; they called this pattern the Hype Curve.

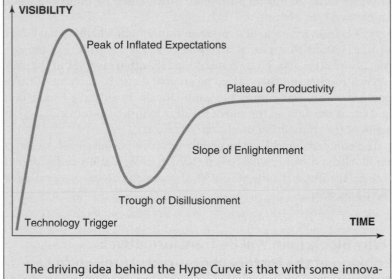

The driving idea behind the Hype Curve is that with some innovations, people are very quick to grasp its transformative potential, but

---

1 Gartner Hype Cycle: https://www.gartner.com/en/research/methodologies/gartner-hype-cycle.

because the innovation is so new and so radical, it takes longer to figure out how that potential can be realized, longer yet to build solutions that make use of the innovation, and longer still for people to adopt those solutions in daily use. This gap between the cognitive understanding of an innovation's potential and a practical realization of its benefits, when viewed through a behavioural lens, makes Gartner's 'Peak of Inflated Expectations' and 'Trough of Disillusionment' eminently predictable phenomena.

The term 'Hype Curve' may have first been invented by Gartner in 2002, but the phenomenon has been around a lot longer. At the height of the South Sea Bubble in 1720, a newspaper carried a solicitation for investment 'for carrying-on an undertaking of great advantage but no-one to know what it is'. In less than a month, they raised over £210k in today's money.

The Hype Curve doesn't happen with every transformative innovation. Sometimes the depth of impact that an innovation will have isn't truly understood until its wide-scale adoption is already well under way. Reliable contraception followed this pattern, as did smart phones. But there is very clear evidence that Blockchain is adhering much closer to the Hype Curve adoption pattern. As of late 2018, there are over 16,000 Blockchain start-ups trying to capitalize on this potential. Having performed due diligence on a few and read about a good deal more, I can personally attest that more than a few of them are the same sort of 'solution in search of a problem' ventures that dotted the landscape of Silicon Valley in the 1990s, while even more are solutions that don't actually require DLT's capabilities at all. If any more proof were needed that Blockchain is tracking to the Hype Curve, consider the case of the Long Island Iced Tea corporation.

The Long Island Iced Tea corporation was an unprofitable manufacturer of powdered drink mixes in Hicksville, New York; it had been in business since 2011. In December 2017, the Long Island Iced Tea Corporation change its name to the Long Blockchain Corporation. They didn't change anything about their business model, just their name. The market's reaction was almost instantaneous; their valuation rose as high as 289% in one day's trading. Eventually, the market recovered from this hysteria and their stock was subsequently delisted by NASDAQ, but it provides a vivid account of the Hype Curve in action.

But underlying most bubbles and their respective Hype Curves is a core assertion that, more often than not, makes sense. During the South Sea Bubble, people in Britain were accurate in foreseeing that dominance of trade with East Asia would lead to over a century of global hegemony. Likewise with the dot-com boom; I had the privilege of working in Silicon Valley during the 1990s, and we were all galvanized by the idea that this thing called the internet was going to change everything. Looking back 25 years, there is no question that this fundamental belief was correct, but we had no idea exactly how that transformation was going to happen, which strategies would prove successful, or which entirely new business models would emerge. And there is no question that understanding the core idea that the internet was going to change everything did not prevent us from spending untold amounts of money on foolish ideas that, in hindsight, never stood a chance of delivering any results.

This, in a nutshell, is exactly where we are with Blockchain today. And the point of this chapter, if not the entire book, is to understand – at an intuitive level – more about why Blockchain is so transformational. If we are able to articulate that core assertion clearly up front, we have more potential to make smarter decisions up front about where to focus our energy, our money, and most important of all, our time. As with most innovations, the key to that understanding lies not in the future but in the past.

Part 2: The World's First Business Requirement

At its core, the value proposition that makes Blockchain so transformational is its potential to solve one of the world's oldest business requirements, one that predates the dawn of recorded history: the need for multiple people to share a single version of a future commitment.

Despite predating recorded human history, this business requirement was still quite a new one compared to the several million years humanity has existed. For most of this time, the human 'business model' was based on hunter-gatherer technology. In this world the notion of a contract in which goods or services were deliverable at a future date was not very relevant. Individual tribes could not reliably predict their location or circumstances from one season to the next, and there had yet to emerge a reliable mechanism for measuring the passing of days with precision.

The advent of agriculture changed both of these things. Staying in one place made it possible to measure the passage of time with much greater accuracy, and planting crops made it far more important to do so. But measuring time did more than make it possible for farmers to know the best time to plant their crops; it also enabled them to come up with new ways of being more productive and more successful.

Let us imagine a business deal between two Sumerian men some 12,000 years ago: Enlil has a farm on which he plants barley, his brother has a farm of similar size next to his, and they each have an ox to plough their respective fields. But one day, while using his ox to take his grain to market, bandits kill Enlil's brother and steal his brother's ox. Enlil inherits his brother's farm, and also the responsibility to look after his brother's family, but his own ox can't plough both fields in enough time to do the planting, which puts both families at risk of starving next winter. So Enlil makes a deal with his friend Enki. Enki agrees to lend Enlil one of his oxen to plough his brother's field in exchange for 10 bushels of barley at harvest time. The fields are ploughed, the barley is planted, and when harvest time comes, Enlil delivers the 10 bushels of barley to Enki. But Enki protests, he swears that the deal called for 12 bushels, not 10. Without a way of verifying which of them was right, trust breaks down, and the next season they refuse to do business with one another. This lack of trust means a crucial opportunity for both Enlil and Enki to grow their respective enterprises is lost.

Needless to say, the Sumerians did not complacently accept this loss of opportunity. As people would today, some of the entrepreneurs of that day came up with a new technology to make it possible for people to take advantage of the opportunity afforded by a reliable future commitment. Our modern term for this technology is a contract.

How were these first contracts expressed? Writing was still 4000 years into the future. As with most successful innovators, these Sumerian entrepreneurs made the best with the resources they had to hand, and the one resource that Sumerians had in abundance was mud. The first form of externally verifiable contract we are aware of now is called a bulla. A bulla is essentially a hollow ball of clay. The two parties of a contract would place inside this hollow ball a number of tokens (yes, tokenization also predates recorded history) representing the number of units – bushels of barley in our example – to be delivered. At an agreed time in the future – harvest time in our example – the two parties would break the bulla open together and settle the debt. This problem, reconciling two versions of an agreement, was the world's first business requirement. And the bulla was the first attempt we know of to solve it.

The bulla didn't solve the problem of reconciliation completely, but it was a huge breakthrough, nevertheless. It made it possible for farmers to grow their farms significantly larger than needed for subsistence and to start accumulating wealth, which in turn made it possible for people to specialize, research further innovations, and so on. But as is still true today, every time a constraint is solved, it uncovers another constraint that nobody realized was there because the first constraint is more restrictive.

Let's look back in on our friend Enlil 10 seasons later. Because he can now make trusted deals with Enki and others, he has been able to grow his farm to the point where it now takes 20 oxen to do his ploughing, and herein lies the new problem. A week before harvest he tries to figure out how many bushels of barley he needs to pay out in order to fulfil his commitments. So he goes into his storehouse, and there in the storehouse are the different bullae he executed with others in order to borrow the oxen from their various owners, but try as he may, he cannot remember how many tokens are in each. Until he breaks the bullae open, he is reliant on his own memory to have a record of his indebtedness.

The problem, then, is one of scale. With the invention of the bulla, we have our first independently verifiable contract, but no way of handling more than a few instances of those contracts reliably. But once again, this is a business problem that the innovators of the day were able to solve. Not long after the earliest bulla prototypes, we start to see bullae that have indentations on the outside. Apparently, what started happening was, when people initially formed the bullae, they would use the tokens to make indentations on the outside of the ball representing the number of tokens that were inside. With this innovation, Enlil could go into the storehouse at any time, and see exactly how many bushels of barley he owed to Enki and the rest of his creditors.

Here is an early Sumerian bulla, photographed along with the tokens that were found inside it. Notice that there appear to be three different types of tokens, and that they make easily distinguishable impressions on the outside of the bulla. This represents the next innovation in our story: the ability to use a single contract to represent different kinds of commodities. Perhaps Enlil's son started planting spelt or oats in addition to barley.

This complexity continued to grow over time. Over the centuries we see bullae and the impressions made on their surface getting more and more complex. Eventually, some 4000 years after the first bullae were created, an innovator is struck with an epiphany. They realize that the impressions on the outside have become so complex and full of meaning that the tokens on the inside are now largely superfluous. So instead of forming the clay into a ball, this innovator flattens it out into a wide sheet in order to have more surface on which to make the impressions. And with more surface area, these impressions continue to grow more complex, and to convey more meaning, until they reach a form that we would recognize as writing.

The evolution from bullae to writing took 4000 years, and for a further 1000 years writing was used for only one purpose: recording contracts. It took a full millennium for people to realize it could be used for law, history, religion, literature, music, etc. In thinking about Blockchain, this is worth reflecting on: The need for a way to independently verify a commitment between multiple parties was the fundamental driver behind the development of writing, and therefore of every aspect of human civilization that writing made possible.

As an aside, bullae are still with us today in vestigial form.

Part 3: From Bullae to Blockchain

Written contracts on clay tablets were a huge step forward from bullae; they enabled much more complex business arrangements. Written contracts like this had their own limitations, however. One of these constraints was that, unlike the bulla, it was difficult to verify that a contract was the original copy agreed to by both parties; only one person had possession of the master, and both seals and signatures could be forged. But a bigger problem with contracts was that only a very few individuals knew how to read and write. One could hire a scribe, but since there was no way of verifying the scribe's competence or impartiality, this reintroduced the problem of trust.

The solution to this limitation is the next big innovation in the chain of events that leads us ultimately to Blockchain and distributed ledger: the tally stick.

A tally stick is another way of recording a debt or contractual commitment. It usually consisted of a long, thin stick of wood. A series of notches would be carved across the width of the stick, representing the number of commodities in the contract. These notches were called tally marks, and we still use them to this day for counting things.

$$\cancel{||||} \; \cancel{||||} \; ||$$

The stick would then be split lengthwise so that the marks would be present on both sides of the split, and only the two original pieces would fit together cleanly.

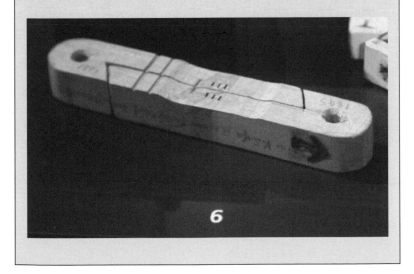

To make clear the relationship between the two parties, the split was made so that the two resultant pieces were unevenly sized. The larger piece was called the stock and the smaller piece was called the foil. The creditor got the larger piece, and was said to 'hold stock', which is where the current use of the term stock as a share in something comes from.

Split tallies had a long run: they were already in use during the Roman republic, and were still valid as proof of debt in Napoleonic law. But as with the innovations that preceded them, tallies had their limitations, most notably their size. As enterprises and governments in particular became larger, holding and making use of an increasingly large number of tallies became unwieldy. It was also exceedingly hard to prepare what we would now call summary reports with them; somebody would have to physically inventory and count each tally to come up with a consolidated position. But replacing tallies with writing was problematic; not only could writing be forged, but unlike the tally there was no way of checking if the individual entries were correct.

The innovation that solved this, and allowed written ledgers to replace tallies as the system of record for most enterprises, is called double-entry accounting. We commonly ascribe its invention to Genoa in the late 1200s, though there is evidence that it was used earlier than this in Egypt and Korea. In 1494, a Franciscan friar named Luca Pacioli published what is now recognized as the first accounting textbook; this book was used as the main reference for the correct way to do accounting for several centuries.

Double-entry accounting resolved at least part of the shortcomings of writing in representing commitments between multiple parties, and most of the innovations over the following centuries were ways of making contracts more secure and harder to forge. But these changes were incremental at best; the next big innovation in contract technology didn't take place for over 600 years, and the fundamental problem with writing as a form of contractual representation – someone needed to reconcile two versions of a contract or ledger to make sure both were accurate – still remained unsolved.

This next innovation in contract technology came in the middle of the last century, and it was not intended to solve the problem of reconciliation. Like the impressions on the outside of a bulla, it was intended to solve the problem of scale. Commercial enterprises and governments alike were growing larger and more complex, and they entertained ambitions of growing larger still. And perhaps the biggest impediment to these ambitions was the need for manual record keeping. As companies tried to grow from thousands of employees to tens of thousands, the sheer volume of bookkeeping required held them back. The next innovation was the one that solved that problem of scale, and made what we would now recognize as a multinational enterprise possible: the digitization of contracts and ledgers. The first digital ledger to be used in production was a payroll application running on a Univac computer for the General Electric Corporation in New York. It went live in 1954.

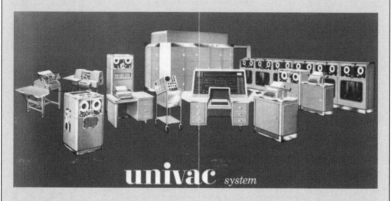

The history of digitally represented contracts and ledgers from 1954 until now, of the migration from mainframes to PCs, and from simple ledger accounting systems to supply chains and ecommerce solutions, is worthy of a book in itself.

All of these innovations, from bullae to fully integrated supply chains, have tried in one way or another to solve this very first business requirement. But even with modern digital solutions, the reconciliation problem still exists. Two enterprises may have digital ledgers, but they each have their own version, and need to verify each other's accounts in order to do business on a trusted basis. Some of this reconciliation is now automated, but even in the most modern trading networks, much of it is still done as it was in the days of the tally stick: manually. This is where Blockchain – finally – comes into the story.

When I am asked to describe Blockchain in a single sentence, I say that Blockchain is, in essence, Dropbox for ledgers. A member of a trading network writes a transaction to a ledger. Provided that the other members agree the transaction to be valid, that transaction is automatically synced across the ledgers of each other party in that network. The result is a single source of truth that is still the distinct, separate, and legal system of record for each party in the trading network.

Part 4: Using History to Filter Hype

Understanding the role of DLT in meeting the world's oldest business requirement, while certainly interesting enough to be studied on its own merit, is more than just an amusing diversion; it becomes a valuable perspective and tool we can use to do a better job of assessing which of the DLT solutions being put forward today are likely to deliver value, and which of the more than 16,000 Blockchain start-ups in existence today are likely to have any chance of succeeding.

Consider some of the 'gold standard' use cases; the ones most commonly put forward as exemplars of the value DLT can deliver

- Supply chain provenance
- Trade settlement
- Medical records
- Land registry.

All of these use cases have something in common: it is easy to see the potential value from having a single version of the truth that every party in a trading network can agree on and legally own. The same can be said of the original Blockchain use case: digital currency. On the other hand, there are any number of Blockchain solutions being put forward today that do not meet this simple sense check. To be sure there are other critical success factors, but just thinking about this one superannuated business requirement can go a long way in separating wheat from chaff.

This, then, is the true transformative potential of distributed ledgers. They are the most significant innovation in contract technology since the invention of double entry accounting over 600 years ago, and they have the potential to finally solve the world's first business requirement: the need for multiple parties to reconcile a commitment over time.

This is the potential that has everyone so excited.

New Business Models and Opportunities

One of the most exciting, and unexplored, areas of Blockchain technology is the new business models and opportunities this new technology-driven transformation will unleash.

The fundamental changes to organizational processes will open up new doors – if you take the 'front to back' thinking, then you will now have a whole set of business processes which get the information 'right first time' as much as possible. This will allow much better decision-making, but allow for more time for analysis.

One of my challenges to organizations over time has been to 'do less processing' and 'do more analysis'. Analysis is looking at the data and drawing out themes and conclusions from this data, on which you can then make an informed decision. Too often, I see organizations that spend too long collating the data, and the decision-making process is often rushed and incomplete.

Imagine a world where the data is correct at the beginning, your team has chance to analyse this data, and you have used the data real time from the Blockchain parties (whose data you would not normally see). This has to make a better, more rounded and well-researched decision and I would go so far as to say, this would allow new opportunities which had previously been lost in the data be surfaced and put into action.

New business opportunities will come from the new landscape. New organizations will be needed to take existing organizations through the Blockchain transformation, and new organizations will be needed on the other side to help organizations best utilize this transformation.

Here are a few new business models that will be driven from the adoption of Blockchain technology:

- Entities that can help organizations through the consensus challenges (and maybe even being an independent part of the consensus mechanism).
- Entities that can develop the Blockchain technology and implement it.
- Parties that can train the entire organization on the best way to implement and use Blockchain technology.
- Consultancies that can take organizations through the initial Blockchain transformation and further into the Blockchain world as the technology matures, and the benefits grow.
- Legal companies that audit/check smart contracts for legal compliance.

MonoChain: A Blockchain Start-Up Building the Circular Economy

A great example of a new industry is how MonoChain was formed and I asked Geri Cupi to share the journey of his current Blockchain technology based start-up MonoChain, which is building circular economy solutions.

Where Do Ideas Come From?

By Geri Cupi

In order to understand how Blockchain start-ups have developed, it is a great start to look at the history of where ideas and opportunities come from.

Recognizing opportunities, entrepreneurs need prior knowledge which is complementary with the new information that triggers an entrepreneurial conjecture (Kaish & Gilad, 1987). Ardichvili et al. (2003) argued that three major types of prior knowledge are important:

1. Prior knowledge of markets
2. Prior knowledge of ways to serve markets
3. Prior knowledge of customer problems.

Markets prior knowledge includes supplier relationships information or sales techniques (Hippel, 1988). Some individuals can recognize opportunities which others overlook, as they possess the cognitive frameworks (i.e. prototypes, exemplars) needed to perceive patterns among seemingly unrelated trends/events (Baron, 2006).

According to Josh Wolfe of Lux Capital, there are two forces that propel human progress:

1. We go from manual to autonomous

   i.e. In the assembly line from human labour to Human/Machines to Humanless Assembly line of Robots;

   i.e. In the taxi space from expert Cab drivers (Black Cabs/Addison Lee) to Every Licensed Driver (Uber) to Autonomous Vehicles

2. We go from isolated to networks

   i.e. computers: from isolated mainframes to network PCs, laptops and phones.

These forces can make a new start-up solution inevitable. For us, we have identified that the current secondary retail market is manual and isolated, which we believe eventually will move to autonomous and networked.

How Did the MonoChain Idea Start?

Back in 2014, the VC firm where I used to work was looking into Bitcoin technology use cases in other industries. (Bitcoin was the only working Blockchain at this time, hence the reason why we refer to it as Bitcoin technology – we now have many other Blockchains, which led the term to 'Blockchain technology'.) At the time, we thought that the gaming space would be an early adoptor after the financial services industry. I left the VC at this stage to start my own entrepreneurial journey.

Since 2014, I've co-founded two start-ups in the fashion space and had a successful exit. At Social DNA, we up-cycled used jeans and jackets, by redesigning them and offering customization capabilities.

I was shocked to see the lack of transparency in the fashion supply chain and how primary and secondary market happens in silos. Despite the fact we were using old jeans, the brands were not receiving any income from this trade. Also, we were tricked several times into buying fake products, which was very frustrating.

As part of JOOK[2], we built a sensor to solve counterfeiting which we filed patents for in 2016. Dr Chris Archer-Brown was my professor at the University of Bath, an early backer of JOOK. Chris co-founded ClarityBlue, a big data company which he sold to Experian in 2006 for more than $100m and since then has been an academic. Both Chris and I were having a lot of conversations about Blockchain over the last two years, as he was doing some academic work at the time. At one of our meetings we were discussing the impact that the circular economy can have on the fashion industry and the presence of counterfeiting. We identified a solution which could tackle both of these problems by utilizing Blockchain technology.

I passionately wanted to work with Chris because we shared a belief that a new type of Blockchain-powered, transparent, and social-impact-driven company could fundamentally change the customer relationship

---

2 https://medium.com/@jookjams/the-story-behind-jook-the-first-virtual-mall-for-instagram-influencers-45a4f3a6a63e.

with a brand, and the products it created. If you are not both excited and scared in equal measure, you are not trying hard enough. With those emotions deep within us, we decided to build MonoChain.

Challenge/Opportunity

We believe the fashion industry will be transformed by the Fourth Industrial Revolution through:

1. Pervasive computing enhancing customer experiences
2. Transformation of supply chains
3. Smart systems mitigating wastage.

This is where we started to look at how we could tackle the issue of counterfeiting and clothing waste (second-hand resale markets).

Deceptive Counterfeiting
Deceptive counterfeiting, (the customer is not aware that they have purchased a fake product) is a major cost to the global economy. In the luxury market, deceptive counterfeiting creates significant costs of deterrence throughout the supply chain: e.g. the global fashion group LVMH spends €15m p.a. in legal costs and The RealReal marketplace must inspect every item passing through their online market to remove fakes.

The opportunity for luxury brands to reduce legal costs in fighting counterfeit fraud is significant: this costs the European economy €43.3bn and over 500,000 jobs as well as the retail value of counterfeit.

Together with the designer resale market online growth, this poses a serious threat to both brands and consumers. 'Folks will be shopping on marketplaces and think they're buying a second-hand, expensive handbag and it's a fake,' explains IACC President Bob Barchiesi.

Grey Market
Sharp drops in exchange rates increase the risk of goods entering the grey market. There is an incentive to buy goods in a cheaper market and resell them in countries where the retail price is higher, resulting in lower profits for the original manufacturer.

For instance, consultancy Bain & Co estimates that daigou (grey market in China) accounted for Rmb34bn–Rmb50bn ($5.1bn–$7.5bn) of sales last year, equivalent to 12% (at the upper end) of Chinese luxury spending. Monitoring the grey market can be challenging and companies must have the ability to trace where each of their products originally entered the market place. This can be both expensive and difficult to manage.

Second-Hand Market

The second-hand market for luxury apparel, accessories, watches, and jewellery was valued at $25bn in 2017 (FT, 2018).

Some brands have already started to embrace the market. For example, Audemars Piguet is jumping into the resale space, planning to open standalone stores to buy and sell second-hand timepieces. Jean-Claude Biver, head of LVMH watch brands TAG Heuer, Hublot, and Zenith, has said they are considering entering the market.

Another evidence of the growing second-hand market is the proliferation of resell start-ups. To give you a brief idea of the scale, consider this example where venture capitalists poured $65m into just two start-ups — The RealReal, which raised $40m, and Poshmark, which raised $25m.

Nowadays, more and more people sell their second-hand clothes and accessories online, and even more are going to buy these second-hand products.

The US second-hand apparel industry as a whole – encompassing both offline and online – is expected to be worth $33bn by 2021. And online resale is growing much more quickly than its offline predecessors (meaning thrift stores, Buffalo Exchange, Beacon's Closet, etc.). While offline resale has been growing at an 8% CAGR (compound annual growth rate), online resale has been growing at a rate of 35% over the last few years.

Environmental Sustainability

There are ~21 billion tons of textiles sent to landfill every year. The fashion industry's CO_2 emissions are projected to increase by more than 60% to nearly 2.8 billion tons per year by 2030 – equivalent to nearly 230 million passenger vehicles driven for a year, assuming average driving patterns.

Having multiple owners of each clothing item, the need for buying new clothes decreases and you do not waste clothing life cycles. Research by Ipsos MORI has shown that more than half of us own unworn clothing that no longer fits, 10% hang on to worn out favourites, and 36% own items that they consider have gone out of fashion.

As an illustration, increasing second hand sales by 10% would decrease the UK's carbon footprint by 3%, water footprint by 4% and waste footprint by 1% per tonne of clothing (WRAP, 2017). As the extent of waste in the fashion industry increases in prominence, it will become clear that the circular economy offers a potential solution, meaning that the provenance of the product becomes critical. MonoChain will facilitate the selling of second-hand products, creating opportunities for its partners to extend customer relationships and increase profits. This results in prolonging the clothing life cycle and reaching a circular fashion industry. Having multiple owners of each clothing item, the need for buying new clothes decreases. Our approach solves needs for both businesses and consumers:

1. Luxury brand manufacturers can validate the authenticity of the product throughout its life cycle (factory, distribution, retail, first owner, secondary markets).
2. Consumers can remove risk of purchase via access to product history and provenance.

Retailers and secondary markets can reduce costs to serve customers.

MonoChain Solution in a Nutshell

MonoChain offers a ledger based on Blockchain technology that shows who owns what, who is an authorized licensee, and so on; it would enable everyone in the supply chain, including consumers and customs authorities, to validate a genuine product and distinguish it from a fake. MonoChain allows for provenance authentication, since verifiable details can be recorded objectively about when and where products are made, and raw materials used.

Fashion companies have the opportunity of extending their relationship with the customer and monetization of the product well beyond current limits by providing a value-add service of reducing the risk of being caught out by counterfeit fraud and facilitating opportunities to resell the product at the end of its life with a particular customer.

MonoChain is a B2B solutions partner for global fashion companies, providing them with the opportunity to extend relationships with their customers (and – vitally – their lifetime value). Specifically, MonoChain can transform the secondary market but allowing firms to facilitate the onward sale of fashion items.

How does MonoChain work now? Every time a user buys an item, he/she receives his/her Certificate of Ownership, a Non-Fungible Token (NFT). The user has the opportunity to enter it into the MonoChain wallet.

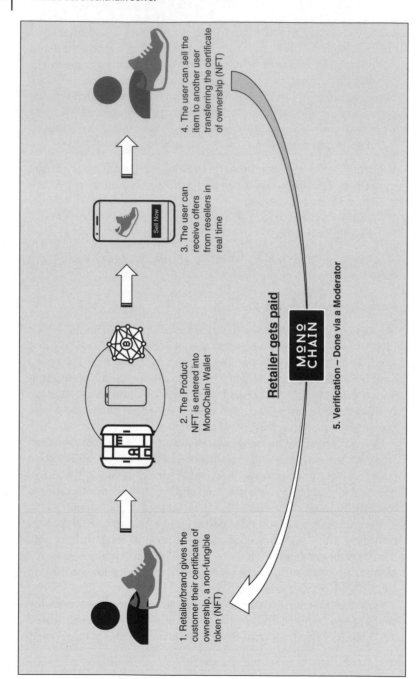

1. Retailer/brand gives the customer their certificate of ownership, a non-fungible token (NFT)

2. The Product NFT is entered into MonoChain Wallet

3. The user can receive offers from resellers in real time

4. The user can sell the item to another user transferring the certificate of ownership (NFT)

Retailer gets paid

MONO CHAIN

5. Verification – Done via a Moderator

When that is done, the user can receive offers to sell them on real time. If user 1 (seller) decides to sell this item to user 2, the item is sent to a moderator for verification first. There will be a Ricardian contract using a multisig escrow. This means that the NFT and money will be held in a separate wallet. If the moderator verifies that the item is authentic, the NFT and the product moves to the buyer and the seller receives the money. Every time ownership changes this will be recorded into a private Blockchain (Hyperledger Sawtooth), but eventually we plan to move into the public Blockchain.

MonoChain Value Proposition and Business Model

At the moment, the customer journey on the primary market happens as follows:

1. The user discovers an item they like.
2. They evaluate and decide to purchase it.

As far as retailers are concerned the customer journey ends there. However, for approximately 1 out of every 6 items, their owner decides to sell them after a while entering a new customer journey. Resale marketplaces have no idea where this item has come from and whether they are stolen or from the grey market. They verify the item authentication and then send the item to the buyer.

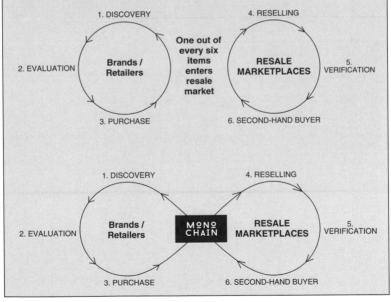

We have built MonoChain to be a bridge between the primary and the resale markets in order to facilitate reselling. We make it super simple; a frictionless experience for users to sell an item they own and to enable fashion retailers to enter the circular economy.

Our solution will have a great sustainability impact. Firstly, it will lead to an increase in the ability to track the source of materials to be used in production (e.g. provide traceability). Secondly, it will increase utilization rate and decrease the risk of throwing away clothes after minimal use. Thirdly, it will enable easier recycling and automated sorting of clothing based on textile components (e.g. easier to separate polyester clothes from cotton clothes).

MonoChain facilitates selling and buying second-hand items. For sellers, they know that they can get a price premium on items proved to be authentic, so they are incentivized to sell. Protecting branded product from grey market and diversion activities is of continued concern to all luxury brands, and MonoChain can be an effective tool in identifying grey market product, to whom it had been sold originally, and how it may have ended up in the grey market. MonoChain is not creating a coin/token to monetize it's solution, but instead it makes money through transaction fees and revenue share. Every time an item changes hands, it gets paid.

5

Blockchain Powering the New Marketplace Model

A Fundamental Foundation: Marketplaces Built Using Blockchain Technology

Blockchain as a marketplace is a very interesting concept, which I have thought long and hard about. On the one hand, a marketplace built on Blockchain technology makes complete sense – after all Blockchain is about decentralization and removing the middlemen. On the other hand, marketplaces today are globally complex beasts, which need significant management and administration. For that reason, I am not putting marketplaces into my use cases, as I do believe this is a fundamental foundation of Blockchain technology use cases.

My questions start to grow when you look at the reality of servicing a marketplace and the high customer expectations set by the current retail world leaders. There are many questions which affect the customer services, around delivery, marketing, quality and many other issues.

I do believe Blockchain-based marketplaces will grow (and there are some already operating) but will they become global giants, with extensive product ranges? This will be difficult to achieve, given the current marketplace giants.

Amazon and Alibaba are founded on two key aspects:

1. Customer service
2. Wide product range.

These are critical to the success of these marketplaces and something that is very hard to get right with a decentralized Blockchain-based marketplace.

Commercializing Blockchain: Strategic Applications in the Real World,
First Edition. Antony Welfare.
© 2019 John Wiley & Sons Ltd. Published 2019 by John Wiley & Sons Ltd.

I believe we will see many smaller Blockchain-based marketplaces grow, focused on a particular product or range, over time these could merge and grow into a global marketplace – it will be interesting and exciting to see this world progress.

Marketplace for Anything

As I discuss in the previous section, there are major challenges for a marketplace built on Blockchain technology, but there are also an unlimited number of options for a marketplace built on Blockchain technology.

The current marketplace landscape – remember that we are including services as well as products in the marketplace sector – Amazon, eBay, Alibaba, Uber, Airbnb, etc., are all current marketplace giants who can be changed by Blockchain technology.

If we look at the discussion above, you will see that the big challenges for a successful Blockchain-based marketplace are the same as the current challenges for a marketplace:

1. Customer service – how to service the buyers of your marketplace.
2. Marketing the products and services – how to find buyers for the marketplace.
3. Seller on-boarding and management – how to attract the right sellers and products/services to your marketplace.

This is where Blockchain technology comes into its own – trust, transparency, and immutable data are all factors which will help solve these challenges.

- Trust and the Blockchain marketplace – trust in any transaction is critical and with current marketplaces, you give your trust to the corporate owner of the marketplace (Amazon, Alibaba, Uber, etc.). *Do the ratings on these marketplaces reflect the truth of the satisfaction of the buyers?*
- Transparency and the Blockchain marketplace – transparency of products/services quality and the ratings customers give is critical in a marketplace. The current marketplaces may or may not check the quality of the product/service and you may find that the product is not how it was described. Often marketplaces will

facilitate a refund, but this is difficult for a service and can cost more than just the price of the service. *Is the product/service what it says it is?*

- Immutable data and the Blockchain marketplace – without trust and transparency, you cannot trust the data regarding your product or service – you have to trust the centralized marketplace provider of the seller. With immutable data, all data and transactions are final and the history is there for all to see – nobody can delete the bad feedback or the record of poor quality products. *Do you know that the data about your product or service is correct?*
- Big data or 'value' and the Blockchain marketplace – as the users become more aware of the current marketplaces who use and sell their data and analysis, Blockchain marketplace, could allow the users to each own their own data, and choose where the data is used and for what. Users could even get 'paid' to share their data, to be given product and service offers from vendors, based on what data they choose to share about themselves. *Who owns (profits from) MY data?*

In my view a marketplace will benefit significantly from these four factors, and all these factors (plus more) are benefits from implementing Blockchain technology.

If we get the first four issues correct, then I believe you will see marketplaces that sell many different products and services succeed based on their use of Blockchain benefits.

Decentralized Utopia – Reality or Dream?

It is probably a great point to look at the reality of a decentralized marketplace – I am in two minds as to whether this is a dream, or in fact, a new business model reality. On the one hand, Blockchain technology gives three beneficial factors to improve the current marketplaces (trust, transparency, and immutability) and on the other hand, there needs to be an agreed consensus or central point to deal with marketing, seller on-boarding, and customer service.

The idea of complete decentralization would not work with a marketplace, but the benefits will still be achieved by implementing the Blockchain technology, and the parties involved can work on a consensus agreement for the 'central' processes which need to happen.

Example of a Product Marketplace: Replace Amazon, eBay, or Alibaba

Let us explore how a marketplace built on Blockchain technology would work – building a disrupting Blockchain-based marketplace to take on the Amazon, eBay, and Alibaba current models.

In the current model with most of these marketplaces:

1. Sellers list products onto the centralized system.
2. These items are then marketed by the centralized owner.
3. Buyers buy the products either via auction or fixed price.
4. Delivery and logistics could be included.

How this would work with a Blockchain-based marketplace:

1. A group of entities/people need to form the Blockchain marketplace team.
2. The team need to agree the 'rules'/principles around consensus, operations, customer service, etc.
3. There would need to be investment in the marketing of the marketplace to both sellers and buyers.
4. Sellers then list their products using the agreed consensus mechanism, to ensure the products are correct and verified.
5. Buyers enter the marketplace and buy the product.
6. It would be assumed that payment is made via a token or crypto currency.
7. The seller dispatches the product and the buyer confirms arrival.

This is very simple to write down, and the technology is actually a simple set of Blockchain technology and smart contracts. Add to this an agreed 'centralized' consensus process to deal with the three major challenges, and I believe you would have a very efficient and effective marketplace.

Example of a Service Marketplace: Replace Uber or Airbnb

Much the same as a product marketplace, the sellers will list their services and the buyers will purchase them.

The difference, and important benefit, with a Blockchain-based marketplace would be more checking and vetting of the service provider at the start of the process. The marketplace will need to be sure that the service provider is able to provide the services offered to the specifications agreed. Smart contracts could be used to check certain information and the use of customer feedback would be critical. This, again, could easily be automated via smart contracts, enabling bad feedback to be seen and actioned across the marketplace at speed.

Real Use Case: Blockchain Product Marketplace – OpenBazaar

OpenBazaar is a retail marketplace without fees or restrictions, powered by the cryptocurrency Bitcoin as a payment method. Individuals and businesses can trade with each other without any middleman or third trusted party involved.

The platform is a Blockchain marketplace alternative for today's centralized services such as eBay, Amazon, and other platforms that usually charge fees for listing and selling products online.

- OpenBazaar connects people directly via a peer-to-peer network.
- Data is distributed across the network instead of storing it in a central database.
- OpenBazaar isn't a company nor an organization; it's free open source software.
- It was built to provide everyone with the ability to buy and sell freely.
- Nobody has control over OpenBazaar.
- Each user contributes to the network equally.
- Each user is in control of their own store and private data.

The store is very practical and not a great-looking platform from a customer experience point of view, but it is a great example of how a marketplace can be built and run successfully using Blockchain technology.

Real Use Case: Blockchain Marketplace to Replace Uber – EVA

I recently met the team behind EVA, which is a Canadian Blockchain project positioned as a next generation of Uber and built using Blockchain technology. EVA offers a platform for direct interaction between drivers and passengers, to book rides and use the car sharing service exactly like they would with Uber.

The application is based on Blockchain technology, the core of which is the EOS Blockchain. The company's goal is to develop decentralized technologies for moving around the city.

The business model makes sense to me – in the current model, Uber retains around 30% commission from the drivers to pay for its service, marketing, and to fund the giant business that is Uber.

EVA aims to share that 30% in three ways:

1. Cheaper rides for the customer – who doesn't want to save money on car sharing?
2. More income for the driver – better paid drivers means happier drivers mean happier customers.
3. Low costs to run the EVA business – because it is based on Blockchain with no significant central costs.

The team suggested they were already live in NYC and San Francisco – so let's see how they progress. This is one of many new marketplace Blockchain companies that will start to disrupt the disruptors.

Summary

Building a marketplace on Blockchain is a great opportunity to benefit from the assets of Blockchain technology: trust, transparency, and immutable data. These are key to a fully functioning decentralized marketplace and where Blockchain technology can greatly benefit a marketplace.

The world of marketplaces is globally significant and any new marketplace will have to beat the significant giants that exist today. I believe this can happen and with Blockchain technology as the enabler, we will see many more marketplaces based on Blockchain technology.

6

Where Can Blockchain Technology Be Applied?

We have covered a lot of information about how Blockchain technology can be used, the different types of Blockchain solutions and how Blockchain solves the biggest organizational challenges.

It is important to remember that Blockchain technology is not a solution to all problems in your organization; there are many other solutions which can be applied. I will discuss how artificial intelligence, the internet of things (IoT), and process automation are all important emerging technologies. Importantly, these will be made even more useful when they are put together with Blockchain technology – I will discuss this exciting area in a later chapter.

I now want to talk through where Blockchain can be applied, and importantly, the challenges and issues around Blockchain adoption.

Please note that these examples are not exhaustive; they are designed to give you some areas to start to look at – areas where implementing Blockchain technology will help you improve your organization in some way.

I have purposely left out the use cases for government and communities, for a couple of reasons: (1) government (despite my being a government advisor) is not my area of expertise – commercial business is my area, and (2) all of the use cases I discuss can be applied to government and community use cases.

The last section of the book looks at the real-life use cases for Blockchain technology; this is where I reference real examples of work that is happening now, as well as discussing how the use cases are being implemented.

Commercializing Blockchain: Strategic Applications in the Real World,
First Edition. Antony Welfare.
© 2019 John Wiley & Sons Ltd. Published 2019 by John Wiley & Sons Ltd.

Industries

The purpose of this book is to focus on organizations using Blockchain technology and there is plenty more information in the following chapters and the very important use case section at the end of the book.

In industry the following areas are key beneficiaries for the implementation of Blockchain technology:

1. The retail and supply chain industry (the total retail value chain from raw material to end customer).
2. The financial services industry.

Let's look at each of these two areas in more detail.

The Retail and Supply Chain Industry

This is my industry, where I have spent my entire life, so I will dwell a little more on the retail industry. This is not due to my laziness – quite the opposite – this is due to the fact that most industries follow retail at some stage and retail is inherently the most obsessed with the customer. All industries should be obsessed with their customers, but in the retail world this is seen in everything they do.

Retail is also a low-profit, high-volume business, which makes the applications of Blockchain technology particularly challenging. In my view, if you can make a Blockchain solution work for a retailer, you can make it work anywhere else.

The retail industry will be greatly improved by the implementation of Blockchain technology and I believe that all areas of a retail business will eventually benefit from this.

In my opinion, the vast complexity of the global retail world is a perfect match for Blockchain technology. There are many parties involved in the business across geographic, language, culture, size, and legal boundaries; all of which need to work together at speed and with high accuracy.

Customer expectations are the highest they have ever been, and whether you agree or not, customers expect extreme levels of service from retailers. This can be one-hour delivery slots, to the latest fashion in two weeks from design to payment via cryptocurrency, to being able to see what components made up the product.

The competition is the highest it has ever been, and Amazon (and other pure play, i.e. online only, retailers) have massively changed the market, and increased the competition and expectations significantly.

Let's look at the main area where Blockchain can improve the retail industry.

Cryptocurrencies

I will not spend much time here on cryptocurrencies, as Chapter 8 is dedicated to this topic.

For retailers there is a simple use case to accept the different cryptocurrencies (e.g. Bitcoin/Ethereum/Ripple, etc.) as a method of transferring value, which is an alternative to current payment methods.

There are many complexities and benefits to this, but there are some countries progressing rapidly with crypto payments, such as in Japan where Bitcoin is accepted in 260,000 stores. A recent survey by NetCents found:

> In 2017, the number of brick-and-mortar retailers accepting crypto grew by 30.3% to 11,291 retailers globally.
>
> At the same time, users have also warmed up to the idea: a recent survey found that 40% of people familiar with the digital currency would be open to using it in everyday transactions.[1]

The adoption of Bitcoin and other cryptocurrencies, whilst great, is not the most important driver of Blockchain technology adoption.

My personal view is that we will see retailers accepting cryptocurrencies once the prices stabilize and the regulations become clearer. Whichever cryptocurrencies are accepted, I do see a world of crypto-type payments across the world in the future.

Identity Management

The management of identity is an entire book on its own. This topic is critical to the future of our lives and to business. By 'identity', I do not just mean our own personal identity, but also the identity of assets and 'things'.

---

1 https://www.visualcapitalist.com/the-future-of-crypto-payments-in-the-retail-market/.

With Blockchain technology you can manage people's identity securely, to be used for simple tasks such as proof of age, proof of address, etc. This is great to start, but there is a much bigger opportunity, where you can use Blockchain technology to allow the entire world to have their own ID – there are millions of people without ID and this means they are unlikely to get access to the financial and support systems set up. If you do not have an ID in the UK, for example, you cannot open a bank account or use a doctor. The opportunities of this are explained well in an excellent article from Berkeley University:

> However, as expressed by BanQu founder Ashish Gadnis, 'Identity on blockchain is old news. The real value of blockchain is its unmatched ability to create and secure an economic identity for the world's billions living in extreme poverty today...this is truly a revolutionary opportunity. In other words, blockchain technology doesn't just allow for the creation of a better digital ID, but rather presents an opportunity to create a 'self-sovereign' identity.[2]

For retailers, having one verified ID is critical for age-related regulations, but makes offering services and other benefits easier. With a verified ID, the retailer can offer personalized shopping suggestions, or offer credit and financial products.

One verified ID for each person is of great value, but the second value is gained from each asset or device having a unique and verified ID. If you can then track the device ID to the person, you can then offer many bespoke and personalized services for that person.

One of the biggest challenges in retail today is online and offline tracking. It is complex to know when your customer is offline and what they are doing – online is much easier to track. With a set of verified IDs (and with the permission to share data given to the ID owner) retailers could personalize their offers to the exact customer using the exact devices. A great solution for the complexities of omnichannel shopping.

Within the supply chain, IoT (internet of things) is a step towards giving the devices used in the supply chain an ID, which is then used to track and monitor. A great example can be seen with aircraft

---

2 https://blockchainatberkeley.blog/the-impact-of-digital-identity-9eed5b0c3016.

engines, which are made up of thousands of parts, all of which need to be maintained regularly. This is done by having many IoT sensors sending data at all times. If this data is written to Blockchain, it can be shared and acted on quickly – for example if a part becomes too hot, an alarm can be raised and the pilot informed.

There is much, much more on identity management and I urge you to research this further, as it will have a fundamental effect on our lives and organizations.

Loyalty

Customer loyalty has become extremely expensive and difficult for retailers to manage. The vast range of loyalty schemes and the lack of clear benefits for these schemes means that most customers, despite being members of many schemes, do not use them often and lack trust in the benefits being offered.

Retailers have reduced the level of benefits over the last few years and the value of data is now starting to be understood by the customers. The realization that 'my data' is of value has given a new challenge to the loyalty schemes.

The management of a loyalty scheme is often quite complex due to its nature across a number of partners, meaning the cost to run these schemes is often offset by any increase in customer loyalty and purchasing.

Blockchain technology offers a more flexible and valuable loyalty service for the customer, as it can utilize the technology to work cross-industry, e.g. across retailer, brands, airlines, and hotels, by using Blockchain technology, all partners will be able to see the data and trust the data.

This opens up the opportunities for many partners to become involved in loyalty and the customer can see the value of their benefits in real time, having the option to spend the benefits when and where they like with ease.

Gift Cards

If you have ever dealt with gift cards and the systems behind these, you will understand the complexity of gift vouchers, especially for omnichannel retailers who operate online and offline. Current systems are great for simple retail models, but the new complexity means that they are struggling to be as flexible and transparent as the retailer, and customer, would like.

With Blockchain technology the whole gift card process can be simplified and automated, allowing cross-industry opportunities as well as better management of expiry and usage controls. The transparency and real-time nature of Blockchain technology will allow better gift carding opportunities, which will help to retain the loyalty of your customers and offer them many more options to utilize the gift cards or vouchers.

ASG Gift Card Blockchain Example

 Let's look at how ASG would benefit with a gift card system using Blockchain technology.

ASG has over 250 UK stores and 300 European stores, which use a bespoke gift card management system. The current process issues gift cards in store and online, with the data being sent to the central database overnight.

The gift cards are only activated every 24 hours, meaning that customers cannot use them immediately. The tracking of the gift cards is then done through a central system, which validates the code overnight.

There is a high level of fraud and poor customer experience, and gift cards are unable to be used with other partners.

With Blockchain technology the solution would be streamlined and offer significantly better customer experience. The process solution suggested the following.

Issuing a Gift Card:

1. The entry to the Blockchain network is made on any node, where the card is issued and the data is certified and validated within a few seconds of issuing the card.
2. This data is held on the Blockchain network and replicated in each store and with the online operations centre, which are nodes on the network. This means that the issuing of cards is shared across the network in almost real time.
3. Customers can then use the card immediately in store and online.

Redeeming a Gift Card:

1. The customer presents the card which is scanned and referenced to the Blockchain network.
2. The validity of the card is verified almost immediately, and if valid, the card is transacted through the point of sale system as payment.

Other Gift Card benefits for ASG customers:

1. ASG customers like to travel and use the gift cards for travel – with Blockchain technology ASG is able to share the data with a travel partner (they become a node on the network) who can access the validation of the card and the balance of the account almost immediately.
2. Allowing ASG customers to redeem their cards with a travel partner increases loyalty and customer satisfaction for ASG.
3. The partner network can be extended as much as the company wishes, to include restaurants, events, and experiences, giving ASG a great customer offer and bringing in new customers via the Blockchain network.

Warranty Management and Refunds Management

Refunds management and warranty management have similar characteristics, which make them a great beneficiary of Blockchain technology. They are currently often slow, paper based, and independent. This makes refunds and warranty issues more complex and time-consuming, while delivering poor customer service.

With Blockchain technology you can gain simple access to sales history, with no need to have a copy of the receipt. Using the data held on Blockchain, the retailer will have a quicker and easier process, with automatic access to purchase history, and confirming entitlements of the warranties, as well as the ownership details.

Warranties can also be exchanged or sold as the asset changes hands through the lifetime of the product. This gives the retailer further data and more information on the life of the product and the ability to become a part of the circular economy.

Improved Sourcing

In the current retail world, there is a big challenge with margins and pressure on retailers to offer ever lower prices. The sourcing of products for a retailer has always been critical, and something I cover in length in my previous book *The Retail Handbook*.

As the growth of online sales and online retailers continues to expand, the management of your suppliers and sourcing strategy becomes ever more critical. With Blockchain technology you can significantly improve your sourcing strategy.

Implementing Blockchain technology across your supply chain will help to develop stronger supplier trust and transparency. If the retailers can see the full supply chain, and all the history is visible across the supply chain, leading to improved and speedier sourcing decisions. Blockchain technology enables enhanced supplier comparisons to ensure that all the options are available and the retailer can choose the best supplier for each product as and when they need this.

A more efficient and transparent supply chain enables quicker transactions with suppliers, a faster supply chain, and a much better supply-chain relationship, as all parties understand what is happening at each stage of the sourcing process.

Inventory Management and Returns Management

Inventory is one of the biggest challenges for retailers. With the growth of omnichannel, where the inventory needs to be in a number of places online, offline, at collection points, with couriers, at lockers, etc., the management of the inventory is critical to an efficient and successful retail operation.

Couple this with the 'last mile delivery', where the omnichannel customers expect their delivery to home, office, or collection point in a short time period, and you can see why this has become an area that needs a better and more efficient solution.

Blockchain technology will improve the management of stock and orders significantly due to its transparent, trusted, and open properties. Allowing your entire complex network of stock data to be placed on a Blockchain will open up transparency across the retail business.

The retailer will be able to view the entire inventory network on one system. This will cover all the stock areas, such as warehouse, stores, collection points, and lockers, as well as stock which is with the couriers on delivery and with the customers. This enables a much more efficient returns management process.

In 2018, up to 40% of online orders were returned (within fast fashion). This is a staggering figure, having grown rapidly over the last few years. Customers often order a few items, knowing that they can easily return them for free. The cost of this to a retailer is significant and this was seen in December 2018, when ASOS (a global fast fashion online business) reported that shocking sales, profits, and returns rates were costing the business significantly.

With Blockchain technology, the entire inventory process, including the returns process, can be made more efficient and effective. The main benefits of Blockchain technology for the inventory and returns management are:

- Improved order tracking.
- Reduced operational costs.
- Real-time, shared tracking through the entire network to customer.
- Customer satisfaction, as they can see exactly where their order is at any stage.

ASG Inventory on Blockchain Example

 Let's look at how Blockchain technology could improve the inventory management and returns process at ASG.

ASG has 5000 clothing SKUs and 1000 clothing suppliers, and operates from 300 stores across Europe. The online business has grown rapidly and returns are now a significant profit destroyer.

Implementing Blockchain technology into the inventory process will bring together the different systems:

- Warehousing management system
- Merchandising management system
- Retail stock and sales system

- Online stock and sales system
- Order management system
- Third party couriers.

We would build the Blockchain technology solution to sit 'on top' of these current systems. This would pull in the data from all these systems on a real-time basis. In the Blockchain solution, we would then see the entire stock pool for ASG at all stages.

We would then share this data with the order management system, which will keep the customer up to date on the their order and the expected delivery. If the customer chooses to return an item, this can be quickly re-entered into the network once it arrives at the warehouse and is ready for resale.

This continuous flow of stock and order data will ensure that ASG understands where all the stock is, where the customer orders are, and can move and manage stock efficiently and effectively.

ASG Returns Blockchain Example

 We have looked at how the inventory management of ASG would be greatly improved, and we can also see that ASG has a high returns rate for the clothing items bought online. This is normal in the sector, but the inefficient process is eating into the company's profitability.

The current returns process is slow and fairly manual:

- The customer will receive a returns list with the items they ordered, which lists each item.
- The items they wish to return can be noted and repackaged in the parcel.
- This parcel is then taken by the customer to a collection point and is collected by a courier.
- The courier delivers this to the returns warehouse.
- Once in the warehouse, the teams open the parcel and check the items.
  - Non-damaged items are set aside and later added back into the warehouse stock.

- Damaged stock is sent to the damaged returns department for repair and then off to be resold in the outlet stores.
- The customer is issued a refund once the items arrive in the warehouse, irrespective of their status.

Let's look at how Blockchain technology can improve the returns process:

- The customer returns the items to the courier and the courier delivers to the warehouse.
- On arrival, the items are all scanned and their status is added to the Blockchain network.
  - This immediately updates the central stock system with the non-damaged stock and this is therefore available for sale.
  - Damaged stock is updated on the Blockchain network and the team in the damages department can see what will be arriving shortly.
- The customer is issued a refund for the non-damaged items immediately, as the finance system picks up data from the Blockchain node. Any queried refunds can then be addressed separately.

This process is not that different to the current process, which is the beauty of Blockchain technology, but sharing the data as soon as the returns hit the warehouse means the stock is on sale immediately and the damages department can get ready to fix the damaged stock.

This benefits ASG. Working capital would improve, as stock would be turned around quicker, and there would be a better customer experience, as the customer would receive refunds immediately.

Supply Chain Industry (Including Brands, Consumer Products, and Manufacturers)

The supply chain industry is highly connected to the retail industry, and most of these applications can be applied in both industries. When you widen the supply chain to include the manufacturing world, consumer products companies, and the global brands, you will see a number of these Blockchain applications apply to many different organizations.

Supply Chain Transparency

The supply chain of any organization is a complex ecosystem of different companies, across different geographies, using different systems and processes to get the products from one place to another. The complexity of an enterprise or government supply chain should not be underestimated, and is one of the main beneficiaries for Blockchain technology.

I will look at a few areas within the supply chain, starting with the overall effect of Blockchain technology providing global transparency to this complex ecosystem.

In the spring of 2017, I visited Nottingham, UK, for an all-day planning session with the European Blockchain teams, which were starting to build our Enterprise Blockchain solution. Our day was tasked to look at what the Blockchain solution would look like for a large retailer and consumer brand.

We started by mapping out a European grocery retailer's supply chain, and then the consumer brand. . .we quickly realized that global supply chains are highly complex and not easy to fix. What we also realized was that Blockchain technology would provide significant benefits for transparency across the whole supply chain. You would not have one Blockchain solution, but a number of interoperable solutions based on the diversity and complexity of the total supply chain.

From this, and many other developments, the Blockchain solutions for transparency have been developed and tested, and are being delivered in many places around the world. We are a long way off the entire supply chain being transparent, but we have started the journey and I hope that this will develop quickly to ensure that the benefits are realized sooner rather than later.

The main benefits of a transparent supply chain:

- Open visibility cross-chain, which speeds up decision-making and analysis.
- Products are delivered more efficiently along the entire chain.
- Enhanced collaborative planning that works across the whole chain.
- Improved and efficient supply chains leading to less waste and more efficient processes.

Global Shipping and Freight

Did you know that for each global cargo shipment, there are around 30 documents which need to be transferred to a number of different parties? That is a logistical nightmare and most of these documents are paper based! Imagine if we could make this paperless? The first question is: Why haven't we already made this process paperless? Great question, as email has been around for 20 years or more! The reason is the lack of trust and the complexity of these shipments.

Each shipment is taking a set of products – many different companies' products – on behalf of those companies, through to another country and different customs regimes. Not only is that complex, but the cargo is often loaded and unloaded by a different organization and taken onto land transport by yet another organization. There are many organizations involved, as well as the governments and regulators, meaning trust must be at the centre of this.

Until now, paper-based documents have been the most trusted method within shipping, but this is changing with Blockchain technology. Remember, trust is the fundamental reason for Blockchain technology, and to implement this across the complex shipping network would be highly beneficial.

Many companies have started this process, but there are many parties involved and it will take a long time to agree the principle around consensus and access to the Blockchain networks.

Once that happens, the global shipping world will be transformed with:

- Enhanced predictability of arrivals.
- Delivery transparency and accuracy.
- Shorter waiting times for all parties.
- Better utilized space onboard and on land.
- More accurate delivery slots to enable retailers to be more reactive and forecast better.
- Less waste from lost shipments and spoiled goods.

Certification and Authentication

Certification and authentication covers many different aspects, from the country or place of origin to individual identification, to certification of achievements and qualifications, to any intellectual property, to digital products and designs.

All of these areas look at how we can be certain that an item, part, or property right, is allocated to the correct owner and this ownership can be proven, irrefutably, using Blockchain technology.

Proof of ownership, entitlement, or achievement is probably the best way to describe this, and these ownerships need proving in many ways for many different reasons. Product certification is an obvious need (and discussed at length in the provenance section).

How about proof of intangible assets, certifications, and rights? If you take any digital product (say, music, or this book in electronic form) how are the rights of the owners secured? This is where Blockchain technology can make a significant impact – by verifying intangible ownership using Blockchain technology, global clarity can be obtained regarding who wrote or authored the asset, and who is entitled to what rights (especially in terms of royalties and copyrights).

There are many ways to use Blockchain technology to certify ownership and rights, some of which are discussed later in this book.

Traceability

Critically important in any supply chain, but especially the food supply chain, is the traceability of all the ingredients from the raw material to the finished product on sale to the consumers.

In today's complex supply chain, there are some excellent solutions for tracking the supply chains, but these are mainly only within certain parts of the supply chain and for certain supply chain parties.

Most supply chains work on a 'one upstream and one downstream' tracking ability. This means that I can tell you who I received my inputs of products from, and where I sent them to next. I know the milk supplier I use for my cheese, and I know the pizza factory where my finished cheese is sent to. I do not necessarily know the farmers whose cows were milked or the company that supplied the food to the farmers for the cows to eat.

Understanding traceability in food is critical, and even more critical in the case of pharmaceutical and regulated products. With these complex supply chains, there needs to be complete and fully accurate transparency of the ingredients added to the drugs, the environment they were made in, and the environment they were kept in. For human prescription drugs, there are many different rules and regulations – all of which add significant complexity and costs through the supply chain.

Blockchain technology has the ability to simplify this supply chain and allow the regulators access to the data held across the entire chain. If you add to this the use of IoT devices, you can track exactly what happens to the drugs, and their current status. In Chapter 14, we will discuss the track and trace Blockchain solutions, which are growing in usage.

The benefits of improved traceability are clearly shown when there is a product recall. It would take an average global retailer around five days to track an entire supply chain for an issue, and this can be changed to minutes – possibly saving lives if there is a health-related recall, and saving a lot of time and resources for a non-critical recall.

The clothing and apparel supply chain will benefit from traceability, but not to the same extent as the food and pharmaceutical supply chains. Provenance and counterfeiting are more important in the clothing and apparel supply chain and I will discuss these two use cases next.

Provenance

To me the best description of provenance is the 'product identification from origin to finished product' where there is complete visibility of all component parts. This could be seen as a dream with current technology, but this use case is one of the most advanced in terms of delivering results. There have been projects working on this for around five years, and they are starting to give some excellent solutions to this use case.

Being able to 'scan' a product and find out the exact make-up of the raw materials, the journey it took, the stages in the production, and the way it arrived in your home, is a significant addition to customer trust and customer loyalty. As I have mentioned many times, the world of today lacks trust and transparency, and this is the same for most consumer products. If a retailer or consumer brand can prove without doubt what the product is made from, a customer could be willing to pay more for the product, but they will most certainly trust you more and become more loyal.

As discussed previously, while customer loyalty is difficult to build and even harder to retain, provenance of products is something the customers are aware of and something they are starting to demand.

There is much more on this in later sections, and in the MonoChain case study, where they are building a company to track the products' provenance, as well as the circular economy.

Counterfeit Products

Preventing counterfeit products is a very difficult task with the global growth of commerce and online shopping. Counterfeit products have always been provided, and online there is very little to stop this happening.

Even on Amazon and eBay, where customers expect the items to be real, there are many counterfeits and Amazon is starting to realize they have a big problem ahead with this. Alibaba in China started to tackle this a few years ago and is making some progress.

With Blockchain technology, you will not stop counterfeiting – bad people will always do bad things – but you can use Blockchain technology to track the 'grey market' and be able to act on counterfeits more quickly and with a higher degree of accuracy.

If we can develop a world where there is 'trust through lifetime visibility of products', then the counterfeiting world will find it harder and harder to grow.

In the luxury products world, these leading brands are acutely aware of this and there are many Blockchain technology projects, looking to help fix, or at least reduce, the impact of this.

The Finance and Financial Services Industry

The financial services (FS) industry has been the industry to develop earliest, and have the most traction with Blockchain technology. This is clearly related to Bitcoin and the fact that after the financial crisis there was a possibility to change the financial systems and currencies across the world.

Of course, this has not happened, and (see Chapter 8) the Bitcoin Blockchain has led to many new use cases for the FS industry and for finance organizations worldwide.

I am not an expert in FS, so I have asked two experts in this field to add their thoughts and details on the use cases and Blockchain technology opportunities in this space. You do not need to be in the FS industry to benefit from these – they are applicable across organizations and governments.

I will first introduce Vikram Kimyani, who will take you through the first use case around payments. This is not a section on cryptocurrency, but how to use Blockchain technology for payments.

Payments Using Blockchain Technology
By Vikram Kimyani

One of the first things taken seriously was whether Blockchain could be used in the payments industry. Traditionally, when banks want to pay each other they send payments through a trusted third party. One of the best known third parties is Swift, which is actually a conglomeration of many banks, and Swift will verify each bank on their network; at the time of writing there are around 11,000 banks on this network. If you were a bank you would want to connect to this network in order to send payments to other banks and there would be a high chance of that bank being on Swift's network. You would then send messages on the network addressed to another member with information on creating a ledger entry.

Not all banks are connected to this network permanently and may only check at set intervals; furthermore, the banks on each side of the transaction would still need to do various checks. At the end of this process it is important to note that these are just instructions about ledger entries and not actually moving money. When money is actually moved, this is a process called 'settlement'. This is another process that may or may not need to be done in order for one person to send money to another person at another bank. At each stage there is an associated fee and time cost.

Now you understand why payments cost too much and take forever using the old method, even though the technology can send information in milliseconds. Enter Ripple.

Ripple

Ripple, as we know it, has had a long journey to come into being. The original idea was formed in 2004 as a peer-to-peer provider, not unlike Zopa, where people with money to save could be connected with people wanting to borrow money. Things didn't really start to gain momentum until Bitcoin started to gain popularity and Ripple Labs came into being in 2012. This is around the time that the XRP token came into being with around 100 billion tokens being created. Ripple Labs rebranded in 2015 and set its focus on protocol; the protocol being different to Bitcoin in that it didn't use proof of work as its consensus mechanism to try and achieve the scale required to handle global payment volumes. Instead, it's very much based on the same as most enterprise Blockchain methodologies to achieve consensus by using policies. This has the effect of making their protocol very fast to confirm transactions via their network.

At this stage Ripple have three products to market, their token XRP of which they hold a substantial amount, RippleNet which is a network designed for payments and settlements, and the protocol, which underpins the other two products. These products can be used together or individually but most of the banks using Ripple's technology are using RippleNet, although they could use XRP at the settlement stage. So what is RippleNet? RippleNet is the equivalent of Swift and is another network designed to send messages about payments with additional features that are not on Swift, such as know your customer data, information on fees, and FX rates. Naturally you can settle instantly by using XRP but you are not forced to do so.

The advantage of the Ripple network over Swift is that Swift is a centralized system and payment is taken for sending each message over this system whereas Ripple uses Blockchain technology to create a peer-to-peer network, or in other words is a decentralized system for sending ledger entries.

What Ripple have done with the technology isn't unique and any permissioned Blockchain could be used to send messages about payments. This was amply demonstrated by the Monetary Authority of Singapore, which ran a successful proof of concept for settlements called the Real Time Gross Settlement (RTGS) on both Corda and Hyperledger as the underlying technology. RTGS is a system that nearly all central banks use with banks within their remit. It won't be long before we see one of these central banks go live with RTGS running on Blockchain technology.

I now want to introduce Nikhil Vadgama, who is an expert in the financial services world, with significant expertise in DLT and Blockchain technologies. He is best placed to take you through the rest of the FS-related use cases and opportunities for Blockchain technology. Nikhil begins back at the 2007/2008 financial crisis and describes its significant impact on this sector. Nikhil will focus on DLT, which is the umbrella for Blockchain technology and other distributed technologies.

Banks Becoming Technology Companies
By Nikhil Vadgama

At the time of publishing, it will have been over 10 years since the world faced economic turmoil. Decisions made within the financial services industry in the prior years were reckless and focused on profit no matter what the cost.[3] During the worst time, those in the thick of it (including the author) felt the entire world's financial systems would collapse. At the height of the crisis, first we saw the implosion of Bear Stearns, then the collapse of Lehman Brothers. Had it not been for the efforts of the world's governments and taxpayers to support the global financial system, who knows to what extent the world economy would have collapsed even further?

To prevent a repeat of the reckless behaviour of the banks, governments and regulators massively increased the level of regulation imposed on them. Curbing bonuses, implementing taxes and levies, increasing capital requirements, increasing reporting, and ring-fencing assets are but a few of the extra measures that have been in place since 2008 in many jurisdictions.

As a result of new regulation, banks have felt pressure on both their revenues and costs. Costs have increased as a result of increased compliance, reporting, capital allocations and liquidity required. Revenues have decreased as the scope to create and trade risky financial products has disappeared. All of this has meant that profits for financial institutions (FIs) have been under pressure.

These extra reporting requirements have required banks to innovate with technology to save on costs. However, they have to do so on

---

3 Some may argue that the banks did not in fact know about the contagion risks of the products they sold and marketed, or perhaps that they didn't want to know.

the back of extensive legacy infrastructure that underpins the world's financial systems. Innovations such as ATMs and credit cards were created in the 1960s; the Swift payment network in the 1970s. These systems have little changed since then. Modern banks are also collections of many different sized entities that have been acquired through decades of mergers and acquisitions. Most of these firms have different information technology (IT) systems, and integrations between systems have taken place without upgrading or unifying them.

The author remembers well the experiences at one of the world's largest FIs, and needing to manually enter information into MS-DOS as this software underpinned billions of dollars of trades globally.

Accenture[4] estimates that investment banks spend approximately two-thirds of their IT budgets supporting legacy infrastructure (the 'back office' as discussed earlier by Antony) and billions of dollars more on attempting to implement cost reduction initiatives.[5]

How can banks innovate using technology to create cost savings and boost revenues? How can they raise their return on equity?

The mantra at some FIs is they now see themselves no longer as banks, but as technology companies first and foremost. This is the new operational model they wish to adapt to. This shift in mindset is now evident amongst their workforces. In mid-2018, the chairman of Goldman Sachs stated that they have more engineers than bankers in some divisions.[6] Prioritizing financial technology (fintech) is a board-level agenda.

Currently, several different technologies are all intersecting at the same time and promise to lead the next wave of fintech innovation. These include biometrics, cloud computing, machine learning/artificial intelligence, quantum computing, robotics, and, of course, distributed ledger technology (DLT).

Focusing on the impact of DLT in the financial services sector (concentrating mainly on FIs), we will consider DLT's impact from an infrastructure and process perspective rather than talk about securities,

---

4 Accenture are a technology management consultancy company: www.accenture.com/.

5 'Banking on Blockchain: A value analysis for investment banks', www.accenture.com/t20171108T095421Z__w__/ph-en/_acnmedia/Accenture/Conversion-Assets/DotCom/Documents/Global/PDF/Consulting/Accenture-Banking-on-Blockchain.pdf.

6 'Goldman Sachs has "more engineers than bankers" in some divisions, says chairman', www.thetradenews.com/goldman-sachs-engineers-bankers-divisions-says-chairman/.

tokenization and cryptocurrency perspective, which are discussed in other parts of this book.

1. DLT Adoption in FIs

DLT has become a rather broad encompassing term for various systems and configurations of electronic record keeping that obey certain principles. Without repeating what has been covered previously, let us briefly examine a technical definition and what properties of DLT suit usage at FIs.

Starting with a somewhat purist definition,[7] one could state that a DLT system is made up of electronic records, which enable a network of independent participants to establish consensus around an authoritative ordering of cryptographically validated transactions, which are replicated across multiple nodes, and tamper-evident through being linked via cryptographic hashes. The ledger of these records consists of the shared reconciliation/consensus process and represents the global version of the truth.

Key properties of any DLT system are principles of decentralization of control, distribution of data, use of cryptography, and programmability/automation (smart contract) functionality.[8] Practically, DLTs are a coordination technology enabling information to be verified and exchanged by multiple parties that are operating in an environment with no central authority and with potentially adversarial parties.

Economically, DLT systems enable a reduction of two costs: the cost of verification and the cost of networking.[9] As DLT systems are designed to operate in trustless environments, the costs of verifying attributes of a transaction are dramatically reduced. One can often take for granted that when you are transferring money, trust and verification is facilitated by a central authority (usually a bank), which ensures that the sender has enough funds or credit and updates the account balances (the ledger) of the counterparties. With DLT systems, this is facilitated by multiple parties who operate nodes and to whom the control of updating the ledger has been decentralized.

---

7 'Distributed Ledger Technology Systems', www.jbs.cam.ac.uk/fileadmin/user_upload/research/centres/alternative-finance/downloads/2018-10-26-conceptualising-dlt-systems.pdf.

8 One may also state transparency and immutability, but these may not necessarily be the case.

9 'Some Simple Economics of the Blockchain', https://papers.ssrn.com/sol3/papers.cfm?abstract_id=2874598.

If we compare the cost of the banking system to the cost of the deployment of the Bitcoin network, the cost of creating the Bitcoin network was far less than a banking infrastructure and took less time. Anyone can join the Bitcoin network as a node. All that is required is a good internet connection and a computer to participate.[10] Compare the cost of this to the set-up cost for a bank. Here we see the cost of networking (which can also be thought of as the cost of setting up an infrastructure to run a network or marketplace without intermediaries) is far cheaper.

DLT use cases in the financial sector can be categorized around cost reduction in the short term and business model transformation in the long term. In the short term, through the utilization of shared infrastructure and process efficiency, various estimates of dramatic cost savings have been predicted. Accenture3 estimates that cost savings could be as much as:

- 70% on central finance reporting: more streamlined data quality and transparency.
- 30%–50% on compliance: improved transparency and auditability of financial transactions.
- 50% savings on centralized operations: better KYC and client onboarding (identity).
- 50% on business operations: on middle and back office functions, clearance, settlement, and reconciliation.

Feasibility studies by McKinsey[11] have identified that the impact of Blockchain technology in the finance industry ranks highest regarding cost reduction in relation to other sectors.[12] They determine the feasibility of adoption of DLT in assets as the highest of any other industry as well.

In the short term, reducing redundant infrastructure and intermediaries can result in a reduction of reconciliation activities between

---

10 At the time of writing, the Bitcoin Blockchain is approximately 185 GB and the hash power on the network is approximately 35 million TH/s. The author acknowledges that although possible to participate in the network, with today's mining difficulty it would not be at all profitable.

11 McKinsey is a management consultancy company: www.mckinsey.com/.

12 'Blockchain beyond the hype: What is the strategic business value?' www.mckinsey.com/business-functions/digital-mckinsey/our-insights/blockchain-beyond-the-hype-what-is-the-strategic-business-value.

different parties involved in financial transactions. DLT's properties of immutability and transparency serve well here to facilitate breaking of information silos and the need for cumbersome inter-firm reconciliation.

Transparency of information and auditability enable the reduction of information asymmetry within the sector. Here, for instance, having more real-time information delivered to the regulator may enable much lower regulatory compliance costs.

Longer term, DLT's promise is for transformational business models to change the nature of the industry. It is because of these transformational business models that DLT is considered a general-purpose technology (GPT), or foundational technology. GPTs tend to have the capability to create substantial productivity gains across multiple sectors, but to diffuse into the economy often takes a long time. Examples of GPTs are the steam engine, electricity, and TCP/IP (the internet). Within the financial sector, DLT may enable transformative business models through utilization of predominantly automation/programmatically executable contracts (smart contracts).

Smart contracts are essentially pieces of code that execute automatically under certain conditions. Their promise is hailed as a means of enforcing business processes and rules such that obligations are automatically fulfilled between contracted parties. They can automate business processes through the codification of business rules and logic. Although smart contracts do not require DLT to exist and function, having them as a part of a DLT infrastructure enables execution of contractual conditions in a trustless capacity. In the context of FIs, smart contracts will allow automation of many financial processes, decrease settlement times and increase accuracy, reduce counterparty risk, and disintermediate many entities, reducing overall costs.

2. DLT Adoption in the Financial Services Sector

There has been much hype regarding DLT as a panacea for many of the problems within the financial services sector. Indeed, the reality is that Blockchain technology, along with many other emergent technologies, is creating the next wave of transformation in financial services infrastructure. Gartner[13] believes DLT is currently in the trough of

---

13 Gartner is a research and advisory company.

disillusionment on their hype cycle.[14] Unlike other technologies, attention on DLT was magnified in the public domain because of the accessibility of the technology through the medium of cryptocurrencies. One may argue that, indeed, cryptocurrencies demonstrated a bubble and in many ways have tarnished the wider potential of DLT.

In the last few years, over $1.4bn has been invested in DLTs by corporates and venture capital.[15] News and media coverage of these investments gave the impression that proof of concept (POC) projects would rapidly make an impact in the industry and society. Unfortunately, the complexity of implementation and the coordination effort required for DLT adoption have meant the adoption of the technology on a broader basis is still several years away. Several hurdles remain for broader adoption. These are primarily around continued legal and regulatory uncertainty, a lack of common standards, the coopetition paradox, and a lack of developer talent. According to CBInsights,[16] several high-profile projects in the sector have stalled, while the success of many are still to be determined.[17] Some of these issues will be explored further in this chapter.

In general, DLT is widely recognized as being a transformative technology. Over 80% of banks are believed to be engaged in DLT pilot projects, and over 90 central banks worldwide are engaged in DLT discussions. According to PwC,[18] 24% of financial executives from all over the world are very familiar with Blockchain technology.[19]

Trends for the adoption of the technology have centred around the utilization of private Blockchain technology and experimentation with consortia in the development of POCs. DLTs can be divided between public and private chains. This division usually refers to the ability to read, write, and commit to the Blockchain. In the case of public chains, usually, anyone can read, write, and commit. In the case of private

---

14 Gartner Hype Cycle: www.gartner.com/en/research/methodologies/gartner-hype-cycle.
15 'World Economic Forum: The future of financial infrastructure', www3.weforum.org/docs/WEF_The_future_of_financial_infrastructure.pdf.
16 CB Insights is a technology intelligence company: www.cbinsights.com/.
17 'Blockchain Trends 2019', www.cbinsights.com/research/report/blockchain-trends-2019/.
18 PwC is an audit and consultancy company: www.pwc.com/.
19 'Redrawing the lines: FinTech's growing influence on Financial Services', www.pwc.com/gx/en/industries/financial-services/assets/pwc-global-fintech-report-2017.pdf.

chains different actors in the system have different abilities to read, write, and commit. This degree of access also determines several critical properties of the system, namely security, scalability, and decentralization. Private chains are more scalable but less decentralized than public chains. Arguably they may be less secure due to more centralized control.

Due to the sensitive nature of transaction data in the financial sector and the requirement for high throughput (many transactions per second), many projects in the financial sector choose to utilize private chains for experimentation and implementation. Public chains are still used at times, but this is mostly when public provenance is required and throughput is not an issue. Private chains are increasingly referred to as enterprise Blockchain because of their general applicability to the corporate environment.

Enterprise Blockchains have also seen what purists would say is a perversion of the dream of decentralization and immutability. Accenture created a Blockchain technology that has redaction properties, or the ability to change what had been written on chain.[20] In an enterprise setting, having to correct mistakes made on information uploaded is a crucial challenge to widespread adoption. Even amongst purists, Ethereum faced its challenge when a decision was made by its community to reverse what some would class as theft from The DAO.[21] Purists opposed to rewriting history continued with Ethereum Classic while Ethereum reversed history and erased the DAO incident.[22]

Several consortia (a consortium is a collection of organizations that work together to implement DLT in a particular industry) have been formed, and Blockchains are being utilized by FIs. Consortia enable the pooling of resources and the setting of common standards, and reduce the risk of running proof of concept projects. Since the benefits of DLT can only be realized through coordination efforts and utilization of multiple members, consortia serve as a facilitator for getting corporates to work together.

---

20 'Blockchain Redaction', www.accenture.com/t20180810T060600Z__w__/us-en/_acnmedia/PDF-44/Accenture-Blockchain-Redaction-Infographic.pdf.
21 A Decentralized Autonomous Organization was called The DAO, and is to date the most famous example of this type of organization: www.coindesk.com/information/what-is-a-dao-ethereum.
22 'Understanding The DAO Attack', www.coindesk.com/understanding-dao-hack-journalists.

In the private chain sphere, R3's consortium ecosystem has over 200 members from multiple sectors. Their enterprise Blockchain solution is called Corda. Hyperledger is another consortium that has some enterprise Blockchain solutions. They have over 200 members from multiple sectors. Enterprise Ethereum Alliance is a consortium that advances the use and adoption of the Ethereum Blockchain (a public chain). Currently, they state they have over 385 members from over 45 countries. JPMorgan has also led the creation of Quorum, a version of Ethereum focused for enterprises. Several banks are working with this technology.

Consortia also help to resolve what is known as the coopetition paradox. DLT's significant advantage in being used is its network effect, with greater benefits achieved the more extensive the network of utilization and adoption. This means that natural competitors need to work together to create common standards for usage. In the case of FIs, R3's consortium consists of over 70 global banks that are collaborating on their open-source platform. Both governments and regulators are also participating and demonstrating signals, and in some cases leadership. Only by working together can the sector move forward to adopt this technology faster.

Generally, the strategy for adoption so far is through the utilization of POC projects between several participants to demonstrate use cases. Some of these projects have stalled while others have reached the stage of live deployment. Some of these will be explored in the proceeding sections. The development of a POC is just the first part of broader implementation. At scale, decisions on standardization, governance, investment, and interfacing with legacy infrastructure need to be agreed.

Due to this coordination complexity, adoption at the intra-firm level is far easier than at the inter-firm level. FIs can utilize this technology internally faster than externally. Information remains limited about the extent to which FIs are adopting these technologies, but the market is full of rumours of adoption.

Interoperability of different DLT systems is also a feature that is being actively worked on. Different DLTs are not able to communicate with each other. Transactions on the Bitcoin Blockchain cannot be transferred to the Ethereum Blockchain and vice versa, but in the private chain sphere firms are working on enabling chains to talk to each other. This helps reduce the risk of having potentially picked the wrong platform. Accenture has developed an interoperability node that can connect Quorum, Hyperledger Fabric, and Corda.[23] The key to avoiding trapped assets and silos of the past is interoperability.

The financial services sector has also led the way for patent filing for Blockchain technology. Looking at the top five global Blockchain enterprise patent filings as of September 2018, Mastercard, Bank of America and the People's Bank of China (PBOC) are present.[24] Of note is that the top 100 ranking consists mainly of Chinese and American companies, with China taking 57 of the top 100 places. FIs are both genuinely filing patents as a result of innovation with DLT but also as a means of being prepared for future uses. Cynically, one may argue that patent filing serves as a means of media attention – part of the hype issue that has tainted the industry and deepened because tangible public utilization has not been seen.

FIs are not only betting and investing in their projects but are also investing in the equity of many other Blockchain businesses. For instance, Citi,[25] Goldman Sachs,[26] and JP Morgan[27] have all invested in Digital Asset Holdings[28] and Axoni.[29] Citi and Goldman Sachs both have many more investments, in companies such as Cobalt,[30] Setl,[31] Circle,[32] and BitGo.[33] In general, FIs have been investing in many different Blockchain businesses that include segments such as wallets, money services, exchanges, and capital markets.

The rationale for why FIs are investing in these businesses is they cannot experiment in all the different areas of DLT innovation. Talent

---

23 'Accenture Tech Now Connects Corda, Fabric, DA and Quorum Blockchains', www.coindesk.com/accenture-launch-interoperability-node-connects-corda-fabric-da-and-quorum-blockchains.

24 'China takes 57 of 100 spots in global top 100 blockchain patent ranking', https://technode.com/2018/09/03/blockchain-patent-china-tech/.

25 Citi is a bank: www.citigroup.com/citi/.

26 Goldman Sachs is a bank: www.goldmansachs.com.

27 JP Morgan is a bank: www.jpmorgan.com/.

28 Digital Asset Holding are developing blockchain infrastructure for FIs: www.digitalasset.com/.

29 Axoni are developing blockchain infrastructure for FIs: https://axoni.com/.

30 Cobalt is providing post trade infrastructure in foreign exchange markets: www.cobaltdl.com/.

31 Setl is utilizing blockchain for the financial services industry: www.setl.io/.

32 Circle is a crypto finance company: www.circle.com/.

33 BitGo are an institutional cryptocurrency financial services company: www.bitgo.com/info/.

and culture also play a role. Creating innovative and transformative products in a traditional FI environment where there are internal parties who are resistant to change is not conducive to success. Indeed, at several FIs, innovation internally in DLT-related products come from hackathon challenges rather than from any organized research unit.

When Blockchain businesses interface with large FIs, the scope to work together can be extremely onerous. Blockchain businesses operating in the financial services sector either come in the form of consultancies who are facilitating product build or actual DLT infrastructure companies that wish to onboard FIs onto their infrastructure. Usually, these infrastructures are on critical operating systems that cannot fail. Therefore, for an FI to become a DLT business's customer, there is a significant barrier to adoption (financially) regarding satisfying all the onboarding and compliance requirements. Before any revenue is even received from a business working with an FI, several hundred thousand dollars may need to be expended upfront to pass the adoption barrier.

Investing into these young DLT businesses make sense from a utilization perspective. By making an investment, due diligence and onboarding procedures have to some extent been mitigated. A more unique and more in-depth understanding of the businesses and its innovation can also be seen. Finally, this also opens up a route to acquiring technology and talent.

This discussion on DLT businesses interfacing with large financial services firms leads us to the broader question of how firms succeed in this sector. With fintech in general, the regulatory and infrastructure barriers for start-ups have meant there was an initially large capital hurdle to overcome even to begin to compete. With DLT the initial coin offering (ICO) mechanism seemed like a new way to raise capital by offering tokens that could be redeemed for services provided by the firm. Essentially this is pre-revenue for services provided that could be utilized to build the infrastructure required. Since DLT infrastructure needs multiple users to demonstrate benefits, onboarding multiple users as an outsider or new player to an industry can be particularly tricky. Here one might argue that incumbents themselves are the only ones that can foster adoption, as they can require all those in their ecosystem to garner adoption to work with them. Here, investments in DLT businesses enable a smoother journey for working with incumbents.

One might argue that given there is such a high regulatory burden in the financial sector, it may be regulators that instruct adoption. We have seen the playing field in the financial services sector become far more open with the regulator wanting to embrace innovation through sand-box environments and the implementation of regulation opening up markets. Regulation such as PSD2 open banking will open customer's account information to new entrants and start-up businesses. In general, though, regulators prefer to take a technology-neutral approach, and do not stipulate which technology must be used to comply with its edicts.

Instead, it may be the very intermediaries themselves, whom many have stated will be disintermediated by DLT, which foster innovation. These players are tried, tested, and trusted by the banks. They have the capabilities and relationships as the connections that will tie financial service firms together via DLT. The argument that they will be putting themselves out of business may be too naïve. There will be a reduction in costs as reconciliation efforts and information asymmetry are reduced. Simultaneously, with more efficient systems, transaction frequency may increase, and the net effect could be a better financial position overall. It may be better to lead and channel strategic disintermediation, rather than this approach be pushed aside without any consideration.

3. Use Cases

So far DLT applicability and implementation in the financial sector has been described in a general way. In this section, we will examine a few selected applications of DLT to various, more specific areas in the financial industry.[34] These areas include payments, regulation, clearing and settlement, insurance, and trade and supply chain finance.

For each use case, we will describe how the regime currently is, how it could be transformed and where we stand today regarding the adoption of DLT.

---

34 There are an extraordinary number of use cases in the financial services sector and indeed a book could be written on these cases alone.

Payments

Payments form a core function of many FIs and are essential for the global economy. They involve the transfer of monetary value to pay for goods and services, and the transferring of value and money across geographical borders. Global payment volumes have grown by approximately 5% per annum and are currently over $600bn for remittances, according to the World Bank.[35] Margins on global payments made are high, at about 7.68% on average of the amount transferred. It is estimated that about 10% of Santander's profits in 2016 came from international money transfers.[36] On average it takes nearly three days for a transfer to reach its destination. For this section, we will focus on global cross-border money transfers.

Current System Payments occur broadly following the process in Figure 6.1. At the Initiation stage, the process begins when someone who wants to send money (the sender) interfaces with a bank or a money transfer operator whose function is to perform KYC/AML (know your customer/anti-money laundering), process fees, and deal with customer service. After initiation, the Transfer stage occurs where the funds are moved via the SWIFT[37] network or through correspondent banks.[38] After funds have been transferred, we come to the Delivery stage where funds are paid in the local currency to the beneficiary. KYC/AML processes may also be carried out at this final stage. Afterwards, certain actions may occur at the Post Process stage, when information is submitted to the regulator.

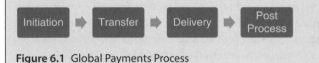

Figure 6.1 Global Payments Process

35 Migration and Remittances Factbook 2016: www.worldbank.org/en/research/brief/migration-and-remittances.

36 'Revealed: the huge profits earned by big banks on overseas money transfers', www.theguardian.com/money/2017/apr/08/leaked-santander-international-money-transfers-transferwise.

37 SWIFT is a payments network: www.swift.com/.

38 A correspondent bank is one that provides services on behalf of another FI: www.investopedia.com/terms/c/correspondent-bank.asp.

The current payments process has several issues in connection with the Transfer stage and the Post Process stage. At the Transfer stage, transfer fees for utilization of the payment network are large and the time to pass through is long. As we have mentioned, fees for transfers are as high as 7.68% and on average transfers take three days to reach their destination. SWIFT is the primary messaging network that is used to inform about money transfers around the world. This network has over 24 million messages sent through it a day and has over 10,000 financial institutions using it.[39] If two financial institutions don't have an established financial relationship, then they must search the SWIFT network for a correspondent bank that can settle the transaction. Given each of these banks maintain different ledgers, they all need to be reconciled at the end of every day.

This can also lead to issues with information that is passed through the system with high rejection rates for transfers. Approximately 60% of B2B payments require manual intervention, each of which takes on average between 10–20 minutes to deal with. Banks also bear the cost of liquidity for holding and funding nostro accounts[40] which results in hedging and opportunity costs. Reporting to the regulator is an issue, as often many disparate systems are utilized and reconciliation of all of these to send a unified reporting to the regulator can be costly and inefficient.

DLT System   Facilitating international transfers through DLT can reduce costs, enable new business models, and create new regulatory oversight.

The utilization of a shared ledger infrastructure between players involved in the transfer process can create a direct link between FIs either side of the transfer process. One benefit of this would be ensuring that all players have real-time reconciliation of records of transfers potentially in real time and with lower liquidity and operational costs.

Smart contract technology can also be utilized as the means of facilitating the transfer between the beneficiary and sender subject to KYC/AML checks automatically. This smart contract could also inform the

---

39 'How Blockchain Could Disrupt Banking', www.cbinsights.com/research/blockchain-disrupting-banking/.
40 A nostro account is one that a bank holds at another bank in a foreign currency: https://www.investopedia.com/terms/n/nostroaccount.asp.

regulator automatically if required, with the regulator sitting as a node on the network.

DLT could be used through already existing cryptocurrencies. Here, the sending institution and the receiving institution utilize the cryptocurrency network to facilitate the transfer of value. At the initiation stage, institutions exchange the sending currency for a cryptocurrency through an exchange, and then transfer the cryptocurrency to the receiving institution, which then changes this back into local currency.

The benefits of adopting DLT for this process are, of course, primarily reduced cost and reduced time of transfer. If one takes Bitcoin as an example, transactions effectively clear every 10 minutes[41] and <1% of the transaction amount[42] is charged as fees. Liquidity requirements are also reduced because the need to maintain balances at other institutions is not required, as you are only dealing with an exchange. Alternatively the utilization of shared ledger means liquidity is managed through smart contracts where foreign exchange can be sourced from parties who are willing to fund these transactions. The regulator can also be an integral part of the entire process sitting on both the shared infrastructure and being able to audit transactions on a public ledger, if that is utilized.

DLT Adoption Examples, where this is currently being utilized, can be seen in many places. Ripple[43] is using DLT specifically to replace payment rails for FIs. Ripple has several solutions in the market which compete with SWIFT as a messaging protocol. They also have a cryptocurrency called XRP that can facilitate the transfer of value in seconds across their network. Ripple currently has over 100 financial institutions as customers of their products, with over 75 of these deploying their products commercially. Customers include the likes of MUFG, Santander, Standard Chartered, American Express, and RBC to name but a few.[44] Currently, it seems that adoption of XRP for transferring funds between financial institutions is primarily utilized in the

---

41 Strictly speaking, one should wait 60 minutes for finality.
42 Under conditions where the network is not congested. For more information on real-time Bitcoin fees see: https://bitcoinfees.earn.com/.
43 Ripple is a blockchain company focusing on FI payments. They also have a cryptocurrency called XRP: https://ripple.com/.
44 From Ripple's website: https://ripple.com/.

remittance segment (where XRP may have better liquidity than exotic currencies[45]). For instance, Cuallix[46] is utilizing DLT to facilitate remittance transfers between the US and Mexico.[47] SBI Holdings[48] have also announced that their mobile money remittance app is using Ripple technology.

BitPesa is also utilizing the Bitcoin Blockchain to improve B2B payments in countries such as Nigeria, Kenya, Tanzania, and Uganda. The company boasts fees on average of 1%–3%, which is 90% cheaper than other traditional payment providers in the region with transfers taking as little as 1–24 hours compared to 2–14 days. With over 25,000 customers and $340m transacted over 85+ countries, they are seeing good adoption of their technology, growing nearly 20% month on month.[49]

IBM has launched a new product called Blockchain World Wire that is utilizing the Stellar Blockchain for transfers.[50] Alibaba has launched a Blockchain-based cross-border remittance service for transfers between Hong Kong and the Philippines.[51] Goldman Sachs has led a $25m investment funding round into a Blockchain payments start-up called Veem, which is offering a multi-rail payments platform that includes both traditional SWIFT and Blockchain-based transfer networks.[52] JPMorgan, in partnership with ANZ and RBC, has also announced that over 75 banks are now participating in their Quorum-based solution called the Interbank Information Network (IIN). Currently, there are over 14,500 USD denominated payments per day made on the IIN.[53]

---

45 An exotic currency is one that is thinly traded.
46 Cuallix is a FI engaged in loans and remittances: http://www.cuallix.com/.
47 'Ripple Event Reveal: 3 Companies Are Now Using XRP for Real Payments', www .coindesk.com/ripple-event-reveal-3-companies-are-now-using-xrp-for-real-payments.
48 SBI Holdings is a Japanese FI: www.sbigroup.co.jp/english/.
49 BitPesa is a blockchain payments firm: www.bitpesa.co/.
50 'IBM Debuts Stellar-Powered "Blockchain World Wire" Payments System', www .coindesk.com/ibm-debuts-stellar-powered-blockchain-world-wire-payments-system.
51 'Alibaba's Ant Financial Launches a Blockchain-based Cross-border Remittance Service', https://blokt.com/news/alibabas-ant-financial-launches-a-blockchain-based-cross-border-remittance-service.
52 'Veem & Goldman Sachs Announce Partnership for Seamless Small Business Payments', www.veem.com/blog/veem-goldman-sachs-partner-for-seamless-small-business-payments/.
53 'Over 75 New Banks: JPMorgan Expands Blockchain Payments Trial', www.coindesk .com/over-75-new-banks-jpmorgan-expands-blockchain-payments-trial.

The Outlook for DLT DLT adoption can help to enable faster and cheaper payments for the entire sector with the direct transfer of value bypassing intermediaries. Utilizing DLT can create transformational business models in many industries through facilitating micropayments (currently they are too expensive to implement). DLT adoption may also lead to the disintermediation of correspondent banks as intermediaries are bypassed.

The biggest challenges for DLT adoption in this sector are, of course, the setting of common standards and systems for different players involved in the value chain (in the face of the coopetition paradox). R3 has shown leadership as a consortium focused on FIs, but several large banks have left because of the lack of control they could exert on the consortium.[54]

Regarding utilizing cryptocurrencies for payment transfers, the biggest issue in using these as a bridge asset is the volatility of the instrument. This is somewhat mitigated by the introduction of the concept of stablecoins, which fix their value to an underlying asset (other major currencies, commodities, or real estate, for instance) or algorithmically, thereby avoiding the volatility in price. Numerous projects utilizing stablecoins are beginning to emerge.[55]

For DLT to succeed in this sector, standards and interoperability must be ensured, and also the interfacing of current practices with KYC incorporated into the DLT system.

Regulation
A vital part of any regulated FI's obligations is compliance and reporting information to the regulator. This information ranges from audits, tax, filings, and general reporting of any compliance-related activities (transfers of funds above a certain size, etc). Compliance costs are high with estimates ranging at roughly $100bn being spent by FIs worldwide per year.[56] This is estimated to increase from 4% to 10% of revenues by 2021.

---

54 'JPMorgan Chase & Co leaves blockchain consortium R3', www.reuters.com/article/us-jpmorgan-r3/jpmorgan-chase-co-leaves-blockchain-consortium-r3-idUSKBN17T2T4.

55 'Report: Stablecoins See Significant Growth in Adoption Over Recent Months', https://cointelegraph.com/news/report-stablecoins-see-significant-growth-in-adoption-over-recent-months.

56 'Taming The High Costs Of Compliance With Tech', www.forbes.com/sites/tomgroenfeldt/2018/03/22/taming-the-high-costs-of-compliance-with-tech/#24f496335d3f.

Current System The current system for audit and regulatory reporting relies on FIs reconciling information for reporting processes, often interdepartmentally, and then submitting to the auditor or regulator when required. In the following example, we will look at an auditing process of the financial position of an FI for tax or regulatory capital reasons. Typically, an auditing process can be broken down into three stages, as shown in Figure 6.2.

Figure 6.2 Compliance and Regulatory Reporting Processes

At the Planning stage, a request for information required is made, and access to those records is arranged and granted. After the Planning stage, the process moves to the Assessment stage, where auditors examine the information submitted. This information is checked for accuracy and completeness. In this part, there is also communication back and forth between both parties concerning any errors or questions about the supplied data. Finally, the audit is signed off, enabling continued operations during the Reporting stage.

This process is by its nature resource intensive. Firstly, from the perspective of the FI, this is a burden on employees' time to supply the requested information and deal with multiple departments internally to coordinate information that is required. Secondly, data is often sampled for audit as there is just too much information to analyse. This means the analysis is only as good as the sampling. The entire process often has a poor integration of technology, meaning a lot of the process is still entirely manual.

DLT System Placing FI records on a DLT and incorporating the auditor and the regulators as nodes would lead to fewer errors, reduced costs, improved efficiency, and more profound regulatory insights, potentially on a real-time basis.

With all parties being on a shared ledger, there would be direct access to the data instead of it being manually handed over and then requiring follow-up and querying. Because the data is transparent and immutable, there is a trail of information visible. The entire process would be less prone to errors and faster, because less incomplete information would appear and one would be able to look deeper into the data. Smart contracts could also automatically transfer this information as and when required to the regulators and auditors. Various filings and returns could also be automatically filed for purposes of renewing licenses and registrations when conditions on regulatory compliance were met. This could apply to reporting of tax, reporting of regulatory capital, reporting of unusual trade activity, etc.

The cost savings for the FI of adopting these technologies would be massive, through the reduction of headcount deployed purely to deal with manual interventions that could be automated.

DLT Adoption   University College London (UCL) has been involved with leading a regulatory technology (RegTech) project called Blockchain Technology for Algorithmic Regulation and Compliance (BARAC).[57] This is the largest publicly funded research project to investigate the benefits of deploying DLT for regulatory compliance. BARAC's first success has been with Project Maison, where the UK Financial Conduct Authority (FCA) worked with R3 and two major banks to develop a prototype application for the regulatory reporting of mortgage transaction data. Here, the FCA sat as a regulator node on the DLT network and were able to receive continuous real-time data from two banks regarding mortgage reporting. This project demonstrated that continuous regulatory reporting could be achieved at a comparatively low cost.

UBS, along with Barclays, Credit Suisse, KBC, SIX, and Thomson Reuters have worked together on a project called the Massive Autonomous Distributed Reconciliation platform (MADREC).[58] This is used to enable banks to reconcile a wide range of data about their counterparties, which is legally required as part of the Markets in Financial Instruments Directive (MiFID) II regulation.

The Outlook for DLT   Although regulators take technology-neutral approaches to regulatory compliance, the increasing burden and costs of compliance have meant that FIs must look to implement cost-reducing technologies to meet their regulatory compliance duties. Part of getting this right is that not only must FIs work to adopt DLT for cost-saving purposes, but also that they must ensure that the regulator can

---

57 Find out more about the BARAC project at http://blockchain.cs.ucl.ac.uk/barac-project/.
58 'UBS to Launch Live Ethereum Compliance Platform', www.coindesk.com/ubs-launch-live-ethereum-platform-barclays-credit-suisse.

interface with this technology. As we have seen, the regulator is keen to look at this technology because of the promise of real-time reporting capabilities. What remains to be seen is whether the benefits of adopting DLT for potentially continuous auditing will materialize. The thinking behind this is that it would help prevent conditions such as systemic risk developing and repeats of previous crises.

It is important to note as well that there are challenges for designing systems such that only compartmentalized access is provided. For instance, for wider security and privacy reasons, auditors and regulators should only be able to access the information that they need, not all the information available. Ensuring interoperability with various systems as well as those used by auditors and regulators is essential.

Clearing and Settlements

Clearing of securities is the process of reconciling orders before their settlement. Settlement is the act of transferring securities and funds between counterparties. Clearing is the process of determining obligations, and settlement the process of fulfilling those obligations. The foreign exchange market on average needs to clear and settle trades amounting to approximately $3 trillion every day. This is just one market of many and does not include all the derivative products that are related to this. The Depository Trust & Clearing Corporation (DTCC) settles approximate 1.5 million transactions per day with a value of approximately $650bn.[59] The NYSE processes millions of trades and billions of shares every day.[60]

Currently, it takes anywhere from one to three days to clear and settle a trade. There are many intermediaries involved in this process who generate multibillion-dollar revenues which could be saved. DLT has the potential to dramatically improve how assets are transferred by streamlining the clearing and settlement process.

Current System   Looking at the equity trading clearing and settlement process, there are three stages of executing and transferring ownership of shares, as shown in Figure 6.3. Firstly, a trade is executed at the Trade Execution stage. Here, an investor or trader places an order through a bank or broker that executes the order on an exchange. The exchange facilitates matching of buy and sell orders in real time and

---

59 www.dtcc.com/.
60 www.nyse.com/index.

initiates real-time post-trade processes. After the trade is confirmed on the exchange, the Clearing process occurs. Here custodian banks[61] (CB) send the trade details to the central securities depository[62] (CSD). Next, the trade moves on to the Settlement stage and to the central clearing counterparty[63] (CCC) who nets trades across all CBs and simultaneously transfers the shares and cash amongst the CBs. They then notify the traders and investors and update their account balances.

The current system typically enforces settlement three days after trade execution, meaning investors are limited in their actions until

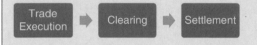

Figure 6.3 Clearing and Settlement Processes

settlement. There are often instances where manual intervention is required because of frequent changes to counterparty bank details. Settlement risk is also present and must be accounted for by CBs. Asset servicing that also occurs to initiate corporate actions, distribute income (dividends), and facilitate voting usually involve many intermediaries, all of which take fees.

DLT System   Utilizing DLT would see smart contracts used in the clearing and settlement part of the process. DLT would enable a disintermediating process, reduce operational and counterparty risk, and reduce settlement times.

During clearing, smart contracts would validate the information sent by CBs and match all parts of the trade. The smart contract would then determine the 'net transaction' and simultaneously execute the transfer of ownership and funds. Confirmations at all stages of the clearing and settlement process would be on the Blockchain enabling asset servicing to be simplified and to occur automatically.

DLT here has the promise of creating a decentralized database of ownership of these assets and thus enabling seamless transferring

---

61 Custodian banks store the assets and facilitate trading.
62 Central securities depository validate the trade details and match all parts of the trade.
63 The central clearing counterparty manages counterparty risk during settlement.

without the need for multiple intermediaries. This reduces the settlement and custody risks and errors involved. Utilization of DLTs would lead to reduced settlement time potentially leading to real-time settlement if desired. Counterparty risk would also be reduced through automatic validation of the ability to settle. Operational risk is lowered, as processes are automatic, reducing the need for manual interventions.

Current Implementations One of the biggest projects actively being worked on is by the DTCC, which is utilizing DLT to provide life cycle processing for roughly 98% of all credit derivative transactions worldwide (worth $11 trillion). DTCC's customer base includes over 2500 buy-side firms and other market participants in over 70 countries. This project has now moved from development to testing with estimates that it will go live in 2019. Several large banks are part of this project including Barclays. DTCC has also used a multi-vendor approach in building this system, which includes IBM, Axoni, AxCore, and R3.[64]

UK-based settlements infrastructure company SETL has been granted permission by the French regulator to operate a central securities depository (CSD) using Blockchain technology.[65] SETL has a multi-asset and multi-currency institutional payment and settlements infrastructure and is backed by Citi.

Abu Dhabi Bank has successfully settled $500m of bonds on the secondary market. Benefits of doing so were cited as being more efficient and reducing overhead costs.[66] The World Bank has also had a recent bond offering settled on a Blockchain. A private Ethereum Blockchain was used to settle the bonds, which were worth $81m.[67]

The Outlook for DLT For DLT to be adopted, CBs, regulators, CCCs, and exchanges will all need to work together to move this complex process onto a Blockchain. Indeed, the Australian Securities Exchange (ASX) has pushed back the launch of its Blockchain settlement system, citing the complexity involved in implementation requiring further

64 '15 Banks Join DTCC Post-Trade Blockchain as Project Enters Testing', www.coindesk.com/15-banks-join-dtcc-post-trade-blockchain-as-project-enters-testing.
65 'Setl Receives Central Securities Depository License from Securities Regulator in France', https://bitcoinexchangeguide.com/setl-receives-central-securities-depository-license-from-securities-regulator-in-france/.
66 'Abu Dhabi Bank Settles $500 Million Bond on a Blockchain By CoinDesk', www.wiredfocus.com/abu-dhabi-bank-settles-500-million-bond-on-a-blockchain-by-coindesk/.

time.[68] There may indeed be disintermediation for CCC occurring for several of the players involved in the process, and, of course, this will be met with some degree of trepidation. CBs will also need to develop standards to match trades. They must overcome issues to standardize attributes that are not prone to change.

It is a matter for discussion as to whether there are benefits in moving to near real-time settlement and what the implications of this would be. Having a slow settlement system enables plenty of time to correct errors. With real-time settlement, if records were indeed immutable and final, it would be difficult to account for this. With real-time settlement, netting of trades would not need to occur unless there were predetermined clearing times (i.e. every hour).

Insurance

Insurance serves as a means of managing risk whereby one can protect against loss, be this on property, health, or assets for instance. Global insurance industry premiums total approximately $4 trillion growing at a rate of greater than 4% annually.[69] At a segmented level, health insurance and property and casualty insurance have had the highest growth at approximately 6% and 4.2% from 2015 to 2016. The insurance industry's most significant pain point is claims processing, where about 11% of the cost of the premium is spent.13 In this section, we will look at the impact of DLT on the claims management area of the insurance industry and how the industry could be transformed.

Current System Examining the claims management process, we can divide this into the three stages shown in Figure 6.4. In the Submission stage, an insuree reports a loss and the insurer or broker takes details about the claim. This then moves on to the Assessment stage, where the claim and the submitted information are verified. Here, additional follow-up may be required as the claims agents may seek verification

---

67 'CBA chosen by the World Bank to deliver world first blockchain bond', https://www.commbank.com.au/guidance/newsroom/cba-picked-by-world-bank-to-deliver-world-s-first-standalone-blo0-201808.html.

68 'ASX Postpones Roll-Out of Blockchain Settlement System', www.coindesk.com/asx-postpones-roll-out-of-dlt-settlement-system-to-2021-q2.

69 'Global Insurance Industry Insights', www.mckinsey.com/~/media/mckinsey/industries/financial%20services/our%20insights/global%20insurance%20insights%20an%20overview%20of%20recent%20trends%20in%20life%20p%20and%20c%20and%20health/global-insurance-industry-insights-an-in-depth-perspective-may-2018.ashx.

on the validity of information provided. If additional information about the claim is necessary, this can be requested as well. Finally, the claim is passed to the Decision stage, where a conclusion about the claim is made and a payment initiated (or not) to the insuree.

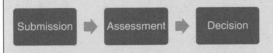

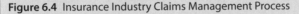

Figure 6.4 Insurance Industry Claims Management Process

There are several problems involved in the current process that start at the Submission stage. Often the reporting process is manual, and a lot of information is required to be submitted (paper-based receipts for instance). This can often be an undesirable process for many insurees. If brokers are utilized, this also adds an intermediary to the process and increases the end cost. In the Assessment stage, often relationships must be established individually between insurance companies and third parties. Usually, very little information is shared between insurers about claims. This means that there is fraud risk there, as processes are usually per-insurer and per-claim. Finally, at the last stage, the Decision-making process is manual.

DLT System With DLT, insurance policy information would be linked to smart contracts that would automatically trigger claims management procedures. Business rules for claims due diligence would be codified into these contracts. Oracles[70] would submit information utilized through external source information or automatically through IoT[71] devices (sensors) and dependent on the complexity of the claim, the smart contract could automatically calculate the payout or refer a human to take the case on. In some instances, a claim would not even need to be submitted, depending on how sensor information is linked to a policy.

Utilization primarily of smart contracts would seek to automate much of the claim's submission, assessment, and decision-making processes. This would enhance the customer experience streamlining the entire process and reducing the time and cost to process the claim. Fraudulent claims would also be reduced if multiple insurers all sat on a DLT system to share

---

70 An oracle in a DLT context refers to a source of information provided to the Blockchain. This may come from a sensor, or be inputted manually.
71 Internet of things (IoT) definition: https://en.wikipedia.org/wiki/Internet_of_things.

information about historical claims, and sensor and asset information. This would reduce costs all round as there is no duplication of efforts to access information required to assess claims. Claims assessors would still be required, but only in circumstances where claims were complicated.

DLT Adoption There are many consortia in the insurance industry that are experimenting with DLT, and several projects have now gone live. Two prominent consortia are the RiskBlock Alliance[72] and B3i.[73] Both consortia are utilizing R3's Corda Blockchain. R3 now count all the major insurance Blockchain consortia as using their Blockchain. Since Blockchain interoperability is an issue, the fact that all the major players are employing R3's Blockchain is positive in some respects.[74]

One of Japan's largest insurance companies, Tokio Marine & Nichido Fire Insurance, and IT firm NTT DATA have put the paperwork for marine cargo insurance claims on a Blockchain during a POC. This project had participation from eight overseas claims-settling agents and surveyors from Europe, Asia, and America. Utilizing a Blockchain system enabled insurance payout periods to drop from over a month to one week at most. Work is continuing on the platform and expectations are that it will go live in 2019.[75]

Metlife has also rolled out an automated insurance product that utilizes DLT to offer financial protection to women with gestational diabetes. Here, DLT is used to securely connect insurees' medical data to their insurance policy and automatically issue payouts should their medical records update and show they suffer from gestational diabetes. All of this will automatically occur without the insuree having to file a claim. This is currently rolled out in Singapore.[76]

Microinsurance is also being trialled with the utilization of DLT. Etherisc and Oxfam have partnered to cover people on very low incomes in Sri Lanka. Paddy rice farmers will try this product and farmers will automatically be paid out in conditions of bad weather. Weather indexes that are already supported by Oxfam in the country will be utilized as the oracles informing claim verification. Typically,

72 RiskBlock Alliance: www.theinstitutes.org/guide/riskblock.
73 B3i: https://b3i.tech/home.html.
74 'Big Insurers Are Uniting Behind R3's Blockchain Tech', www.coindesk.com/all-big-insurers-are-uniting-behind-r3s-blockchain-tech.
75 'Japanese Firms Claim Success in Marine Insurance Blockchain Trial', www.coindesk.com/japanese-firms-claim-success-in-marine-insurance-blockchain-trial.

microinsurance is not provided because of the cost of processing claims, but through automation, it can be offered.

The Outlook for DLT   It can be seen how implementing automation through smart contract technology can lead to enormous process benefits in the insurance sector for claims processing and management. However, this does require some intermediate steps before being rolled out. Primarily this means getting all the different sources of information involved on to a ledger. This can be somewhat straightforward when talking about IoT and sensor data, or anything that is publicly available online or via APIs.[77] In the case of signing up car garages and car mechanics, for instance, this would be a more manual and complicated process.

Similarly sharing insurance claim information would go a long way to reducing fraud in the industry and help to bring down premiums. Ultimately, the most prominent benefits would come from enabling asset profiles and history to be placed on DLTs and available for all insurance parties. Through digitizing this information, the efficiency for claims handling would be vastly improved.

Trade and Supply Chain Finance
Some sort of trade finance is required for 80%–90% of world trade. Trade finance exists to mitigate risks, extend credit, and to enable importers and exporters to work together through trusted third parties. It is part of the global financial system, but still very much operated with paper documents and manual and old-fashioned processes. FIs serve as the trusted third parties that for a fee will take oversight of the payment terms and take the risk between counterparties for them engaging in business. It is estimated that $18 trillion of trade transactions involve some form of trade finance[78]. DLT promises to optimize the entire trade finance process by providing a means of enabling trust throughout the process.

Current System   Figure 6.5 illustrates a typical process by which trade financing occurs on exporting and importing of goods. In the Negotiation phase, two counterparties, an exporter and an importer,

---

76 'MetLife's New Blockchain Health Insurance Product Eliminates Claims', www
.businesswire.com/news/home/20180820005644/en/MetLife%E2%80%99s-New-Blockchain-
Health-Insurance-Product-Eliminates.
77 An Application programming interface: https://en.wikipedia.org/wiki/
Application_programming_interface.
78 How Blockchain Could Disrupt Banking: https://www.cbinsights.com/research/
blockchain-disrupting-banking/.

agree to transact for a product to be sold, including where and when it will be delivered. An agreement is made to this effect, and the importer then provides his bank (the import bank) with a copy of this. The import bank will then, if acceptable, issue financial credentials for the importer. This is then passed on to a correspondent bank who has an established relationship with the exporter's bank (export bank). At the Delivery stage, the export bank provides the exporter with the financing details and then enables the exporter to make good on delivery by initiating shipment. The final phase is the Settlement phase, where goods are received by the importer, and subject to notifying the import bank of receipt, payment for the goods is fulfilled and rendered via the correspondent bank.

Figure 6.5 Trade Finance Process

Trade financing processes are extremely old-fashioned with documentation often being paper based with manual processes, and intermediaries utilized in the entire process. For instance, bills of lading are paper-based and often may be financed multiple times due to the difficulty in authenticating them. Since there can be various versions of the truth and fragmented information silos, the entire process is prone to errors, delays, and risk.

DLT System DLT technology can improve processes in this space by incorporating all the players and intermediaries onto a shared ledger, utilizing IoT and smart contracts to automate manual processes and improve transparency. Smart contracts can be used to codify the agreements for the import and export banks. This record can then be updated by every party involved in the delivery and settlement process to make sure terms of the financing are met for the shipping of goods and final delivery. This information can be manually entered on the Blockchain or can be automated through the utilization of IoT. If there is an underlying ledger system utilized between the import and export bank, this also facilitates a faster flow of payments through the network without intermediaries.

The benefits that DLT bring are of course improved transparency and an understanding of what is occurring in real time. Utilizing DLT may also lead to disintermediation of the various middlemen involved in processes meaning a reduction in cost and less risk in the system, including counterparty risk and contract execution risk. Settlement will become faster and transaction fees reduced. Multiple financing based on duplicated bills of lading can be minimized, as information is available on chain to facilitate trust and decentralized control. Better regulatory and customs oversight will also be possible.

DLT Adoption There are several trade finance consortia, which include Voltron, Batacia, we.trade, HKTFP, and the Marco Polo consortium. Marco Polo is led by R3 and has banks such as ING, BNP Paribas, Commerzbank, and Standard Chartered to name but a few. Many banks are members of all the other trade finance consortia.

There exist several examples of POCs and some deployment of trade finance initiatives. Reliance Industries recently executed a live Blockchain powered trade finance transaction in collaboration with Tricon Energy. Major banks such as HSBC and ING participated in this trial on R3's Corda Blockchain. UK-based Bolero International issued and managed a digitized bill of lading in this POC. Here, Reliance was the exporter and Tricon Energy the importer. Reliance commented that there existed significant potential to reduce timelines involved in the exchange of export documentation from seven days to less than one day.[79]

The Voltron consortium successfully utilized Corda's network to complete a letter of credit for Cargill to ship soybeans from Argentina to Malaysia. This was facilitated by ING and HSBC. This experiment cut down the number of days for processing from 10 days to 1 day. The next phase for the Voltron consortium is to expand the number of banks participating in POCs.

We.trade is operational across 11 European countries and claims to have successfully executed seven live trade transactions between 10 companies on the platform.

The Outlook for DLT DLT promises to disrupt the trade finance segment through utilization of letters of credit through smart contracts and via payments networks that can bypass correspondent banks.

---

79 'HSBC, Reliance Industries execute first blockchain trade finance transaction', https://yourstory.com/2018/11/hsbc-and-reliance-industries-execute-first-blockchain-trade-finance-transaction/.

There is also promise for new business model creation, as global networks for trade change, so will new opportunities reveal themselves. Several steps need to be achieved for successful adoption of this technology. Firstly, many of the manual processes, especially those involving paper, need to be digitized. Secondly, those assets that are moving through the platform need to be digitized. It is only through digitization of these assets that the process of large efficiency gains can be realized through utilization of DLT.

Both the regulatory and customs frameworks will also need to be incorporated in rollouts as these bottlenecks could become more efficient if digitization and interfacing with their legacy interfaces were possible.

4. The Future for DLT in the Financial Services Sector

DLT must be adopted within the financial services sector for traditional FIs to survive. The sector has seen by far the largest investment in Blockchain projects. Now we are beginning to see some POCs start to emerge into the mainstream and move on to live deployment.

One should not be in a rush to push POCs into live testing and then full production. Let us not forget that financial service infrastructure underpins the economy of the entire world. This is not something that can fail. Any movement to a new technology must be gradual and done with certainty that there will be no errors. The process for this should start with POCs, and then move to small live tests, followed by an expansion to parallel production (where legacy systems work at the same time as new technology). Only after successful parallel production should we switch, when one is sure about the stability of the technology.

Multiple challenges for the adoption of DLT have already been covered previously. The biggest is, of course, the 'coopetition' paradox. For the technology to be adopted, financial institutions must work with each other such that they can set standards for technology that can be utilized between them to enable the benefits that DLT purports. For natural competitors, this can be a difficult thing to abide by.

Some may say that the regulators would be the perfect vehicle to force adoption and get the banks to utilize this technology. This may be possible in China with the PBOC and their system. In the UK this wouldn't be possible as the regulator takes a technology-neutral approach in adhering to compliance requirements. Instead, it should be the very intermediaries, the centralized players who look to reposition themselves as nodes in the system to facilitate increased efficiency for the entire system. They are the ones that we should look to for adoption, as they are trusted already within the system and provide services to the whole FI segment.

One must also solve the issue of interfacing with legacy technology. Banks have systems upon systems of legacy infrastructure that in some cases cannot be removed. Any implementation of DLT must be able to interface and communicate with legacy technology. DLT systems must also be foolproof. For all the shortcomings of the global payments network based on SWIFT, by and large, the system has not failed.

The cryptocurrency markets have not helped with the adoption of the technology either. Extreme volatility, scams, and ICOs have served to bring media attention on cryptocurrencies but focused attention away from what is arguably the most useful part, which is the underlying infrastructure. Indeed, perhaps more so in other more traditional sectors than finance, DLT's reputation leaves executives with a sense of trepidation.

Executives themselves have also felt that Blockchain technology is difficult to understand. This should not be the case, but perhaps educators have a part to play in this. As with most new technologies, this technology has moved much faster than the business and economic study of it, meaning that education has come from technically minded individuals rather than business-minded ones. All too often this has meant that DLT is explained from a technical perspective rather than a business benefits perspective. Executives should easily be excited about the business benefits, certainly enough to make them feel passionate about the technology.

By far the biggest impact will come from one thing – the digitization of assets and their placement onto Blockchains. The purported economic value increase can only come to fruition once the ability to trade and fractionalize assets into pieces can be realized. The first issue with doing this is legal and regulatory. However, this is something that will soon be solved. Then, it is the effort to digitize all the assets in the world. Once this is accomplished, then DLT, as the new economic transfer layer, will be evident and global economic value magnified manyfold.

Transformational business models will also be opened up. Micropayments are currently too expensive to support with the present infrastructure. Blockchain technology will enable micropayments for the first time to be implemented, and we will see new business opportunities created. With most new technologies, as the cost of using them decreases, their use increases. Then, as the cost becomes sufficiently cheaper, they are utilized for purposes that at first weren't obvious.

As Blockchain technology gradually gains adoption in the future, it will be seen as another tool that can be called on for use in any system. As the internet has become ubiquitous in our lives and is now taken for granted that it is the communication layer the world operates on, so too will Blockchain technology become the ledger regarding value transfer – the economic layer underpinning the world economy. How far away that is depends on how quickly the world can work together to implement it.

7

Blockchain Adoption

This is an interesting area to discuss – where will Blockchain technology be adopted and how? This is a key question for any organization embarking on a Blockchain journey – whether your staff and customers will adopt the technology and what you need to do, to make the adoption easier.

How Will Blockchain Be Adopted?

There are five areas where I believe the adoption of Blockchain technology will develop:

1. The user interface.
2. The understanding of Blockchain technology.
3. The killer app for Blockchain.
4. Daily life use cases, especially payments and contracts.
5. Winning business models make Blockchain technology the hero.

Blockchain Adoption: The User Interface

The biggest barrier to Blockchain adoption will be the user interface – the way that a human interacts with Blockchain technology will be critical to adoption. If we look at the current applications of Blockchain (namely cryptocurrencies) you will see that we have a concept of 'wallets'.

A wallet is the interface between the Blockchain technology (the transactions) and the human interface. This is often very basic and

Commercializing Blockchain: Strategic Applications in the Real World,
First Edition. Antony Welfare.
© 2019 John Wiley & Sons Ltd. Published 2019 by John Wiley & Sons Ltd.

complex for the end user to make use of and benefit from. Wallets are evolving quickly, and the technology is improving to allow the wallet to be more intuitive and customer friendly.

User experience is often the make or break of adoption, so any Blockchain interface must operate 'like normal technology'. If you look at the enterprise Blockchain solutions, the large organizations are integrating the technology into current systems, or alongside current systems and retaining the same user 'look and feel'; this ensures the end user is able to maximize the use and benefits of the Blockchain technology.

Smartphone as ID

The smartphone is becoming the human's natural interface with all technology. We use our phones to pay bills, order food, book time off, submit expenses, watch a movie, chat with our friends, video chat with our colleagues, and sometimes we even use them to chat to another human!

We are at ease with smartphones and the wide variety of apps allows us to conduct our daily business using the smartphone. This could be a massive opportunity for Blockchain technology – we could use the smartphone as our 'digital identity'.

Every interaction we have requires some form of ID – name, email address, date of birth, IP address, etc. – all our interactions are based on an ID. With Blockchain technology, we can securely use our smartphone as an ID device. We can keep our data secured, and use Blockchain technology to secure our transactions with other parties.

This is a powerful way to adopt Blockchain technology and something which large organizations and governments around the world are looking to implement. Imagine using your smartphone ID to validate transactions using cryptographic Blockchain technology – your ID will be safe, and you can interact more quickly and simply compared to today.

For example, you can have one ID for online shopping – you never need to give out your personal details – they will all be held securely on Blockchain and only the data needed is shared securely with the transacting party. You will never have to give your email or credit card details out again.

QR Code World

You can take the digital ID one step further and use QR code technology to scan the ID for any transaction – like you would swipe a credit card or use NFC for Apple Pay, you can use a Blockchain-secured QR card to pay for items or share data.

This gives the adoption of Blockchain technology a large benefit – we all understand a QR code; they are secure and there are billions of possible combinations (to prevent fraud). I can envisage a world where we scan a QR code on our phone to open the door to our home, pay for the taxi and order the takeaway food. All the transactions will be seamless for the user, but the data will be safe and secured – ensuring the safety of the customer identity, but delivering the service they expect.

Real Use Case: HTC Launches a Blockchain Smartphone in December 2018

HTC unveiled its Blockchain-focused smartphone in December 2018, which it aptly named the 'Exodus 1', and which was launched to shift its strategy to focus on new technology.

HTC is a Taiwanese phone maker, which has developed its own cryptocurrency wallet called Zion to make its new phone function as a hardware cryptocurrency wallet – exactly what is needed to improve the experience I talked about earlier.

The Exodus 1 comes with a secure enclave — a secluded area on the phone's chip kept separate from the Android operating system that the phone runs on. This 'area' uses technology made by SoftBank's Arm Holdings to keep a customer's cryptocurrency safe.

It is basically a cryptocurrency wallet which holds your private keys. Private keys are lines of code which are meant to be known only to the owner of a cryptocurrency to allow them access to their funds. The significance of integrating Blockchain technology in the phone is that it improves the security and privacy of a user's data and their own 'value'.

As I have mentioned before, the large companies 'own' our data and with this phone it is one step forward to helping users own their own data using Blockchain technology.

To help with the user experience, the phone comes with a 'social key recovery' function that lets a user regain access to their funds if they lose their private key, via a select number of trusted contacts.

Exodus 1 will support multiple Blockchain protocols, such as Bitcoin and Ethereum support, Lightning and Dfinity network support. This will be brought together through universal crypto wallet which will permit its users to ensure the safety of their virtual currencies. The phone also boasts a key management API which helps users manage their own wallet keys and secure their applications.

At the global launch in Berlin in October 2018, Phil Chen (the inventor of the phone) demonstrated how the world's top tech minds are coming together to make the 'next big thing' in the crypto ecosystem. He mentioned that this is being fuelled by social backing, especially of the younger generation. It is the general public that adopts and adapts with cryptos and thus the movement is mostly a down-up one.

'And the reason why you do a Blockchain phone is . . . for everybody just to own their own keys,' Phil Chen told CNBC in an interview. 'Everything starts there. When you start owning your own keys, then you can start owning your own digital identity, then you can start to own data.'

Blockchain Adoption: The Understanding of Blockchain Technology

Do people understand Blockchain technology and do they need to understand Blockchain technology? These are two questions I am often asked and often reflect on.

Let's tackle the first question. Do people understand Blockchain technology? My answer is a categorical – 'no'. We are in a world of 'fake news' and misinformation where Blockchain is frequently misrepresented. Most press coverage of Blockchain technology surrounds Bitcoin and the cryptocurrencies. In January 2018, the value of these hit a record high due to the 'mass hysteria' around the potential of this technology.

This spawned the 2018 'death of the ICO' (initial coin offering) where millions of pounds were raised by over a thousand projects to fund 'Blockchain ideas'. As I will discuss in Chapter 8, most of this was raised for ideas and not real projects; often there was not even a need for Blockchain technology.

In 2019, this hysteria has calmed down. I hear more and more people discussing Blockchain technology and that it is more than just Bitcoin and the crypto market. The conversations are often misinformed and often take the Bitcoin price graph as a reflection that Blockchain technology is dead.

I fundamentally disagree, and this book gives you hundreds of reasons why Blockchain technology is not dead; in fact, it is quite the opposite and the start of the next revolution.

Most people do not understand what Blockchain is, but why should they?

On to the second question: Do people need to understand Blockchain technology? And the answer to this is again a categorical 'no'. Why do people need to understand how this works? Do you know how a database works? Or how your car works? Or how the 5G network operates? In most cases we do not – and, more importantly, we do not need to – we just need to know it works.

The information that people need to know is WHAT can Blockchain technology be used for? Not so much about how it works. As you will know, this book is written for that exact reason – to inform people as to what, how, and where Blockchain technology can be used, and why Blockchain is at the start of a revolution.

I believe that once people understand what the technology can do, they will adopt it quickly. Once we see the impacts of Blockchain technology, we will naturally adopt this and take it for granted that it works.

My last point is that, because trust is replaced by technology, we need to rethink what this means and how this affects our lives. Trust is an emotional word, and is linked to our deep seated beliefs and culture. To suggest that this can be replaced by technology is a fundamental shift in our understanding of trust and its emotional impact.

Over time, it will be clear how trust is replaced with Blockchain technology, and it will become proven, via real uses of Blockchain technology, that trust can be automated and improve our lives.

Note that I am not talking about all forms of trust; I am focusing on trust between interacting parties in a complex enterprise, both internally and externally – this is not about whether you trust your friends and family, etc.

Blockchain Adoption: The Killer App for Blockchain

It is very important that we find a 'killer application' for Blockchain technology. For the internet it was email which made the internet as expansive and proliferated as it now is. The internet was not built for this purpose; the email was built after, but it could only exist because of the internet technology.

What can be the killer app for Blockchain? I have no idea. . .email was poorly received at the start – we had wired connections, poor interfaces and very few users. . . .

Isn't this how we think about Bitcoin? Most people do not believe it, the user interface is difficult, and to look after your own private keys is something new to us. . .but this is how email became adopted and developed the internet to where it is now.

I am not saying that Bitcoin is the killer app – I do not know, but it is only here because of Blockchain technology and it is being adopted more and more each day (by adoption I mean people using it for transactions, not its actual value).

I would love to hear your thoughts on this – message me or connect using #CommercializingBlockchain and we can further this very important adoption of Blockchain technology.

Blockchain Adoption: Daily Life Use Cases

One of the best ways to help any technology to become widely adopted is for it to help us in our everyday lives. Blockchain technology has many use cases, which will transform our lives over time and this is when we will start to adopt Blockchain technology without even knowing.

At a recent conference, a fellow delegate of mine said, 'We will know when Blockchain is adopted when we don't know we are using it' – a really great way to describe where we need to get to with this technology.

Imagine a day in our life where we are going to finally buy our dream home in Barcelona:

1. Wake up – IoT device detects right to time wake.
2. Shower – IoT device sets perfect temperature in the bathroom and shower.
3. Breakfast – avocado and eggs – Blockchain provenance shows their history.
4. Autonomous car arrives.
5. Car arrives at solicitor's office – route committed to Blockchain.
6. Takes auto payment in 'Acoin' for journey.
7. Auto scan walking in – using digital ID on Blockchain.
8. Main task: document for a purchase of property in Berlin is sent for signature – using digital ID.
9. Payment made in 'Acoin'.
10. Celebrating drinks – Digital ID scanned and green tick applied for correct age.
11. Scan champagne glass to see the grapes, the location, and an animated history of the champagne.
12. Payment made in 'Acoin'.
13. Car arrives to take me home and records journey to Blockchain.
14. Takes auto payment in 'Acoin' for journey.
15. Message appears on phone – title deed for property in Barcelona.
16. Digital keys sent via secure Blockchain wallet to phone.
17. Open flights app and book flight to Barcelona using 'Acoin' and digital ID for details.
18. Celebrating owning a property with Blockchain confirmation.

A massively important day, powered by Blockchain technology and you never even realized!! Visit my website Commercializingblockchain.com to see a very cool animation for a day in a life on Blockchain.

Blockchain Adoption: Winning Business Models

Winning business models make Blockchain technology the hero and the best business models and ideas will win. This has always been the case in life, business, and in government. The best solutions will win and this will make the adoption key and important to the users.

Focusing on the real use cases, where the Blockchain technology makes a difference to the current enterprise process or helps develop new business solutions will automatically embed Blockchain technology.

In the book, my sole purpose is to help you understand how Blockchain technology can help develop enterprise organizations – follow the use cases, and the expertise from myself and the other contributors, and you could become the team to develop the next Blockchain-driven solution for your enterprise.

8

First Use Cases

Cryptocurrency, ICOs, and Tokenization

This chapter will look at the start of the Blockchain world as we currently see it – starting with the synonymous white paper from Satoshi Nakamoto in 2008. Nobody knows who he/she/they are. . .and to be honest, I do not care.

The important understanding in this chapter is that this paper started Blockchain adoption and all which has happened since the paper was written. In my view, this is where Blockchain has been initially developed, tested, and destroyed. Most people still think that 'Bitcoin' is Blockchain and vice versa – Bitcoin is a use case of Blockchain technology not the other way around.

After looking at the quick history of Bitcoin, I will move onto the very interesting world of Cryptocurrency, ICO's, and Tokenization – all of these areas which we hear about every day in the news, and areas which are changing the Blockchain world at speed.

This chapter is in no way a guide to any of these areas – there are literally hundreds of books on these subjects. My slant on this is to take you through the story so far, and why I believe this has influenced greatly where we are with Blockchain technology in general and with Enterprise Blockchain.

History of Bitcoin

The history of Bitcoin and the Satoshi Nakamoto paper is fundamental to Blockchain technology. There are many people who tell me that Blockchain or distributed ledger technology (DLT) in its wider

Commercializing Blockchain: Strategic Applications in the Real World,
First Edition. Antony Welfare.
© 2019 John Wiley & Sons Ltd. Published 2019 by John Wiley & Sons Ltd.

context has been around since the beginning of time. That may or may not be the case. The importance of the paper is that it was written anonymously in 2008, at the height of the financial crisis and as an alternative to the current financial system (which was – and is still – fundamentally broken).

Here is the abstract from the actual paper:

> Abstract. A purely peer-to-peer version of electronic cash would allow online payments to be sent directly from one party to another without going through a financial institution. Digital signatures provide part of the solution, but the main benefits are lost if a trusted third party is still required to prevent double-spending. We propose a solution to the double-spending problem using a peer-to-peer network. The network times-tamps transactions by hashing them into an ongoing chain of hash-based proof-of-work, forming a record that cannot be changed without redoing the proof-of-work. The longest chain not only serves as proof of the sequence of events witnessed, but proof that it came from the largest pool of CPU power. As long as a majority of CPU power is controlled by nodes that are not cooperating to attack the network, they'll generate the longest chain and outpace attackers. The network itself requires mini-mal structure. Messages are broadcast on a best effort basis, and nodes can leave and rejoin the network at will, accepting the longest proof-of-work chain as proof of what happened while they were gone.[1]

The paper introduced the concept of transacting value via peer-to-peer nodes – missing out the financial system as it stands and allowing the mathematical computational power to secure the network and assets.

The introduction discusses commerce and transactions:

> Commerce on the Internet has come to rely almost exclusively on financial institutions serving as trusted third parties to pro-cess electronic payments. While the system works well enough

---

1 https://bitcoin.org/bitcoin.pdf.

for most transactions, it still suffers from the inherent weaknesses of the trust based model. Completely non-reversible transactions are not really possible, since financial institutions cannot avoid mediating disputes. The cost of mediation increases transaction costs, limiting the minimum practical transaction size and cutting off the possibility for small casual transactions, and there is a broader cost in the loss of ability to make non-reversible payments for non-reversible services. With the possibility of reversal, the need for trust spreads. Merchants must be wary of their customers, hassling them for more information than they would otherwise need. A certain percentage of fraud is accepted as unavoidable. These costs and payment uncertainties can be avoided in person by using physical currency, but no mechanism exists to make payments over a communications channel without a trusted party. What is needed is an electronic payment system based on cryptographic proof instead of trust, allowing any two willing parties to transact directly with each other without the need for a trusted third party. Transactions that are computationally impractical to reverse would protect sellers from fraud, and routine escrow mechanisms could easily be implemented to protect buyers. In this paper, we propose a solution to the double-spending problem using a peer-to-peer distributed timestamp server to generate computational proof of the chronological order of transactions. The system is secure as long as honest nodes collectively control more CPU power than any cooperating group of attacker nodes.

This is where the Blockchain community started to look at this paper, discuss it, and, importantly, they worked together to create Bitcoin.

Over the following five years, the community built, tested, broke, fixed, and used the Bitcoin network. In the early 2010s, the adoption started to grow exponentially and the dollar price of a Bitcoin grew accordingly.

The adoption, as with any new innovation adoption, led to many new Blockchain cryptocurrencies to appear.

Cryptocurrency and Crypto Assets

So what is a cryptocurrency?
Let's use Wikipedia's definition:

> A **cryptocurrency** (or **crypto currency**) is a digital asset designed to work as a medium of exchange that uses strong cryptography to secure financial transactions, control the creation of additional units, and verify the transfer of assets. Cryptocurrency is a kind of digital currency, virtual currency or alternative currency. Cryptocurrencies use decentralized control as opposed to centralized electronic money and central banking systems. The decentralized control of each cryptocurrency works through distributed ledger technology, typically a blockchain, that serves as a public financial transaction database.[2]

Cryptocurrency is a means of exchanging value – what is the value? This is the interesting question and discussion. There are currently over 1800 cryptocurrencies listed on CoinMarketCap (an aggregator of crypto trading information[3]).

These crypto assets are often called Altcoins – alternative to Bitcoin. These are the 'currencies' which are being traded and there are many more in the ICO stage (see next section) and many more not listed yet.

How Are Crypto Assets Classed?

A very interesting discussion is how do you classify these crypto assets. In Alex Tapscott's book *The Blockchain Revolution*, he splits the crypto assets into seven categories. The crypto taxonomy is as follows:

1. Cryptocurrencies – The main category at the moment, and includes Bitcoin, as well as the smaller players, such as Monero, Zcash, and Dash.
2. Platform tokens – These are the tokens that power the decentralized platforms such as Ethereum, NEO, and ICON. On each of these platforms the token is used to pay for dApps (decentralized apps) that use the network and to fund new dApps and network uses.

---

2 https://en.wikipedia.org/wiki/Cryptocurrency.
3 https://coinmarketcap.com/all/views/all/.

3. Utility tokens – These are used within the dApp to access services or to be given discounts, etc. Many of these tokens come from the ICOs (see next section) and have mainly been used to raise funds for the projects on Blockchain.

4. Security tokens – These are tokens that represent value in the same way that the current securities (stocks and shares) do. There are usually no physical assets involved and the tokens are exchanged via contracts between parties. These could replace all current securities which are traded around the world.

5. Natural asset tokens – There have been a large number of tokens where they are backed by natural physical assets, such as gold or oil. The token is used to transfer this value and settling the trade.

6. Crypto collectibles – These are the functional tokens such as the infamous CryptoKitties and new tokens like Aircoin.

7. Crypto fiat assets – A very controversial, but obvious use case, using cryptocurrencies instead of traditional currencies. In early 2018, Venezuela launched its own cryptocurrency – Petro – aimed at avoiding the US imposed sanctions. The Petro was backed by the country's oil supply and mineral reserves.

Will the Bank of England or the Federal Reserve launch a crypto-pound or a crypto-dollar? At the moment they clearly say no, but why wouldn't they? After all a crypto currency is a digital asset – if you look at the current banking system, your dollar or pound is now a digital asset.

The difference is the current digital dollar or pound is not yours, and there are more of them than the real assets that back them. This is why we have inflation, deflation, and quantitative easing – all mechanisms for the control authorities to take your money.

A decentralized currency will remove the control of the centralizing authorities and give you control of your money – why would you not want that? Remember, in the EU, the government can take 30% of your cash assets if they choose. . .and there is nothing you can do about it! And if they don't take your money that way, they will take it via inflation and taxes!

The Tapscott crypto taxonomy is one of the first and is a great way to start to classify this new set of assets.

The complexity will be to get all entities, authorities, and parties to agree to a new classification, and then the regulation to follow and build on this. We have a long way to go, and I am sure there will be a few false starts, but the crypto market is here to stay and will change and morph over time.

ICO – Initial Coin Offering

Welcome to the new world of funding a business or project. ICOs have taken off in 2017 and 2018 with billions of dollars being raised this way.

An ICO is a cross between an IPO (Initial Public Offering – shares issued in a new company) and crowd funding. With an ICO the business produces a 'white paper', which details the project and the plans. A white paper varies in quality from one or two pages to hundreds of pages and plenty of detail – if you are looking into ICOs read the white paper and then do further research.

Have a look at the image of white papers online where on the left-hand side it is titled 'White Paper' and shows a high quality image of a horse, the centre is titled 'Production', which shows the high quality image of the back of the horse, with the rest of the horse as a lower quality sketch, and the right-hand side is titled 'Actual Product Release', which shows a child's drawing of a horse's head.

What this shows is that the ICO promises the world, but once they start to build the project, they end up delivering something of poor quality, at best, and often they deliver nothing at all.

The white paper is published and it will list all the details of how the tokens will be sold and how you can buy the tokens. There is a complex process of pre-ICO and stages during the ICO, where often discounts are given for buying a larger volume.

Once the ICO closes, the company then looks to list the tokens on an exchange, where they can be bought and sold like an old-fashioned security. There are lots of issues around this which I will cover later.

ICOs Often Raise Money via Crypto

An interesting new problem to emerge is the finding of these ICOs. They are often built on the Ethereum network, and as such, they often raise most of their money via Bitcoin and Ethereum.

This needs to be managed well – when you raise your funds in crypto, you need to transfer that back to fiat currency – until your teams take Bitcoin and Ethereum as their salary.

There are exchange rate risks here as well as tax implications that must be understood and plans built for it.

A great example is an ICO which raised the equivalent of $12m in spring 2018 – mainly from Ethereum. By summer 2018, Ethereum had fallen 70%, meaning the funds in dollars were now more like £4m – a big impact on their plans. This means that the company had to drawdown more Ethereum each month than they had planned, meaning their funding window was shrinking. Worst case, you could argue that they halved their funded period – which could lead to the company failing when they have not built up the new income streams.

Why Use an ICO?

As anybody launching a new business or project will understand, raising money in the beginning is extremely difficult. The current ways to raise money for a business are:

1. Friends and family
2. Crowd funding
3. Loans and banks
4. Angel investors and high-net-worth individuals
5. Venture capitalists
6. Large funds
7. IPO

Whilst all of these options are open, they often take a lot of time and the business must give away lots of equity and often has to give personal guarantees. Any funding from these sources will often be at a low level and money businesses fail to raise the amount they really need.

This is where ICOs have moved in and transformed the fund-raising world. They have completely turned the old system on its head – you can now raise millions from a white paper and a few meetings. In the past, you would have to raise a small amount, test and build, then raise more – with many companies failing on the way.

With an ICO you can basically raise a few million for any crazy idea – and this is where the problem lies. If people were raising the ICO money for real projects and businesses, this would be a great new world, but there are always bad people in the world.

A large number of ICOs have been blatant fraud and scams – literally people just raising money to steal it. Some ICOs have raised money with no real plan and have not delivered anything to the investors, and the Securities and Exchange Commission (SEC) has challenged a number of ICOs as there have actually been securities funds raised.

The ICO world is new, and with any new process there will be teething problems. The value of the ICOs and the Altcoins market plummeted in 2018 from crazy highs at the end of 2017.

This was a good thing in my view; the market was pricing the value of these businesses on nothing – just hype and excitement.

> The world needed to 'wake up' and the businesses (just like in the old world) should be valued on their own merits and their own success or failures.

The ICO world is moving quickly that way, and I would estimate over 90% of the current crypto assets will be gone. There will be many new ones to take their place, and some of these second generation will build some exciting and scalable Blockchain technology companies.

STO – Security Token Offering

You will notice that many of the ICO advisors on LinkedIn are now STO advisors – in my view there is little difference between an ICO and an STO. Technically, with an STO you have to follow the securities regulations and register with them. This is a great step forward, as with an STO you need to know your customer (KYC) and act more like a listed stock market company than a Wild West company.

I mentioned the LinkedIn advisor at the start; this is a little tongue in cheek, but it is important to understand what to look for in an ICO or STO.

What to Look for in an ICO/STO

The ICO market is maturing and over the next few years we will see some fabulous companies built through the ICO world. As with all new businesses there is a high degree of risk – over 90% of companies fail in their first year. That statistic is unlikely to change – often these businesses fail because of bad ideas or badly executed ideas – not through lack of cash.

When you look at an ICO/STO look for:

1. Whether Blockchain technology is needed to solve this project or business issue. Too many times I see ICOs where Blockchain is not a solution – steer clear of these.

2. A track record – has the management team done anything like this before?
3. A strong white paper – actually, you want to see a business plan, a white paper is not enough – you need to see a plan and realistic estimate for time and resources.
4. A good advisor team – too many ICOs have an advisory team that has no relevance to the project and are only trying to make a quick profit. If they have advisors, ensure they have the skills they say they have and ensure that they are real (yes, there have been a number of fake advisors. . .maybe we should build a Blockchain to verify the genuine ICO advisors!).
5. Meet the team – if you can, physically go and meet the team. There is nothing better than looking the team in the eye to ask them about their project. If they cannot answer your questions, or you do not 'get the feeling' then walk away.

Tokenization

Tokenization is an exciting new world powered by Blockchain technology. When we mention tokenization, we are talking about using a token for transactions and converting rights to an asset into a digital token on a Blockchain.

We are in essence 'digitalizing' an asset current or new onto the Blockchain where it can be referenced, shared, sold, transferred, and tracked indefinitely.

The process of asset tokenization creates a number of benefits:

1. Tokens for liquidity
2. Tokens for globalization
3. Tokens for global commerce
4. Tokens for new assets
5. Tokens take us beyond money.

Tokens for Liquidity

Tokenization of assets will create a more liquid world and change the dynamics of global trade across the globe. All economic assets exist on a spectrum of liquidity. Once an illiquid asset (e.g. buildings, cars, land, etc.) is tokenized using Blockchain technology, it instantly becomes easily tradable and becomes as liquid as an asset like fiat currency or securities.

This process of tokenization has great advantage for illiquid assets, the tokens can be divisible into a number of fractions or decimals. By the tokenization of an illiquid physical asset, you can now be a proud co-owner of a fraction of a valuable piece of art, like a painting, a diamond, or a chandelier.

Importantly, your ownership rights are recorded (immutably) using Blockchain technology, which tracks and records the history of the asset every single time it changes hands. Our ability to trade real-world assets on a global scale will massively increase due to this opening of asset liquidity.

Tokens for Globalization

When tokenization of assets starts to become further adopted, the global trade of illiquid physical assets will become an everyday reality. We have already made the first steps towards global commerce with the ICO funding model, which removed many of the bureaucratic barriers of IPOs and made funding simpler, borderless, and direct.

As assets become increasingly tokenized, global trade becomes less difficult, and, with the help of smart contracts, will create a new asset class of *smart assets* with embedded features like voting, distribution of dividends, and fast transfers of ownership.

As a result, people from all over the world will be able to own fractions of the same physical asset or exchange different kinds of assets directly and instantly, opening a new and global asset world.

Tokens for Global Commerce

Using Blockchain technology means that once an asset becomes tokenized on the Blockchain, we can now add all sorts of data to it; for example, we can track previous owners, locations, add images, reviews, videos, opinions, and legal documents such as insurance policies, contracts, land titles, etc.

Remember that as Blockchain technology is immutable, censorship-resistant, and transparent, this makes Blockchain technology the perfect platform for the facilitation of global commerce.

Tokens for New Assets

The most disruptive feature of asset tokenization is its potential to create new kinds of assets. We can tokenize intangible assets like intellectual property, and artistic creations such as writing, music, paintings, or videos.

Tokenizing artistic creations helps to develop individual artists while reducing the power of large publishing corporations, giving creators better control over their finances and direct contact with their customers.

Furthermore, we can, theoretically, tokenize 'assets' that are not traditionally considered assets at all.

Imagine being able to tokenize your future time, your medical data, the data containing your shopping preferences or your social network, and then make different industry stakeholders bid for it? This is possible using Blockchain technology – whether we want this to happen is another question.

Tokens Take Us Beyond Money

Tokens mean that we do not need money to transact – money and money prices are just an enabling technology. Tokens – the digital representations of assets on Blockchain – can now accomplish all three functions of money with ease.

A tokenized, highly liquid global marketplace may reduce the need for money as trade intermediary. We can, hypothetically, completely eliminate money (even money prices) from transactions.

Tokens enable us to swap, or barter exchange across two or more items or sets of items directly. Any piece of data that can be permissioned and controlled with a private key within this crypto ecosystem can essentially become an exchangeable property.

I have covered a number of the current tokenization areas, and I would like to bring in a guest contributor (Geri Cupi, CEO and Founder of MonoChain) to discuss the non-fungible tokens – these are being used as the next generation of tokens and cover a few previously mentioned, but Geri discusses how these can be used for the next stage of Blockchain technology development.

Non-Fungible Tokens – The Next Iteration
By Geri Cupi

By now, you have heard about digital cash. The usage of distributed ledger technology (DLTs) goes beyond cryptocurrency. Another usage of DLTs is using non-fungible tokens (NFT) to secure uniqueness and identity. NFT enable certificates, real estate data, people ID, and physical assets to be added on the Blockchain. Imagine having your university diploma issued directly on the Blockchain like University of Nicosia does, and it gets directly recognized by all institutions. This section will explain NFT in detail, including what they are, how they work, how they differ from fungible tokens, what can enable, and different use cases.

Non-fungible it may sound like a type of mushroom that you should know from biology. In fact, the concept is very simple. Fungible refers to goods that are interchangeable or equivalent with other units of the same commodity. Let's use some examples to get a better grasp of this concept using some modern commodities such as USD and potatoes. If Alice lends to Bob, 100 USD, it doesn't matter whether Bob returns the same 100 USD bills or other ones. The same applies to 1 kg of potatoes, it is the same as another 1 kg of potatoes. Potato, potatoes – the same thing! Fungible goods have no uniqueness and are perfectly interchangeable between each other. For fungible goods only the number of units (quantity) is important. If Bob and Alice swap a tangible asset, they don't lose or gain anything, so far as it is the same quantity. Fungibility is a very important attribute for any currency. Fungible tokens include the likes of Bitcoin, Ether, EOS, XRP, or any type of ERC20 tokens. If you send someone 10 Ethers, and get 10 back, you will not be better or worse off.

On the other hand, non-fungible tokens (NFTs) mean they are unique, different from one another despite sharing common attributes. A real-life example are tickets. If you have a ticket to watch Real Madrid–Juventus and you have a ticket to watch Everton–Fulham. Both will give you access to an event at a place and particular time, but they are not transferable. So, NFTs can standardize ownership of a certain asset category, but those assets don't necessarily have the same market value. Other examples include collectibles, such as baseball cards, autographed football shirts, your ID, and diplomas.

Below is a summary of their differences.

Fungible Tokens	Non-Fungible Tokens
Interchangeable	*Non-Interchangeable*
A token can be exchanged for any other token of the same type and keep the same value. A 1 USD bill can be used for another 1 USD bill without making any difference to the holder.	NFTs cannot be replaced with other NFTs of the same type and keep the same value. If you lend a token to someone, you would expect to receive the same token back. You cannot exchange your driving licence with the driving licence of another person.

Fungible Tokens	Non-Fungible Tokens
Identical	*Unique*
All tokens are the same and have the same specifications.	Each token has unique attributes and is different from tokens of the same class. This makes them irreplaceable or impossible to swap.
Divisible	*Non-Divisible*
Tokens can be divided into smaller units and the unit you get is not important as far as it has the same value. For example, changing USD bills with coins.	NFTs cannot be divided into smaller units as the NFT is the elementary unit and one token only.
Ethereum Standard used: ERC-20	*Ethereum Standard used ERC-721*
This standard on the Ethereum Blockchain allows the issuance of tokens.	This is a new (2017) standard on the Ethereum Blockchain which enables the issuance of NFT.

The launch of CryptoKitties, the first use case of NFTs on Ethereum, took the crypto world by storm in 2017. There were some kitties selling for $300,000 and transactions slowed down the entire Ethereum network. CryptoKitties are collectibles assets, which are unique and stored in Ethereum wallets. The players can buy, sell, and breed digital cats, with each cat's digital genetic material being stored on the Blockchain. Some of them are rarer and they can be bought and sold using ETH. In 2017, their sales hit over $12m, just 3 months after the launch. (Source: https://www.cryptokitties.co//.)

However, until recently, there were no standards for NFTs. This changed with the launch of ERC-721 in late 2017. This standard allows the creation of NFTs on Ethereum and opened up the possibilities for digital collectibles.

One of the key features of NFTs is the ability to create digital scarcity which can be verified without needing or trusting a central authority to confirm this authenticity. The amount of NFT on Blockchain is visible to everyone. In the past there have been attempts to offer and manage digitally scarce items, such as avatars in Warcraft or other games. However, this scarcity wasn't cheap to manage and depended on the validation and security of game creators. In the real world, companies try to keep scarcity of their product by limiting the number of hours it sells their product. CryptoKitties are a good example of how this token can be used to create scarcity and therefore value for a digital asset. With ERC-721, both the uniqueness and scarcity of an item is provable.

NFTs go beyond digital collectibles. NFTs give the opportunity to tokenize real-world goods, which can be much more fruitful from an investment perspective. There are many projects happening in art (Artory with Christie's), Real Estate (BlockSquare), ticketing (Upgraded), and high-end fashion (MonoChain). NFTs can be the backbone of a new Blockchain-powered economy. We will explore below more potential use cases.

Use Cases:

1. Collectibles

   We've already talked about one example of NFT collectibles – CryptoKitties. Other examples include Pokémon cards, baseball cards, stamps, autographed football shirts, or any other collectible you can think of. Factors that determine a baseball card's value are condition, age, origin, scarcity, and the featured individual.

2. Fashion

   Another avenue is fashion. Luxury fashion is prone to counterfeiting. Through MonoChain once an item is verified and authenticated, an NFT is created. The buyer receives the NFT when they finalize the purchase. When the owner wants to sell this item, they can simply list the NFT on MonoChain as proof that they own the real asset and receive offers in real time. Data about an item, i.e. Certificate of Ownership, is digitized, stored into MonoChain wallet, and owned by the users. Only the owners can access the detailed data. However, its existence and provenance can be examined by other parties.

3. Art

   Art is another industry which is a target of forgery, scams, and frauds. Similarly, the art world has the chance to transfer the ownership onto a system, which cannot be altered or falsified. Companies working on this space are Rarebits and Artory.

4. Identity

   Every person has their own characteristics, which can be represented by an NFT. There can be an NFT as your passport, driving license, or ID. This cannot be traded, but can be used to interact with authorities or to share this information voluntarily with whoever needs your proof of identity, such as doctors, employees, banks, etc.

5. Academic Credentials

University of Nicosia in Cyprus issues all their diplomas on Blockchain. Users can keep a decentralized record of their certificates they receive from academic intuitions and can be easily attested if required.

6. Real Estate

Another use case is in the real estate industry, where a building can be tokenized. Some tokens can grant ownership of the building and facilities, while others enable only access.

7. Tickets

NFTs also find another use in the tickets industry. Every ticket has its own NFT and is given to the buyer. Upgraded is a company which does exactly this and recently was acquired by Ticketmaster.

8. Licensing

Software licensing is another usage of NFTs. This can reduce piracy and allows people to trade their software licences. Users can potentially avoid yearly subscriptions when not required anymore. The licence can turn into an asset for the user.

9. Video gaming

The first uses of NFTs have been in gaming (CryptoKitties and Decentraland). We have talked about CryptoKitties. Decentraland enables users to purchase, develop, and sell land using NFTs. Users have full control over their land and can build anything, making it unique and adding value to it. Characters in video games acquire different items, i.e. weapons. Through NFTs these assets can become tradeable for in-game credits or cash.

10. Fractional Ownership

Tokenizing physical objects enables owners to receive more liquidity when they need it or even acquire an asset which they cannot fully afford. For instance, the owner of a Picasso painting might want to liquidate some of its value, but keep the physical control of the item itself. Also, the users who cannot afford an item can use this as a form of crowdsourcing.

NFTs are still in their early days and quite likely the best use cases haven't been imagined yet. It will be quite exciting to see how the ecosystem evolves in the next few years.

Benefits of Tokenization

- Opens markets to smaller players, through larger segmentation and removing the need for transportation of physical assets.
- Ability to trade fractional ownership on assets that are not possible now (real estate, art, diamonds, etc.).
- Increased global trade and the opportunity to develop new markets with direct and instant trade.
- Opportunity to monetize assets which were not possible before.

9

What Makes It Work? Blockchain Best Practice

What makes Blockchain technology work? This is a question I often receive and the answer is the same as any new project or idea: follow the usual principles of best practice transformation, development, and project management. Just because the solution is Blockchain technology does not mean there is a different transformation process.

Using the basic principle that you already have in place within your enterprise will be the key to unlocking the best practice for Blockchain technology in your enterprise. In this chapter, I will concentrate on the key areas specifically related to Blockchain technology to be successful – these are over and above your current transformation best practice.

Consensus

I have already covered consensus in the early chapters, but want to discuss further here as I believe this is critical to the success of Blockchain technology use cases.

Consensus involves agreeing at the start of a project how the participants in the Blockchain network wish to work together; i.e. how the data will be entered into the Blockchain in a way that all parties are happy with that data quality. This will not eliminate mistakes, but it will help develop trust between all the parties that the data is correct and can be used for analysis or other purposes agreed by the network.

Agreeing the consensus rules at the start is hard, but it gets easier with time and also as the different consensus principles become more and more common. At the beginning, they all seem quite difficult, but consensus has always been around in our world and is used in all our daily lives.

Commercializing Blockchain: Strategic Applications in the Real World,
First Edition. Antony Welfare.
© 2019 John Wiley & Sons Ltd. Published 2019 by John Wiley & Sons Ltd.

Consensus should be implemented with a business process transformation mindset. This is not about the technical rules of consensus – this is about how you want to run the network and the process the network will deliver. Concentrate on the process side of the Blockchain network and the technology will easily fit what you require the consensus technology to deliver.

Be flexible and open to change with your consensus rules. We are still new to Blockchain technology and we will, and we are, iterating continually. The consensus mechanisms for a Blockchain network of 50 entities is not the same as one with 500 entities across 500 enterprises.

You will need to be flexible and adaptive as learning grows and the network grows. Having a great network management and administration plan is key to keeping the consensus up to date with your requirements, as the Blockchain network changes over time.

Governance

As with any transformational project, you must start the process with a clear plan and strategy. This needs to be managed with an exceptional governance process. The setting up of project/programme plans, a steering committee, regular milestones, and other best practice project management skills are needed.

Due to Blockchain technology crossing many parties, this governance is even more critical. You could be dealing with hundreds of different entities within the project, and this needs careful and thorough project management.

If you do not have the buy in from the senior stakeholders, and a clear set of milestones, you are unlikely to deliver a transformational Blockchain project. The actual technology side of the transformation is not the biggest challenge.

In my experience, the people and process part of the transformation is critical in any project, but with Blockchain projects this is key. In theory, with a Blockchain technology-led transformation, you are taking some of the processes from the 'back' of the process to the 'front' of the process – you are in essence reconciling and auditing the data, before it enters the Blockchain. This is a change of mindset and thinking for the people involved and needs to be clearly managed, explained, and governed.

Agile and Iterative Approach

Blockchain technology is new; it may be at version 0.7 or 0.8 – in my view it is not yet 1.0 – I do believe this will happen in 2019 as the trials and proofs of concept grow exponentially though 2018 and 2019.

In order to succeed, with Blockchain technology moving so quickly, you need to adopt an agile and iterative mindset to the Blockchain technology. There will not be one stable solution which is implemented easily in a period of time – you will be implementing a number of versions and variants as the process and the technology develops, and you learn from these stages.

Concentrating on your minimum viable product (MVP) is key – you cannot afford to perfect the Blockchain technology solution on day one – too many changes are happening to do this. You can, however, adopt a number of MVPs which you develop quickly and test quickly.

Test and learn takes on a critical role here – there are many moving parts around this technology, so you need to be quick to test and quick to record the learnings. Iteration then becomes a way of life as you develop the MVP into a better solution each day.

As with any technology development, do not be afraid to throw out what doesn't work. No matter how much time and money you have invested, if it's not working change it or throw it out.

Learning from mistakes is normal and some of the best inventions have come from the mistakes of previous projects. Did you know that the Amazon Fire Phone failed spectacularly as a smartphone, but led to Alexa voice controls, which is a significant and growing part of the Amazon empire?

Be clear what you are trying to achieve with the MVP and test it as soon as possible; learn from the results and change the process and technology as required to meet the needs of the results you desire.

Solution Driven

Blockchain technology is not a solution for all processes – it has some great benefits for certain process and use cases (as described in an earlier chapter) As with all good developments, you need to start with the use case or requirements first.

What problem are you trying to solve? What issue or process are you trying to improve? This is where you start and you develop the solution to deliver the results required.

When you ask your customer what they *want* you get a different answer to when you ask them what they *need*. Concentrate on what they need – this is the important part for them and this is where you can add value. Most customers still do not understand Blockchain technology enough to be able to understand what the solution is. As long as you work back from the use case and need, you can build a suitable Blockchain solution for your customers.

Collaborate

Team work is dream work. No idea who said this, but this is true of any project in life, and with Blockchain projects this is a must. The technology is new. The white paper that launched Bitcoin was written in 2008 and it took until around 2014 for a bigger network to be built around the technology. Ethereum went live in 2015 and grew over the next couple of years.

As I mentioned a few times, we are still at 0.6 or 0.8 in terms of Blockchain technology development. This means that it is impossible to have lots of experts – there just isn't enough time and people involved to do that.

New uses, platforms, regulations, hacks, updates, cryptocurrencies, etc. are appearing daily – set your news feed for Blockchain and you will get new news throughout the day. This is why you need to collaborate and work with as many people as possible.

When I talk about collaboration, I also mean to work across boundaries internally and externally. Start-ups need to work with enterprises, enterprises need to work with government, and government needs to work with academia...we all need to work together on Blockchain technology solutions.

The early stage of the technology also needs to mix experience and youth – people who are experienced in technology, business, government, etc., need to work with the youth of today, to find out how each other thinks. I know that the younger generations adapt to Blockchain thinking more quickly than older generations. That does not mean either has a better opportunity, it means both can add value equally to this exciting new revolution.

Blockchain is not a place for ego – nowhere is in my view, but not in the exciting new world. Nobody can control this, nobody can own this – we can all benefit from this if we work together. Being a specialist in one area is great, but trying to own Blockchain is not going to help you or the development of Blockchain technology.

If we move to a sharing economy, we can achieve more together. Pool our ideas, our thoughts, and our experiences around Blockchain technology, to help build something better and stronger for the future.

My final point on collaboration is to 'practise what you preach' – use Blockchain to record the ideas and source the solutions. Share the ideas and expertise on Blockchain and you will be able to see who came up with what idea, and who is the expert in which area within the Blockchain ecosystem.

Teams Need to Be Fully Bought In

Alongside collaboration, you must buy in your entire teams – this is cross enterprise and not a siloed operation. Blockchain spans the entire enterprise and beyond, ensuring that everybody is brought into the projects and process is very important.

To do this you will likely need to train the teams. As I discussed previously, most people do not understand Blockchain technology and therefore need to understand the basics before they can add value and start to further the Blockchain technology solutions.

When I am meeting people new to Blockchain technology, I often take them through 30 minutes of what it is, use cases, etc., and advise them to spend the next three months researching and discussing with people. I believe it takes that amount of time for people to action the different processes and opportunities that Blockchain technology can offer.

Not everybody needs to be the expert, but they do need to appreciate what the technology can do, and how it will impact their lives over the next few years.

Open-Minded to Everything

There is no right answer at this stage; Blockchain technology is too new. You need a fully open mind to the possibilities of Blockchain technology – ignore the fake news and bad press, read the stories about how Blockchain technology has changed things, made things better, and added value to lives. Think about these and how your life and enterprise can benefit from this revolution.

Be open-minded to all the new opportunities. I have no idea what Blockchain technology will solve in 10 years' time; I have been part of it for over four years and it has transformed and changed a number of times. It will continue to do so, and along the way there will be countless opportunities – be open to these and you can learn more than you ever imagined.

I am often sceptical when I am shown a totally new idea, solution, or plan, but I am open to the discussion and, often after actively listening, I can see the opportunities and embrace the potential that this offers.

We are in the stage of rapidly morphing Blockchain technology and this, together with other emerging technologies, is opening a world of possibilities beyond today's vision and dreams.

Mixing emerging technologies with current technologies and life offers completely new opportunities which we will no doubt be shocked and amazed with. We will never think that they are possible when they are launched, but we will start to embrace them and after a few months or years, we will wonder how we lived without them.

Learning Mentality

The final and most important key to best practice Blockchain is the learning mentality. If we are constantly learning and evolving we will keep up with the pace of change both technically and life-wise.

Blockchain technology is new and changing every day. We need to keep up with this and be open to all people and all ideas. Once you start on this journey you will never end, but you will have an immensely satisfying journey and expand your mind beyond what you currently believe is possible.

Blockchain Best Practice Summary

Blockchain best practice is no different to our current world of best practice – the main driver is to be open and collaborative. Work with your teams and other teams on the solutions, think of the customer end use and ensure that you have an open mindset along the entire journey.

10

How to Commercialize Blockchain/Reach Its Potential

We have looked at the foundation of Blockchain technology, some use cases, and best practice around Blockchain technology. In this chapter we will look at how you use Blockchain technology to its fullest.

Blockchain Is a Network Play

The biggest way to reach a successful Blockchain transformation is to remember that this is not a one entity issue. Blockchain inherently is a decentralized network – with network meaning lots of other parties and entities involved.

Many people talk about the Blockchain ecosystem and I think this is a great way to look at this. 'You cannot Blockchain alone' may sound comical, but it is true – a Blockchain network is an ecosystem of interrelated, but separate, parties. These could be suppliers, partners, customers, governments, etc., but they are all separate entities, which we are using Blockchain technology to connect and interact with on a trusted basis.

The benefits will only come from working together with all these entities. The mindset is to build solutions together, not separately, and you will gain the biggest benefits. If you include all the ecosystem, and work with all parties in the ecosystem, you will ensure that you are part of the future of Blockchain technology benefits.

We live in a world of 'platform economy', where much of the technology is cloud based and usage is based on taking the modules or elements that fit your business needs. Blockchain technology is no different. As discussed previously in this book, there are a number of Blockchain technologies, and there are many more in development.

Commercializing Blockchain: Strategic Applications in the Real World,
First Edition. Antony Welfare.
© 2019 John Wiley & Sons Ltd. Published 2019 by John Wiley & Sons Ltd.

These work on the basis of a platform on which you use or build the modules and needs for your business.

Inherently, this helps to standardize the process and protocols around the technology and the business process. In order to establish a common set of standards for each ecosystem, there are a number of consortiums or alliances that have been formed.

Much like the ISO standards for business, or the IFRS accounting standards, there need to be more Blockchain technology standards developed. Most of these alliances and consortiums have a very clear focus on developing standards for a certain sector, use case, or Blockchain technology. They often are comprised of end users, entities, technical developers, and other partners, to ensure the standards developed work for the intended target.

One of the most useful aspects of these, and something I would encourage you all to get involved in, are the working groups that these consortiums develop. The concept of these working groups is to develop a very specific standard or best practice for either an end use case or a process.

Real Use Case: Retail Blockchain Consortium

A great example of a Blockchain technology consortium (and one that I have co-founded) is the Retail Blockchain Consortium (RBC).

The RBC explores and advances the usage of distributed ledger technologies (DLT) within the retail value chain. The RBC facilitates collaboration, the pooling of resources and platforms, knowledge transfer, and mitigation of risks in the adoption of DLT for its members.

The consortium is a global collaboration led by UCL, Oracle, and MonoChain, and includes leading retailers, universities, technology companies, Blockchain companies, and service providers.

Mission and Vision

The aim is to share deep knowledge of Blockchain technology via the Retail Blockchain Consortium. This will enable key players in the retail value chain to understand the practical challenges of the deployment of Blockchain technology at scale across global organizations.

The consortium will provide resources for academic and commercial partners, to leverage this innovative transformational technology for specific retail value chain use cases.

How You Benefit by Joining RBC Executive Forum?

As a retailer, brand, supply chain provider, or partner, you can become a member of the RBC to benefit from the following:

- Access to workshops run by industry thought leaders.
- Intensive educational and technical accredited courses run by experts.
- Participation in members-only events and committees on Blockchain applications within the retail value chain.
- Helping to drive CSR and improve the environment, through the relevant use of Blockchain.
- Access to the latest academic retail focused research on Blockchain from the world's leading universities.
- Opportunity to lead working groups, focused on your business challenges.

Real Use Case: UK Government APPG Blockchain

I am privileged to be a Board advisor to the UK Government APPG Blockchain group. For those of you who do not know what APPG is, let me briefly explain: APPG stands for All-Party Parliamentary Group, and is set up to advise the entire government on issues, irrespective of their political party, or their position in either house.

Set up by The Big Innovation Centre, and with a comprehensive two-year programme, the aim is to give the government advice on what to do with Blockchain technology for the UK. The chair of the APPG is Damien Moore MP.

The mission of the All-Party Parliamentary Group on Blockchain (APPG Blockchain) is to ensure that industry and society benefit from the full potential of Blockchain and other DLT, making the UK a leader in Blockchain/DLT's innovation and implementation.

We bring evidence, use cases, and future policy scenarios while considering industry and societal implications as well as environmental opportunities.

My role on the APPG is as an Advisory Board Member, where I give my advice on Blockchain from the last few years working with Blockchain technology.

As you would expect, my specialist subject within Blockchain is of course retail. I have extensive experience in Blockchain for retail and supply chain and this advice I bring to the APPG.

Blockchain Business Case

Let's get down to the figures here (and being a qualified accountant for nearly 20 years something that is close to my heart) and look at what is the business case. What are the benefits of adopting any kind of Blockchain technology solution?

I have been a Finance Director in a number of commercial businesses for a number of years and we always measure the benefits cases in terms of financial impact – profit or cash – because at the end of the day, a commercial enterprise is there to add value to the shareholders and build a sustainable business.

It is important to remember that not all benefits have a direct financial impact, and there are good reasons for this, such as customer satisfaction, employee happiness, and sustainability. But all these have an indirect financial impact – happy customers buy more, happy employees sell more, and a sustainable company survives longer.

The benefits which I see from implementing Blockchain technology are split into three areas:

- Efficiency gains – enterprise operations are faster, cheaper, and more efficient.
- Revenue growth – distributed process and systems help to grow revenue opportunities.
- Business growth – disrupted business models build new financial incomes.

We will look at each of these in depth, but first let's look at the complexity of a Blockchain technology business case. In the previous section, we have discussed what is needed to reach the potential benefits of Blockchain technology and we have discussed the network play – the fact that you are not siloed when you are dealing with Blockchain technology. Inherently, you are delivering benefits across a network or ecosystem.

This is a critical point, the benefits of implementing Blockchain technology will be spread across all the participants in the network or ecosystem, with varying degrees of impact – from little impact to significant impacts.

The world of Blockchain technology is complex, the normal rules of looking at 'only my benefits' needs to be challenged, and the entire network needs to assess the benefits.

Blockchain in a multiparty process which means that you must work together to gain the most potential from Blockchain technology – 'you are only as strong as your weakest link' has never been a more important phrase.

Let's look at the financial benefits of implementing Blockchain technology.

Benefits of Implementing Blockchain Technology

As discussed by Nikhil earlier in this book, there are some significant benefits for the financial sector, which can be categorized around cost reduction in the short term and business model transformation in the long term. In the short term, through the utilization of shared infrastructure and process efficiency, various estimates of dramatic cost savings have been predicted. Accenture estimate that cost savings could be as much as:

- 70% on central finance reporting: more streamlined data quality and transparency.
- 30–50% on compliance: improved transparency and auditability of financial transactions.
- 50% savings on centralized operations: better KYC and client onboarding (identity).

Whilst these are aimed at the financial sector, you can apply these to every enterprise – especially the 50% saving on middle and back office functions. Earlier in the book I have discussed ERP and Blockchain technology, together with intercompany and Blockchain technology – both of these add to the compelling use cases to drive out significant savings on the back office.

> 50% on business operations: on middle and back office functions, clearance, settlement, and reconciliation.

Let's look at the efficiency gains in general, as well as the growth drivers and new business model benefits.

Efficiency Gains of Blockchain Technology

With the use of Blockchain technology, enterprise operations will become faster, cheaper, and more efficient, leading to a number of significant business case benefits. I want to start with a very important business case benefit around the finality of the transaction.

Finality of the transactions: an important misunderstanding in today's financial system is that when a person pays using a bank card or electronic payment, that this is finalized and settled there and then. This is completely incorrect; the current financial system takes days to settle a transaction and costs plenty in time and intermediate processes. A normal credit card will take around 72 hours to 'finalize' in today's old system.

With a Blockchain transaction, the transaction is final once committed to Blockchain and cannot be changed. The benefits of this are significant, but clearly misunderstood in the current world.

In today's system, the transaction can be reversed at any stage over the 72 hours, meaning that the whole process can be stopped, reversed, and resent. This is a massively complex task and costs thousands of hours to monitor and work with.

Credit card chargebacks is a big issue in the retail world; this is where the transaction is questioned by the card holder as incorrect for some reason. The current system suggests that the payment provider takes the cost of this, but they will always try to push this back to the retailer.

The current cost of chargebacks has been shown in a recent Javelin Research & Strategy study commissioned by Verifi that cardholder disputes and chargebacks generated $31 billion in financial losses in 2017, of which $19 billion was borne by merchants. The study also noted that for every dollar in a disputed transaction, merchants and issuing banks incur an additional $1.50 in costs due to demands on technology, personnel, and external resources.[1]

These figures are only for the USA, but show the scale of this global problem. For retailers and brands, the loyalty issue is also hit hard – customers are less loyal if they are hit by chargebacks, which reduces loyalty and revenue.

Transaction finality of a Blockchain transaction will remove almost all of these costs (both time and money) and will improve customer loyalty. This business case benefit is significant and something that should be pursued at speed by retailers and brands, as well as the financial services industry.

Let's look at a few more efficiency benefits of using Blockchain technology:

- Right first time data – ensuring that the data is not checked, reconciled, and rechecked, costing time and resources to monitor.
- Less reconciliations – less time needed to reconcile data, especially with intercompany data and across complex supply chains.
- Improved analysis – based on accurate and more timely data, which leads to more time spent analysing data and adding value to the enterprise, versus reconciling and checking the data, as happens without Blockchain technology.
- Increased transaction speed – once the consensus and governance models are agreed and applied, the processing can take place in an automated and seamless process. There will be little requirement

---

1 www.euromoney.com/article/b19y2sl7r93kgg/chargebacks-hitting-merchants-hard-but-they-dont-have-to?copyrightInfo=true.

to check data at every stage and more opportunity to use the data as quickly as it is applied to the Blockchain.
- Faster settlements – with intercompany Blockchain and external Blockchain solutions, payment settlements will be faster (assuming this is agreed by both parties) and there will be a significant working capital improvement.
- More transparency with the data will equal less waste – this is especially important in the supply chain, where the excess parts and raw material build up, in the production process, leads to significant waste. Allowing the entire supply chain visibility on the next stages and prior stages, will allow all participants to plan better and buy in quantities exactly needed, rather than estimating and hoping for the best.

Efficiency gains are important to the business case for Blockchain solutions, and there are many that we have seen and will see over the next few years. There are also revenue benefits which Blockchain technologies will enable.

Revenue Growth with Blockchain Technology

Blockchain technology will allow many opportunities for revenue growth, by utilizing the distributed process and systems of the Blockchain technologies. When you implement Blockchain solutions, you are opening your networks and working closer with your ecosystem; if this is done well there will be new revenue opportunities for many of the participants within this ecosystem:

- More connected systems and entities across your networks open up many more opportunities – working closely with shared and transparent data across your ecosystem, allows new revenue streams to be identified and implemented.
- Tokenization of assets and trading – a big opportunity for the use of Blockchain technology and something I have discussed at length in Chapter 9. The benefits for the business case are still work in progress, but there are many new revenues being seen across the Blockchain ecosystem.
- P2P, B2B, and micro payments – this is a massively exciting area for growing your revenue streams. If you could transact at a level that would be far too small for today's financial system, there would be new options to grow revenue.

- P2P – person-to-person payments. This could include the payments between individuals for bills, payments for meals out, etc., but this can also extend to paying for assets and tokenized assets between individuals.
- B2B – business-to-business payments. This not only includes paying as a business, but also as an asset within your business. Imagine a self-drive car which needs charging: the car can drive itself to the charging point and pay for the energy used via Blockchain payments. Using smart contracts, many payments between entities can be automated and settled finally within a short time period.
- Micro payments – these are something yet to be explored in depth, but a very exciting set of benefits to come. If you can transact to the smallest amount i.e. 0.00001 of a US$ for example, then you can start to make micro payments on a global scale. One great example is the IP world, where copyright royalties are complex and hard to collect. With micro payments, automated contracts can take micro payments at a volume never seen before. This is due to the fact that the transaction fees using Blockchain are so small, micro payments are possible.
- Transaction fees using Blockchain technology are negligible – once the Blockchain technology has matured to great volume and speed, the cost of each transaction will be so small it will not be of concern to any enterprise. This will enable the volumes of payments to increase, and the values of these decrease. This opens up many new revenue streams and business models.
- Improved customer experience – one of the biggest challenges in the world of the internet is creating a great customer experience via technology. There have been significant improvements in this over the last few years, and businesses spend a lot of resources on ensuring this works well. With Blockchain technology you can improve this customer experience even further with the transparency aspect of Blockchain technology. Allowing the customer to see what data you hold about them, where their products were made, where the product is in the delivery cycle or what loyalty rewards they can spend, will help to improve the customer experience, and more importantly loyalty.
- Improved loyalty is critical to any business's success – using Blockchain technology, we could give the customer access to their data and allow them to benefit from their data; via a reward

programme for example, you will find they will happily share their data to enable their rewards to improve. In an Oracle survey in 2018, it was found that '72% desire an effortless loyalty programme where rewards are automatically redeemed'.

I have outlined a few of the areas where implementing Blockchain technology will help to increase revenue, which you can estimate and forecast for your business case.

New Business Growth Powered by Blockchain Technology

An exciting area for any new technology, and especially where the technology is such a disruptor of the existing model, is the creation of new business models – models which have never existed and people had never been able to think of before the technology was created. I will talk about a few of the areas where new business models will be born from the Blockchain revolution.

Business growth via disrupted business models:

- Reduce and better manage middlemen and intermediaries – the classic Blockchain disruption message 'you will eliminate the middleman'. I have to say this is not correct at all, Blockchain technology will not remove the middlemen, but it will change what they do and automate some of their tasks. Understanding this is important – you still need the activities carried out by so-called middlemen, but with Blockchain technology you will automate some parts and change other parts. The basis of Blockchain technology is trust and transparency, and if you apply this to our ecosystem, there is no need for the middlemen, but what you have actually done is automate this via the consensus and governance mechanisms that must be implemented with Blockchain technology. The role of middlemen will change to an advisory role, they will be able to use their experience and expertise to help advise the users of Blockchain technology on how to implement the consensus and governance which replaces them. This maybe a one off task at the start of the transformation, but there will always be business changes along the way and the consensus and governance mechanisms will continually be updated.
- Legal services for automation – the world of Blockchain technology will take off with a lot of automation or smart contracts being implemented across organizations. This automation is not outside

the rules, regulations, and legal frameworks in which the organization operates. This opens a great new business stream around the understanding of the legality and conformity of the smart contracts and other Blockchain automation. In my view, all the code used to write these contract and automation needs to be 'checked by legal'. I am not sure if this means people or machines, but the code that will be delivering the transaction must be compliant with all rules and regulations.

- New services using distributed micro transactions – I talked previously about the automation of micro payments, but there are many other micro transactions which can be developed using Blockchain technology. This could be collecting data from millions of tiny devices or readers around the world, and applying this to Blockchain technology will allow quick and easy sharing and usage of this data. Currently, micro data takes time and is complex to manage due to different systems, processes, and parties within the ecosystem.

- Trusted and distributed means ideas can be tested quicker and rolled out further – if you apply Blockchain technology across the ecosystem, you will be able to test ideas and process much quicker across the entire system. Currently, this would take time and be very cumbersome due to the different parties within the ecosystem.

- Transparent tracking of external spend (i.e. PPC) – the entire digital advertising industry is based on trust of intermediaries and tech giants. This trust is disappearing and companies are starting to question what is really happening with their money spent on digital advertising – did the customer actually see the advert I just paid for? Was the click from my real customer or an automated bot? With Blockchain technology, you will be able to track all your spend and see exactly who and where the click or the view was made. This data is readily available today, but for many reasons it is often not shared or is inaccurate. There are many other areas such as purchasing and expenses where this would significantly improve organizations.

- Monetize IoT and emerging tech – Blockchain technology is not the only emerging technology (as discussed in Chapter 13). If you use Blockchain technology with other emerging technology you will find new business models to develop and grow. For example, using IoT devices and Blockchain technology can enable the information from millions of devices to be shared real time across the ecosystem. Imagine a vineyard, where the harvesting of the grapes and the conditions of the growing season is critical. If you plant an IoT device with every grape vine, you can consistently monitor the moisture, sunlight, chemical make-up, and fertility of the plant and soil. This helps to maximize the water usage during the growing phase, and then gives a clear sign when the harvesting period is ready. The opportunities with other technologies are significant and discussed later.

We have looked at the benefits for the business case from these perspectives:

- Efficiency gains – enterprise operations are faster, cheaper, and more efficient.
- Revenue growth – distributed process and systems help to grow revenue opportunities.
- Business growth – disrupted business models build new financial incomes.

All three of these are valid benefits to apply to your business case from implementing Blockchain technology. All have the potential to transform your organization, and there are already some great use cases and benefits being seen today. As the speed of Blockchain adoption grows, the benefits will become more obvious and exponentially bigger.

My key belief is that Blockchain technology WILL make the organization and ecosystem more efficient, open new opportunities, and bring better control. If any of those happen, then you can put a value on that and you will have your business case benefits.

My last message is to remember that the *estimate of efficiency savings is from 30%–90% – this is significant and something that any organization should look to implement.* The savings are only one side – the transparency and trust, fundamental to Blockchain technology, will also add significant value to your organization either directly or indirectly.

Blockchain Technology Benefits Realization

To realize the benefits of implementing Blockchain technology, you basically follow the same process of project management and digital transformation which has been used for the last few years. Implementing Blockchain technology is no different to any other transformation but you need to ensure that you remember this is not just about technology, but also the people and the process.

People and Process Transformation

The technology transformation is covered throughout this book and is the main part of what we are discussing. The people and the process transformations are much more difficult and need a closer plan to realize the benefits of Blockchain technology.

When you are dealing with a new process, you will find that a large majority of people will be against the new process; this is normal in today's world. You will have the champions who want to help you implement the new technology and processes, through to the saboteurs who will take every opportunity to prevent the implementation of the new technology.

I want to reflect on one of my biggest transformations within business back in my time as Director of Share Service in Brno, Czech Republic. My role there was to set up a new shared service centre (SSC) to run the back office finance, IT support, and customer support for the European retail business. There were already existing teams and I had to make most of the people redundant and recruit a whole new team. We also implemented a new ERP system as an extra complication!

The details of this are in my previous book *The Retail Handbook*, but I want to add the people and process experience I learnt there. In order to transition a European business from one country to another, we first understood every single process which the team carried out today. Once we knew, and documented, each process we were able to streamline the processes which were changing, due to the implementation of new technology, and write the new processes for those.

Once the new processes were written, we used the existing teams to train the new teams on both the old and the new processes. It was important to bring along the current expertise, as this ensured that the service was able to fully function during the transition.

The transition was a success, but this was due to the complete focus on the process and the people elements of the transition. My complete focus was ensuring the new teams were able to complete the processes (new and old) as our clients required and within the agreed boundaries.

The reason to share this is to show you that the implementation of Blockchain technology solutions is no different to previous transformations, and I am sure many of you reading this book have experienced one, if not many, transformations over your working life.

Principles of Transformation

Let's have a look at what makes a transformation a success:

1. Only build what the customer needs – it sounds obvious but we often get lost in the excitement of the new technology that we forget the fundamental reason we exist – to satisfy our customers and clients. We need to ensure that the Blockchain technology solution built is what the customer needs. Notice I use the word 'needs' rather than 'wants', as I often find customers 'want' lots of things, but actually only 'need' a few things.

2. Don't build a solution and then find a problem – a common pitfall in technology development, is to build a solution and then to find a problem, this is the wrong way around and something that you should limit. Work with your customers and find out what their problems and pain points are – work back from these to develop the solution. If the solution uses Blockchain technology great; if it uses other technologies, that's great too – you need to find the solutions and use all the technologies we have to solve these problems.

3. Real and scalable solutions – stop what is not scalable – looking at the scalability of the Blockchain solution is important for us, as we are focusing on enterprise organizations. These organizations require solutions which are scalable and deliver real benefits to their organizations. You must test quickly and stop solutions which are not scalable. It was interesting to see, in late 2018, that the main Ethereum development company (Consensys) actively began to stop projects in which they saw no potential to be a scalable solution. This is important to see, as it shows that the technology is maturing from hype to real scalable solutions for organizations.

4. Listen to the end users to learn what their problems are whilst educating them on the concept of Blockchain technology. If you then work with them, you will find that they often have the answer we are looking for. They need to understand what the technology can do and then apply that to their current process – you will be amazed at how quickly use cases and scalable solutions will appear.

5. Make Blockchain technology user friendly, especially around interfaces, wallets, etc. Humans are all used to dealing with technology from smartphones and laptops; we are used to easy to use interfaces which seamlessly allow us to use the technologies of today.

With Blockchain technology, we must make the solution user friendly, where the end user can easily use the technology via interfaces, wallets, and dashboards. The adoption of the use case will often rest on how easy it will be for the end user to complete the process. If you think about the original wallet technology for cryptocurrency, where you have to remember your private key and wrote down random words – this is not how humans operate, and use case solutions need to be 'human friendly' to be realized.

6. Be focused on the exact results and outcomes you want to test – keeping the focus to the exact results you are trying to test is great business practice. This is even more important with Blockchain technology, where you can easily be distracted by lots of new and exciting opportunities this technology opens up to you. Keep it focused on the use case and the results you want to test; small and focused development is better than longer more complex outcomes.

7. Buy in your teams – your people are key to the development of Blockchain technology and you need them all to help develop the solutions. Educate the teams on the purpose and benefits of Blockchain technology, and work closely with them, and the entire ecosystem to deliver the use case solutions required.

8. Crack the consensus debate early and keep iterating it – in my opinion, the agreement and automation of the consensus mechanism is fundamental to the success of Blockchain solutions. I do believe there is still a long way to go to develop the consensus mechanisms, and we are only just at the beginning of this journey. However, we do have some principles and models we can follow (see earlier chapters) and we can easily take these and iterate as we progress.

Here are eight principles for great transformations, and I know that there are many others out there. You must believe in the technology and sell the vision and the future opportunities. We know that people don't like change, because it is new and scary, but your role is to excite and support the team through this journey.

> The outcome is a new world of trust and transparency powered by Blockchain technology, and this leads to many new and exciting opportunities for the future.

Example Blockchain Implementation Plans in Retail

Let's have a look at where to start with Blockchain technology in retail:

1. Solutions involving transactional trust; various transactions inter company or shared with external parties, e.g. regulators and industry certification bodies.
2. Provenance of high-value or high-risk assets; such as luxury goods, electronics, free trade goods, pharmaceuticals.
3. Supply chain tracking; where existing processes are not, for instance, transparent and timely enough or incur insurance, spoilage, e.g. tracking cold storage supply chain with live record publishing across supply chain parties.
4. New Asset Classes: tokenization of existing goods or creation of new tokenized goods; such as new forms of loyalty, goods like digital collectibles, fractional ownership, etc.

At the moment, these are the 'hot' areas in which Blockchain technology will make the biggest impact to any retailer. There will be many more over time, and these are discussed at length in the use case section at the start of the book and real life ones at the back of the book.

Next I have chosen one example and used ASG Stores as an example of how you might implement a Blockchain strategy for provenance.

ASG Provenance Tracking Example

Let's think about this practically. Here is a high-level process of what to think about if you were to implement a Blockchain solution for provenance of a product for ASG stores:

Six-step guide to a Blockchain implementation:

1. User Interface (UX): Of critical importance for our customers and something which is often poor in Blockchain technologies. For ASG the end goal is for the customer to walk in with a mobile app and scan the product to see the full transparent product history.

   Therefore, one of the key features of mobile app is a read-only application in the first place and will therefore not require any log in (speeding up the process). The customer will then be able to scan a barcode, RFID sensor, or QR-code and access the information related to a particular product, which may involve multiple steps in the supply chain or only the place of production etc.

2. Data Storage: The next component is designing the information storage or database. Typically the information stored in Blockchain includes contract verification, hashes, and identification of who has added this information.

Let us take a simple example of fresh fish and just the recording of the fish itself – if a fisherman at source takes a photo of the fish and tags it at source and adds it to the Blockchain, with the GPS co-ordinates of the catch.

How this data could be stored on Blockchain is a critical solution element and the information needed to be stored will need to be agreed upfront (consensus) – GPS, Photos, Size, weight etc.

There will need to be enough information to satisfy all the following parties in the supply chain that the fish is genuine, from the area reported and then tagged on its way through the supply chain.

3. Blockchain Platform: Choosing the Blockchain platform is the next step in solution design. As mentioned above, the Blockchain platform verifies files, contracts, and stores transactions.

Platform options include public, private, or a hybrid. Platform selection for start-up company is primarily driven by transaction costs and transaction capacity. The public Blockchain platforms include Bitcoin and Ethereum, etc., and due to the transaction costs Bitcoin is not considered as an alternative in this project. Even if the transaction cost on Ethereum is significantly lower, transaction capacity is limited. Both transaction costs and transaction capacity will be a restriction in a price/service sensitive market.

One way to handle this is to opt for a second layer solution, such as Hyperledger. Many companies are building these integrations to help speed up the adoption of Blockchain technologies.

Another option is a private Blockchain, which can be attractive, and where only trusted partners are allowed to validate transactions and blocks. The validated and recorded content of the Blockchain may or may not be published to the public.

4. Application/Smart Contract: The application or smart contract is another key element of the solution. The most well-known Blockchain solution for applications is Ethereum, where the contracts are called as decentralized applications (dApps). The applications are run on the Blockchain by all nodes on which they are distributed.

In some other cases the contracts are not run on the Blockchain – they are confirmed in the Blockchain, and their verifications are embedded in the Blockchain but the entire application is not run by the Blockchain network.

Many technology providers want their applications to be able to run on different Blockchains and this is much easier if the application is not run by the Blockchain.

5. The identity (ID) and authorization: The entities who will authorize the different steps in the process must be identified and some sort of ID solution is required to be built into the overall architecture.

Either the company can handle the ID creation and directory within the Blockchain system, or rather create the ID system and let the administrators of the system be responsible for the ID solution. The system then creates the private and public keys of the participants and may use extra security such as IP addresses to control for authority of the participants.

6. Asset Registry: In the Retail value chain, there are many organizations and authorities who have an interest in labelling the products with their certificates. Hence, in our use case there should exist a public authority to assign a code to keep track of the clothing/food/ art/fishermen, etc. and their production. The amount produced or sold by the producer, will then get this registered ID or document, which is entered into the Blockchain and is live immutable.

This gives you an overview of the basic steps to follow for a Blockchain provenance tracking implementation in a retailer such as ASG. Please remember, I am not a technical architect and there are many ways to build Blockchain technology into your retail value chain.

How to Commercialize Blockchain Summary

A few thoughts to close this chapter on what to look for in your quest to commercialize Blockchain technology solutions:

1. Commercializing Blockchain technology is a network play, across an ecosystem and the benefits will be realized together, not just with one participant.

2. The basis of this is transformation on a global scale, and to release the benefits, you need to focus on the people and the process, more than the technology. The technology will work, if you get the process and the people right and on board.

3. The efficiency gains with implementing Blockchain technology solutions are significant – from 30% to 90% efficiency savings could be achieved.

4. The efficiency gains are great, but the new revenue streams and business models that Blockchain technology opens up can allow your organization to grow its revenue significantly as well as become significantly more efficient.

5. The old rules of transformation and focusing on the end results are critical. Keep the projects focused, and when they do not work, change them, do not just keep following a project, just because it is a Blockchain technology solution.

11

Risks of Implementing Blockchain Technology

Before we look at the relationship between Blockchain technology and other emerging technologies, it is worth looking at the risks and 'perceived' risks in adopting this new technology. As with all transformations, implementing Blockchain technology will not be easy and there will be many issues along the way, but I am 100% confident that the benefits more than outweigh the risks. As with any transformation project, do you own research first.

Change – Inertia of People

People do not like change; 'I like it this way' is a common trait amongst the population. Change is often related to fear and unhappiness, meaning most people are fearful of what they do not understand.

Once you do understand the power of Blockchain technology you then realize that this isn't a quick and easy fix – nothing worthwhile is ever quick and easy.

Thoughts such as 'It's hard' and 'It's scary' appear, and these are strong feelings and reasons to not continue down the road of Blockchain adoption.

As with any change there are always a number of people who want to lead the change, and want to be at the forefront of new technologies (I would argue that you are an early adopter, because you are reading the first comprehensive book on commercializing Blockchain). These people are important to the community and to your organization and you must help them to champion the development of Blockchain technology.

Commercializing Blockchain: Strategic Applications in the Real World,
First Edition. Antony Welfare.
© 2019 John Wiley & Sons Ltd. Published 2019 by John Wiley & Sons Ltd.

In the general media there is too much fake news on cryptocurrency such as Bitcoin, which means that people do not see the benefits of Blockchain technology in the non-crypto world. This has changed slowly during 2018, but it is still the starting point of many conversations about Blockchain technology. I have had many a discussion with C-level executives on the fact that Blockchain technology is not Bitcoin; it is Bitcoin that is the first use case of Blockchain technology. As more and more Blockchain use cases are developed, this misunderstanding will slowly disappear.

Finally, regarding change and Blockchain technology, you have the fact that with Blockchain technology it is a different way to think – from front to back. This is a big change for many people who are process driven, they are used to entering data and then reconciling and auditing post the transaction; as we know, with Blockchain technology, the data is verified and certified as it enters the Blockchain. This 180-degree change is hard to understand after a lifetime of working the opposite way around. Once the users understand this, they will be well on the way to adopting the revolution powered by Blockchain technology.

User's Adoption

Talking about user adoption is critical for the growth of Blockchain technology. If we cannot interact with a Blockchain solution in an easy and intuitive way, we will not adopt this. As I have mentioned previously, the first cryptocurrency wallets are very difficult to work with and result in many people not adopting them. We have to ensure that the end result is useable and what the customers want. The end user needs to be able to use the technology with the same ease they use today's technologies; anything that is more complex is likely to be left on the shelf.

To ensure you have the right user interface you must 'test, test, and test', find out what the users like and dislike and ensure their systems are built for them to easily use the technology.

Education on Blockchain technology is also critical for user adoption, you must educate the users on why Blockchain technology is applicable and on the benefits of using the technology. The better the education, the more the users will adopt the technology and start to develop their own use cases and solutions.

Scale and Complexity

We are focusing on enterprise organizations, which process thousands of transactions daily, which means that the risks around scale and complexity are as big as they can be.

How do you onboard 500 entities? How do you manage consensus? What happens when the consensus mechanism goes wrong? Who do you blame?

These are all questions that need to be answered by the process around the implementation of the Blockchain solutions. As I have mentioned previously, the adoption of Blockchain technology is more around the people and the process, rather than the technology. If you bring the people on board with the journey, using their expertise, as well as the full ecosystem, then you will be able to collectively solve the issues around scale and complexity.

Standardization

With any new technology, there is a period before standards are established, where the technology's competing parties try to be 'the' only standard in the industry. There is a rush at the moment to be 'the' Blockchain solution, which I believe is completely pointless. The fact that Blockchain technology is decentralized means that we do not need one solution and one main provider.

What we need is standards across the Blockchain world. Much like we have standards across the internet or standards across the telecoms industry, we need to agree a set of standards on the operating of the Blockchain technologies. This is the key reason why I say that Blockchain is still at 0.7 or 0.8, we need these standards to take this revolutionary technology to 1.0 and then onwards.

The next stage of standardization is with interoperability and ensuring that there are processes and standards in place for transferable systems and data agreements. These will help to allow all the different Blockchain solutions 'communicate' together and across the entire ecosystem.

Finally, whatever the standard, they have to be easy to implement and understandable across the entire ecosystem globally. The standards and interoperability standards will need to cover all geographies and use cases, which means this will take time and interactions.

A great example of working together on standards is the Hyperledger community and the Enterprise Ethereum Alliance, where they have agreed to pool and share their technical ideas, plans, and solutions. This type of collaboration will help speed up the development of Blockchain technology to 1.0 and beyond.

Government

The government is the biggest beneficiary – but do they see it? I work with the UK government and see lots of other governments 'looking at' Blockchain technology, but do they really comprehend the significant benefits that this will bring to their countries, across all areas of government. From Digital ID to healthcare tracking to digital title deeds to digital payments, their entire system can be revolutionized with Blockchain technology.

I believe that few people in the governments do understand the potential, but they are highly siloed and risk-averse. They lack the correct knowledge and awareness, and unfortunately, they believe the fake news which we see on a daily basis. This will change over time and there are governments in countries such as Estonia, Malta, and UAE, where they are taking Blockchain technology seriously, and will have an excellent head start on the governments who are not embracing this revolution.

We also have to remember that old government systems cannot understand decentralized worlds; it makes sense as they are the complete opposite of a decentralized organization. It is important to understand that I do not expect the world and governments to become decentralized, I expect them to adopt the Blockchain technology based on decentralization and sharing, to help benefit their countries and citizens.

The Control Structures Around the World aka "The 1%"

Let's get a little controversial now, and whether its 1% or just what you call 'the system', there is a world order and there are entities around the world – powerful ones – who may not want a more decentralized and trusted world; they may prefer the status quo and keep the power to themselves. It has been seen many times in history, where the powers that be do what they need to control a new technology or asset.

The oil industry is a classic example, where everybody started to drill for oil until the Rockefellers drove the price so low that all the drillers went out of business, or they were bought by companies connected to Rockefeller. The owner, John D. Rockefeller, become the richest man in American history and was later found to have violated many anti-monopoly and trust rules.

If you look at today's society, we have some very powerful organizations controlling many things that we do not know about. The classic, for conspiracy theorists, is that the Rothschild family own all but three central banks in the world, but they deny this. My view is that there is no smoke without fire and there is always an alternative truth.

Conspiracy aside, with Blockchain technology you are introducing transparency and trust – neither of these two words have been used to describe the 'system' for many years (if ever). My view is that if you are to allow Blockchain technology to be implemented across all organizations, there will be many people opposed to this new transparency. That is why I believe there is a concerted effort to slow down the implementation of this technology, and some of the reasons are bona fide.

I have mentioned the cryptocurrency price crash of 2018, and I do believe some of that is due to the institutions preventing the growth of this. This is proven by the often ridiculous comments, from the leaders such as JP Morgan and Warren Buffet, who resorted to childlike insults about the technology.

These will all wash over and the technology will flourish with the right regulations and the right ecosystem driving the benefits.

Regulations

Regulations are a very complex arena and something that I am no expert in. What I do know is that we do need some form of regulations for the Blockchain technology, and especially for the cryptocurrency world.

National regulations will not work, as this technology is cross-borders and cross-everything; this technology is global and beyond any one government or organization's jurisdiction. Maybe that will change, but as we sit here today, we have a complex mix of national regulations crossing all organizations and borders.

For Blockchain technology to develop, we need 'supranational regulations' and agreements; these crossborders, governments, and organizations. This task is ambitious and complex to say the least, but it will be needed for the longer term revolution that Blockchain technology will bring.

We need to Blockchain the world! (Please see previous caveat that Blockchain is not a verb!)

Millennials and Younger Generations

One interesting experience that I have seen in the Blockchain world is that the younger generations do not agree with the current 'system'. They tend to lack trust in governments, law enforcement, and the large organizations that run the world. They want transparency and trust, and more understanding and a voice in the future of the world. They have unlimited access to technology and are born with the internet – there is nothing that they cannot find out.

Whilst there are many strengths and weaknesses of this, my concern is their understanding of and interest in a world with Blockchain technology. Most of the students and graduates I speak to have a 'standard' interest in Blockchain technology. By 'standard' I mean they see it as an interesting opportunity to change the status quo now, and they view it alongside many other emerging technologies. This healthy attitude has to be countered with the understanding of the practicalities of a decentralized world.

Do they really understand the scale of complexity to make this work? Is there too much idealism and not enough practicality? In my view, their enthusiasm and interest could easily lead to ideological, rather than achieving real, benefits. My focus is to keep the Blockchain technology developing for real use cases, helping organizations around the world to improve themselves, their staff, and their customers' lives.

Ignorance

There is a significant level of ignorance around Blockchain technology, which has been perpetrated by the fake news world. As I have mentioned before, Bitcoin is one use case of Blockchain technology; it is not the Blockchain technology.

There is misinformation everywhere; I have seen Blockchain courses which are completely wrong, I have been to keynote speeches where the presenter has no idea what Blockchain is, and I have met leaders of Blockchain businesses, who have no idea what the technology actually does. This ignorance is widespread and common for any new technology.

My view is that we need to share accurate and educational news and information on Blockchain technology, and I hope this book will help people to start to understand the real opportunity of Blockchain technology.

Remember that all news, and social media in particular, have bias algorithms that play to your view and your previous experiences. Make sure you read as much as you can about the technology, and the best way to learn is to go and work with organizations who have Blockchain solutions. See the technology in action (it is actually quite boring to watch a Blockchain transaction) and learn how it works, and where you could implement this revolutionary technology in your organization.

Quantum and New Technology

My final risk is the unknown, I have no idea what technology is coming next – no one does. That's why the world of technology is so exciting. Who knows what's next? We will embrace the next technologies like we have the previous technologies and I am sure we will see more technologies developing and working in harmony with Blockchain technology.

If we look at Blockchain technology to solve the trust and transparency issues, we can use other technologies to maximize, share, and further develop this. I have no idea what they will be, but I will embrace them when they arrive.

One risk I hear as a question all the time is 'Can quantum take over from Blockchain?' And my answer is simple: 'No, you just develop quantum cryptography to work against the quantum criminals.' Also, how about looking at quantum computing on the Blockchain technology – how powerful is that combination?

I will leave the risks section there and move swiftly onto the final section on the emerging technologies and bringing together all the current and emerging technologies to build a better and brighter future for us all.

12

Blockchain Is Better When Used with Existing and Other Emerging Technologies

In this chapter I wanted to share a few of the other emerging technologies which are important for the future of our enterprise organizations and work with or alongside Blockchain technology.

I will first share my thoughts on this area and follow this with a contribution from a friend of mine, Peter Bambridge, sharing his views on this area. I will then add a couple of examples before I hand over to another friend of mine, Michael Forhez, who has a very interesting view on the future of the consumer brands and retail world, and how emerging technology is key to the future speed and adoption of change.

My final contributor, Eric Wallace, will end this chapter with an interesting look at how Blockchain technologies related to permissioned and public are not fit for purpose for enterprise organizations today. Eric suggests another way and gives some examples of how this can be achieved using Blockchain technology and the other exciting emerging technologies.

Eric studies and researches DLT and Blockchain technologies. Eric's section is a great read to finish off this chapter, and lead us into the final chapter on the future of Blockchain technology.

Commercializing Blockchain: Strategic Applications in the Real World,
First Edition. Antony Welfare.
© 2019 John Wiley & Sons Ltd. Published 2019 by John Wiley & Sons Ltd.

IoT, AI/ML, RPA, Blockchain, AR, VR – Emerging Technologies

The world of emerging technologies covers every type of new technology that you have heard about. The term is widely used and is not that clearly defined – i.e. what is really emerging or what is emerging, or what will actually become a technology used by people and enterprise?

I refer to the Atos view of emerging and transformational technology which is a great visual on the technology of the future, its business impact and when it is likely to happen.

Referring to this, you will see that Blockchain technology is in the high business impact quadrant, which will happen around 2020 and it is in the early adoption phase. If you have kept up with me in this book, you will understand that this reflects my view of the technology today.

There are many technologies on this chart which are exciting and I could devote an entire book to this, but I want to focus only on a couple, which have a real connection with Blockchain and we have seen use cases where these technologies mutually benefit each other.

How Blockchain, AI, and IoT Work in Harmony – 'ABot'

I believe one of the best matches of emerging technology currently is with Blockchain, IoT, and AI.

Let's look at how these work together.

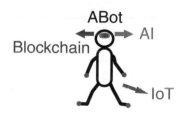

As you can see the technologies work together to make the 'ABot' a powerful asset to any company where:

- Blockchain technology – becomes the memory, storing all the data and analysis in an immutable and shared ledger.
- Artificial intelligence – becomes the brain – this is the logical thought process which analyses information constantly, making decisions based on this continual data flow.
- IoT – these are the sensors that are bringing in the data in the first place, and they share these via Blockchain with AI.

I find this an excellent way to visualize these three technologies working as one.

I will now introduce Peter Bambridge, who shares his thoughts on a few Blockchain and emerging technology relationships.

Powering the Next Industrial Revolution
By Peter Bambridge

Blockchain is currently being adopted to address a wide spectrum of use cases throughout the retail value chain, ranging from financial settlement and payments, to tracking packages through the entire delivery process. In order to achieve this, existing ERP, accounting, and supply chain management systems are being integrated seamlessly with Blockchain.

In addition to addressing the needs of these early use cases, Blockchain is combining with existing operational systems and a growing list of emerging technologies that together will have a significant impact on the way businesses operate. These emerging technologies that can combine with Blockchain include: artificial intelligence/machine learning (AI/ML), the internet of things (IoT), robotic process automation (RPA), and in the future, quantum computing (QC).

The combination of these emerging technologies is now resulting in smarter solutions that predict problems and recommend resolving actions, learning from previous experience, sensing real-world status information and reacting accordingly, as well as automating routine tasks.

One good example of emerging technologies combining in the retail value chain is around the supply chain with the traceability of products. Information can be written securely to the Blockchain at every stage from the initial creation/sourcing of products, right through to the product being in the hands of the consumer. Providing consumers with access to information on the provenance of products can help reinforce consumer trust in the product, as well as ensure food safety standards are adhered to. Using QR codes to provide information on the sustainability of the product directly to the consumer, and also the ethical aspects of the product's creation, provides new ways to interact with the consumer that give far more than the information contained on the product label.

In a recent retail and consumer goods industry solution, we focused on delivering traceability from farm to fork. In this solution we look at the catching, processing, distribution, and retail of fresh fish. The Blockchain platform provides the reliable secure storage of multi-enterprise information on the cloud at every stage from the original fishing boat through to the shelf of the retailer. This integrates with the supply chain management platform that manages every step of the process, and also gathers data from IoT sensors on the boat to capture where and when the fish was caught, how it was stored, and at what temperature, when it changed hands, at each stage of processing, as well as when and where the product was distributed.

Gathering IoT data for location tracking, date and time recording and temperature monitoring, and aligning it with product information is an important capability in the retail value chain, and also in some of the pharmaceutical value chains where temperature-controlled logistics is also a requirement.

Having the Blockchain as a reference it is then simpler to trace products and their raw materials back to their sources. This helps to clearly target recalls when the issues occur, that helps minimize direct recall costs and help protect the brand. Given that the average recall cost now exceeds $10m in direct costs, increasing visibility is a major factor.

A later phase of this solution may extend the scope with how AI/ML capabilities can also be integrated to the process to drive even higher levels of scrutiny and to drive further enhancement in food safety by becoming increasingly predictive. Learning from previous experience and leveraging a growing set of history data to predict potential issues, before the consequences occur.

Another area where there is increasing interest in the adoption of Blockchain is around the management of private brands. There are well-established systems to help coordinate all aspects of private label products that facilitate their sourcing, development, labelling, quality, marketing, and protection. Typically adopted by retailers, restaurants, food service and manufacturers, these systems take advantage of the cloud to audit and manage all aspects of the product specification, creating accurate and certified labelling detail against local regulative and industry policies. It is becoming ever more important to balance the needs of quality and consumer trust, with the ever-present cost considerations. It is key to have a range of audit quality inspection and traceability solutions to check and test each product throughout its production, delivery, and shelf life. The next generation of these tools will become Blockchain enabled. By adding value to users at every level from the farmer in the field to the retailer on the high street, Blockchain represents a new level of trust and reliability that is the key to ensuring product safety and maintaining consumer trust.

This will be achieved by allowing connection and collaboration with the entire supply chain utilizing Blockchain applications that will capture, authenticate, and track trading relationships, accreditations, and movement of product. This data will then allow the sourcing, validating, and managing of the entire compliance lifecycle from farm to consumer. These services will include the ability to authenticate certifications and trading relationships, and track movement of product enabling governance and control with greater due diligence across the entire product selection and development process and provide a faster and more reliable assessment of incidents with the empowerment to drill down and identify the actual batches/lots affected.

Ultimately, adopting Blockchain in this area will help ensure the security, reliability, and management of private brands, and also the ongoing validation and compliance throughout the entire life cycle of these increasingly important products. This combination of Blockchain and major operational systems is another example of combined capabilities that are growing in demand.

AI/ML is increasingly being adopted in retail; a recent Capgemini report identified that 28% of the 'Top 250' retailers are deploying AI in 2018, up from 17% in 2017. (See 'Building the Retail Superstar: How unleashing AI across functions offers a multi-billion dollar opportunity' at: www.capgemini.com/research/building-the-retail-superstar-how-unleashing-ai-across-functions-offers-a-multi-billion-dollar-opportunity/.) At a country level, in the USA, the research suggests

25% AI penetration, whereas in the UK it is already at 39%. When looking at pure-play online retailers, then the AI penetration is already at 68%. If Morrisons reduced stock gaps by 30% during its trials of AI, and if Walmart anticipates saving over $2bn over the next five years by AI-driven image optimization reducing the occurrence of spoilage, then we will continue to see increasing levels of adoption by increasing numbers of retailers over the coming years in these and other customer facing areas.

What is also interesting from this report is the spread of use cases where AI is already being adopted. Examples include the following. In Planning and Procurement: these include stock replenishment, assortment rationalization, demand planning, and sales forecasting. In Production: new product development and in predictive maintenance. In Logistics: reverse supply chain and returns management, route optimization, reducing pilferage, inventory optimization, and robots to manage warehouses. In store operations: customer behaviour analysis, enabling self-checkouts and bots for shelf scanning. In sales and marketing: image recognition to identify counterfeit products, personalization, sales support, and promotion optimization.

A number of these AI use cases also leverage RPA, for example in scanning store shelves and in the warehouse, so there is well-established use of a combination of robotics and AI. IoT sensors in the production environment are also an important part of AI based-predictive maintenance, as they are throughout the supply chain.

As with the adoption of all new technologies, there are some key ingredients to success: having a clear roadmap of how and when to implement, having the data environment to enable the new capabilities and having the skills within the business to exploit the new opportunities.

Whether it is for visual aided picking in the warehouse or recommending alternative products in ecommerce matched to your style, colour, size, and previous buying history, it is important to undertake real-world testing, adopting a 'fail fast' approach, and then reviewing, learning, and moving on in the eternal battle to exceed customer expectations.

Blockchain will continue to expand the portfolio of use cases it is used to address, combining its strengths with those of the emerging technologies will further accelerate its adoption, and lead to further growth in benefits realization.

I will now share a couple of use cases before my final two contributors' sections.

Use Case: Emerging Technologies Working Together in Retail

The current brick and mortar stores will have less relevance in the future, and they will play very different roles. Rather than the standard style we see now, the emergence of new technologies will allow there to be a vastly different set of shopping outlets based on the customers' ever-demanding requirements and the vast emergence of new technologies.

Blockchain technologies will be used as the central 'hub' for all this data, to ensure that the customer facing technologies operate at speed, with accuracy and with a transparent information flow.

There would be three types of stores:

1. The major retailers and brands (Apple, Nike, Armani, etc.) will transition to a 'showroom' type of store, where the customer comes to experience the products in an experiential led environment. These stores will serve several purposes, such as to:

   - Demonstrate the products in an interactive and exciting way.
   - Utilize new technologies which will help the customer select their products.
   - New services such as personalization, or digital approaches to customize clothes will be used – utilizing the new world of 3D and digital printing.
   - Food sampling and tasting - today's food hall trend will continue to evolve into mega stores that sell foods and other items, but with highly interactive presentation and lots of tasting.
   - Virtual Reality (VR) technologies to help you take your imagination to the next level and see what the products will look like in your home or on your body, especially useful in furniture stores.

2. Convenience and top-up shopping will continue to grow for the purpose of 'refuelling' along the lines of the Amazon Go concept. Aided by scanning technologies and wireless wallets for payments, customers will walk in, collect their products quickly and walk out – all seamlessly without any hassle.

3. Pickups, drop-offs (returns) and other 'fulfilment' type services.

The last mile delivery and collection of products is the most complex issue in retail. Using the latest technologies retailers will be able to offer many different options such as:

- Collection points in store
- Lockers
- Drone deliveries
- Driver deliveries
- Deliver to cars
- Deliver to office
- Collect at station.

These are a few of the many options being tested for the last mile, and all of these require a highly coordinated supply chain network. Blockchain, together with other new technologies, will enable retailers the technological solutions to offer customers all the options they want for their own shopping requirements.

Use Case: Waltonchain for Provenance

Let's look at RFID and Blockchain technology and a great use case from Waltonchain, which combines Blockchain technology with radio-frequency identification (RFID) and IoT (internet of things) technologies to improve supply chain management performance.

Waltonchain introduces a new era of value internet of things (VIoT) to produce a decentralized ecosystem of inter-connectivity. It also uses embedded RFID tags for tracking precious goods in the supply chain and then logging product status data coming out from RFID tags to Waltonchain Blockchain. This then becomes an immutable record which cannot be tampered with and can therefore help to identify a product's authenticity.

Waltonchain teamed up with Fujian Skynovo IoT Technology to launch Blockchain based two-way traceability food authenticity platform, WTC-Food.

WTC-Food will achieve mutual benefit for consumers, enterprises, and technology through the powerful and flexible data collection, information traceability, and credit endorsement.

Waltonchain, in association with China's leading high-end clothing brand Kaltendin, has launched Blockchain-based high-end clothing authenticity trace ability platform, WTC-Garment.

WTC-Garment platform not only improves the efficiency of business operations of high-end clothing retailers in manufacturing, logistics, and store management, but also provides an immersive shopping experience for customers.

Platforms like WTC-Food and WTC-Garments use all technologies including; Blockchain, IoT, RFID, AI, big data, analytics, Cloud, mobility, which are converging to provide provenance applications.

Use Case: Convergence of Blockchain, IoT, and AI for Successful Provenance Solutions

Convergence of Blockchain, IoT, and AI is going to be a large disruptive area for the retail and supply chain industry. Blockchain alone cannot deliver total provenance, but an ecosystem, combining the power of Blockchain + IoT + AI is going to build a comprehensive provenance solution.

Let's look at Shanghai-based start-up BitSE, which is instrumental in building the provenance application VeChain, which can track and verify items such as luxury apparel, handbags, wines, and groceries.

Shoppers can use VeChain's app to access product profile and check its authenticity through public key available on VeChain servers and other relevant data fed through IoT sensors throughout the entire life cycle of product.

It is working on next generation Blockchain technology known as VeChainThor Blockchain. The VeChainThor blockchain uses PoA (proof of authority) to maintain the consensus among all blockchain nodes.

The blockchain consists of 101 authority nodes which are controlled by the whitelist. So here there is mix of decentralized and centralized architecture. VeChain has partnered with numerous world leading IoT device manufacturers, RFID, and NFC tags producers, to empower the integrity and accuracy of the dataset stored on VeChainThor Blockchain.

Two current retail and supply chain solutions, where VeChain are working on provenance and track & trace solutions are:

1. Cold-chain logistics
   VeChain's cold-chain logistics solution uses proprietary IoT devices to track key metrics throughout the entire journey. VeChain embeds data management and sharing in every process, making cold-chain logistics transparent, regulated, secure, and reliable.
2. Luxury and fashion
   VeChain embeds smart chips within luxury goods, so brands can monitor their sales channels in real time to prevent illegal overstock trading. Meanwhile, consumers can verify the authenticity of the luxury products through VeChain apps. VeChain puts control back into the hands of brands, making luxury chains transparent, seamless, and data-driven.

Michael Forhez is a global leader in the worlds of consumer products, brands, and retail. Michael has an excellent view on the future of the customer across all emerging technologies and the Blockchain world. Have a look at his thoughts and some really interesting statistics about the world we live in now and what it could look like in the future.

From the Improbable to the Inevitable
Michael Forhez

Looking Around the Corner and Over the Horizon
There are points in time when nothing is as it was before. Currently we are passing through such a time – a disruption and discontinuity we are only now sensing and defining. Old attitudes, long-standing practices, deep-rooted beliefs, assumed 'truths' are challenged, knocked down, brushed aside, crushed. What two decades ago we thought to be impossible, we now recognize as inevitable.

Consumer products (fast-moving consumer goods – FMCG) are increasingly a globally connected network. Customers, brands, and retailers, today, link in both the physical and digital channels. For most, the future will not resemble the past:

- The tech-enabled customer changes faster than brands or retailers do.
- Brands can no longer sell what they make...they must make what they can sell.
- Retailers can no longer sell what they bought...they must buy what they can sell.
- The ability to sense and respond is now a requisite skill set.

To serve today's connected consumers, manufacturing and retailing skill sets must be augmented with new marketing, brand, and retailing concepts based on three factors:

1. Smart data, illuminating the way.
2. Relationships and transactions, happening anywhere, anytime.
3. Frictionless commerce, with focused experiences as requisite.

Current, and future, leadership and management must, in this transformative age, be prepared to look around the corner and over the horizon.

Radical and Rapid Change

Digital technology is enabling consumer behaviour to change faster than the majority of retailers or brands' abilities to serve them. Likewise, consumer expectations have changed. Today, products and services, to be relevant, must be present in the moment, or what we once called 'the moment of truth'.

While the repeated use of the word 'change' makes one's eyes glaze over, it is nonetheless an inescapable disruptive reality and today also the new normal. Accepting change, therefore, requires the systematic abandonment of the old and obsolete because:

- For brands, mass production economies of scale are no longer a guarantee of profitability or growth. As well, centralized manufacturing facilities must evolve to customized quick-change and automated plants, close to differentiated, niche markets they must serve in near real-time.

- Quality is now determined by the consumer's perception of a personal price/value relationship, not, at least not exclusively, a manufacturer's standards.
- Ethical sourcing, fair wage, workplace health and safety, and environmental responsibility are now explicit product attributes, which consumers recognize and are making buying decisions upon.
- Distribution channels are no longer exclusively determined by the brand or retailer. The consumer now decides how, when, and where they wish to buy, what they are willing to pay and how they will take possession.
- Brand and retailer market strategies and decisions must no longer be made solely on cost-based economics. The creation and delivery of unique value to prospective customers is required to acquire a sustainable competitive advantage.

As a consequence, brands and retailers are now engaged in a technology that is enhanced, matching process to their customers, with these customers easily pairing their wants and needs to the capabilities of trading partners, more often one vs. the other.

Scope and Scale
Author and futurist William Gibson noted, 'The future is already here—it's just not distributed evenly'.
Consider these foundational trends:

- In the 1960s, US network television delivered to over 90% of domestic households. Mobile phones, launched in the 1970s, are now owned by 82% of the US population. Given the power of these powerful digital devices to deliver content anytime/anywhere, TV's reach has dropped by approximately two-thirds of these households, and is still declining.
- From the 2000s on, hundreds of millions of e-commerce platforms, services, and apps were created for media streaming, online advertising, online marketplaces, brick and mortar retailers, e-commerce payment systems for online storefronts, etc. Consumers downloaded an estimated 205 billion apps in 2018 alone.
- Today, close to three quarters of all the adults on earth now have a smartphone, and most of the rest will get one in the next few years. However, the use of this connectivity is only just beginning, with 29

billion connected devices forecast by 2022, including IoT devices, connected cars, machines, meters, wearables, and other consumer electronics, according to recent research by Swedish multinational networking and telecommunications company L. M. Ericsson.

- According to IHS Markit research, 82% of mobile operators globally are participating in 5G tests. The US and South Korea are already deploying in 2018–19, and Europe going forward in 2021. With 5G downloads 20 times faster than the current standard 4G, massive bandwidth and super low latency, 5G will accelerate investments in and commercial utilization of AR, VR, robotics, cloud, gaming, immersive education, autonomous vehicles, IoT devices, and more.

- On 31 October, 2018, Rwanda became the first country in Africa to join the Electronic World Trade Platform (eWTP). On December 5, 2018, Belgium became the first country in Europe to become a member of the eWTP. The eWTP led by China's Alibaba seeks to lower barriers to global trade for small and medium-sized businesses via e-commerce. eWTP is a private sector-led multi-stakeholder initiative that offers SMEs support in logistics, financing, cloud computing, mobile payment services, and digitized customs clearances (potential Blockchain applications).

- Euromonitor International predicts that e-commerce will be the largest retail channel in the world by 2021. As technology is adopted globally, by 2020, the US and Europe will account for 16% of total e-commerce sales. Asia and the rest of the world will account for 84% based on a September 2017 Global Ecommerce report by Shopify Plus.

Thinking Differently

The way we were taught to assess and solve problems, for the most part, was designed for a different era. To deal with the problems of today, however, we'll need a quite different approach, with fresh mindsets and skill sets to match.

Why? In reality, there is no mass market, and there never was. Mass media, and particularly network TV, enabled, and sustained for a time, the illusion of a mass-market mentality. The ability to collect, store, access, and manipulate data, to turn data into information, and apply it in the laboratory, factory, marketing department and, yes, in the home, has changed everything. Computers and smartphones gave capital value to information and shifted power from the retailer/brand to the consumer, hastening the development and hyperextension of e-commerce and the digital marketplace with incredible speed and economic consequences. Witness:

- More brick and mortar store closings were announced in 2017 than in any year on record.
- The demography of the US 'family unit' is shifting. In the 1960s, 60% of families included three or more members; 20% had five or more members. As of the 1990s, the family defined as mother, father and two kids comprised only 7% of households. More than half of all households now formed are comprised of singles. The implications for marketers? Basic household needs (i.e. furnishings and kitchen appliances), more lifestyle options considered, more mobility, etc.
- The technology-enabled consumer of today can adapt faster than most retailers or brands. Retailers and brands must develop the new insights and technology required to meet the evolving challenge of selling to individual consumers, small cohorts and a range of changing need states predicated on rising expectations, rather than expanded markets. As we switch from the concept of mass markets to niche markets then, the motto from the age of the retailer/brand, 'caveat emptor' – let the buyer beware – is replaced by 'cave emptorum' – beware of the buyer. Information, therefore, has become the defining element of business strategy.

Building Blocks and Blockchains

The design, manufacturing, marketing, and distributing of consumer products increasingly relies on a globally connected network. Customers, brands, and retailers today are – or must be – linking in both the physical digital channels. This 'linkage', which relies on combination of technology, transparency, and trust, is now the key to payments and provenance moving ever faster, in an increasingly frictionless commercial world. How do we insure its integrity, while nurturing its growth? Most prognosticators see the Blockchain as the best potential solution.

But beyond the promise is the reality. The proof of concept. And today, and for the next several years, Blockchain will be pressure tested to see if all the hype can live up to this promise.

Implementing Blockchain will require partners to remove existing, ageing infrastructure, starting nearly from scratch – a complicated, time-consuming, and expensive process. These partners, justifiably, will be cautious in making real-world, long-term commitments to Blockchain without the technology first proving its ability to deliver at scale. All that said, this powerful solution could prove to be the ulti-mate 'game changer' if it proves trustworthy and commercially viable.

Crossing into 2019 and as we pass through the next several years, can Blockchain move past its proof-of-concept phase? Below, a sam-pling of projects that are providing the foundation for the future:

- Walmart, Kroger, Tyson, Unilever, McCormick, and others banded together in August 2017 for a Blockchain pilot designed to improve food safety through better supply chain tracking.
- Maersk joined Hyperledger to help shippers, ports, customs offices, banks, and other stakeholders in global supply chains track freight and replace related paperwork with tamper-resistant digital records.
- Microsoft, Accenture, and Avanade are creating a blockchain-based identity prototype designed to solve the problem of identity docu-mentation for the estimated 1.1 billion people around the world without legal forms of ID.
- The United Nations is exploring distributed ledger technology (DLT) and Blockchain for humanitarian aid and climate science research.
- Oracle, Amazon, and Google have, or are in the process of, develop-ing Blockchain interfaces that integrate Blockchain services with their respective platforms.
- Tencent and Huawei are leading a Blockchain consortium of over 100 different Chinese companies. The objective is to enable fast transactions while providing 'observatory' nodes for government regulators and auditors.
- United Healthcare, Optum, Quest Diagnostics, Humana, and Multiplan have launched a pilot provider directory on the Blockchain.
- NASDAQ and CITI are teaming up to use DLT to integrate payments between banks. Blockchain technology is being used to automate payment processing worth trillions of dollars per year.

Putting It Together, Making It Work

- Well acknowledged, though not so well understood, the grocery industry is now being fully disrupted. McKinsey estimates that $200bn to $700bn in revenues might shift to discount, non-grocery, and online channels, constituting $1tn in EBIT earning now at risk. Walmart and Kroger are currently making massive e-commerce investments to bridge the physical and digital operating universe, but when the dust clears, likely half of traditional grocery retailers will not be around.
- Zegna's CEO, Gildo Zegna, recognizes that fashion is an ever-changing landscape. 'A global fashion house needs the ability to sense and respond to the variety of needs and tastes of its global customer base', Mr Zegna stated in a recent interview, adding that he now relies on a 'Digital as a Services' model to guide his company '…from Sheep to Shop, From Shop to Screen.' Data input allows this company to approach a collection not by season, but on a project basis, even to release 'capsule collections' at higher introduction frequencies.
- At Nike, combining the online and offline worlds is a key priority. According to CEO Mark Parker, '…the company's Digital Strategy is driving a shift from traditional operating models to a "digitally-powered" future model that builds on the firm's heritage'. Parker further notes that the use of data analytics will be used to inform product design and logistics capabilities in the future.

Again, as we switch from the concept of mass markets, to niche markets, to consumer specific markets; information and smart targeted data becomes the defining element of business strategy.

Restructuring the Structure
Author Saul Bellow said, 'People create a world they can live in….' and that seems to be what we are doing today.

'Change management' is often thought of as transition management. We are 'this'; we need to be 'that'. Then we begin to recognize the breadth and depth of the delta. Brands and retailers need to manage change from 'this' to 'that' without going under in the process. The implicit challenge is to achieve the coherent organizational alignment required, while not losing our shirts in walking the path.

In a data-driven era, powerful systems must be created with completely new processes, skills, roles, assets, and information infrastructures that are flat, team-centred, networked, and highly dynamic.

These newly empowered teams will be a surviving organization's imperative in a world where consumers value a predictable but flexible and frictionless response as premier characteristics of the organizations they want to deal with. A network of empowered teams can be extraordinarily effective, but only if the teams operate in a common, coordinated context.

Consumer first party and anonymous first party data will be the primary resource for brands and retailers to sense and respond to their customers' wants and needs. AI will assist humans in abstracting reality and that reality will be applied to model increasingly large and complex modules of institutional behaviour. However, new regulatory laws like Europe's recently passed General Data Protection Regulation (GDPR) will need heightened awareness and special organizational attention.

Consumer informed insights drive innovation. The simultaneous rethinking of business strategy and business operations is now requisite. Management must weigh the cost of doing something. . .but also of not doing that same thing. For if they don't do it, someone else will; someone else already is.

Will Blockchain technology be the answer? Time will certainly tell, and sooner than we think!

Reprise
The fast-moving consumer goods (FMCG) industry is a marathon without a finish line, which must increasingly be run at sprint speed.

Hail the Consumer!

I now want to introduce the final contributor in this section who is Eric Wallace. Eric has been researching the issues around the current enterprise Blockchain solutions; focusing on the issues, and complexities, with the different types of Enterprise Blockchain solutions, covered by Chris Wing earlier in the book. Eric has researched nearly every Blockchain solution there is and has a few ideas on what the future Blockchain solution could look like, and importantly, how we can use the other emerging technologies with Blockchain technology.

SecureChain: Trustful Decentralized Enterprise DLT Platform for AI and IoT

By Eric Wallace

The Landscape

Bitcoin mining currently consumes more energy for transaction confirmations than 6 million US homes.[1] This is a 7x increase since April 2017, with a current total network hash rate of 45 EH/s (45 quintillion H/s).[2] Given the current task of mining Bitcoin, the world's top 500 supercomputers account for less than 0.1% of the Bitcoin network.[3] Although miners waste the large majority of this computational power through proof of work, the Bitcoin network highlights the incredible power of incentives in a decentralized environment as miners strive for a financial bounty in the form of a block reward. Now, over a thousand cryptocurrencies exist but despite the promise of DLT, few enterprises use this revolutionary technology. DLT projects face challenges related to scalability, sustainability, and privacy, while centralized cloud services allow businesses highly scalable computational power, data storage, and other IT resources. Platforms including Amazon Web Services, Microsoft Azure, and Google Cloud Platform are growing rapidly with widespread adoption while minimizing the upfront costs for users. Although these centralized cloud services provide enterprise scaling solutions, they also come with significant risks, including data breaches, insufficient access management, system vulnerabilities, and denial of service (DOS) attacks. DLT is still in its infancy but as the technology matures, we will see widespread adoption in nearly every market. As the security and performance requirements of applications and devices push further to the edge, many of tomorrow's applications and services will require trustful infrastructures incorporating DLT.

While public DLT solutions like Bitcoin, Ethereum, and NEO advertise large decentralized networks, they have limitations for enterprises, such as

---

1 www.eia.gov.
2 www.eia.gov.
3 www.top500.org.

controlled data reversibility, data privacy, scalability, updatability, integration, and system responsiveness. Most enterprises are unable to use public, decentralized Blockchains for trading and payments; public ledgers could expose customers, suppliers, vendors, service providers, partners, shareholders, bank account balances, and other sensitive information. Furthermore, the clear majority of public DLT networks specialize in the financial sector, leaving production, manufacturing, transportation, military applications, heavy machinery, construction, agriculture, food processing, and cyber security relatively untouched. These deficiencies have led to the development of private DLT solutions.

Private DLTs offer efficient permissioned consensus with increased transaction throughput 500x faster than Ethereum. IBM's Hyperledger Fabric advertises 100k transactions/sec using Practical Byzantine Fault Tolerance (PBFT).[4] This performance increase comes at a significant cost in terms of immutability, reliability, and decentralization. The organization that owns a private DLT network also owns consensus determination and can tamper or edit data [4]. Private DLT networks are partially or entirely centralized with far fewer nodes than public DLT networks, leading to higher susceptibility of attack or failure.[5,6] A derivative of private DLT networks is the notion of consortium DLT networks where preselected individuals or nodes control consensus instead of an individual or single organization. A consortium DLT network may be public for viewing or restricted to its participants. Upcoming projects are looking to solve the problems of public and private blockchains; however, the work is by and large very specific to a singular issue. Filecoin with its InterPlanetary File System (IPFS)[7] is providing a solution for serving billions of files used across a global peer-to-peer decentralized network. ArcBlock is developing an open chain access layer with adapters for interacting between various cryptocurrencies and creating a blocklet specification

---

4 https://hyperledger-fabric.readthedocs.io/en/release-1.3/whatis.html.

5 www.reuters.com/article/us-blockchain-consortium/blockchain-consortium-hyperledger-loses-members-funding-documents-idUSKBN1E92O4.

6 Z. Zheng, S. Xie, H.-N. Dai, and H. Wang, 'Blockchain challenges and opportunities: A survey', *International Journal of Web and Grid Services*, 2017, pp. 1–23.

7 Juan Benet. IPFS - Content Addressed, Versioned, P2P File System. 2014.

for developing microservice-based applications that interact with the blockchain to perform on-chain and off-chain transactions. Telegram is developing a highly scalable network with a multi-chain architecture to provide fast, scalable transactions fully integrated with the existing Telegram messenger application, which has over 160 million users. Hedera Hashgraph is developing the first public asynchronous Byzantine fault-tolerant gossip protocol with advertised speeds like private or consortium solutions. Most of these projects are still in development or in their infancy. Although these projects are groundbreaking, there is still no decentralized solution for enterprises facing complex challenges in the artificial intelligence (AI) and internet of things (IoT) space.

The concept of distributed artificial intelligence has been around since the 1990s but high end AI processing is in the hands of a few elite companies. AI initiatives from Microsoft, Facebook, and Google are published as open APIs, but remain under the control of these large corporations. These systems can solve problems that are difficult or impossible for an individual agent or a monolithic system to solve. Amazon Web Services (AWS) and other cloud computing providers already provide virtualized GPU processors for deep AI processing. Bitcoin proves how millions of people around the world are motivated to provide computing power to solve complex mathematical problems. Though this computing power is dedicated to confirming transactions, the concepts extend to distributed artificial intelligence. DLT can provide the framework and incentive for a distributed location-based AI engine that applies the principles of edge computing to millions of users. Miners with GPUs or other AI processing units can receive a small reward for contributing computational power and solving complex AI problems. DLT can provide easily accessible 'supercomputing power' to ordinary people and entrepreneurs as opposed to research institutions and large corporate enterprises.

The availability of distributed supercomputing will also accelerate the IoT market. IoT devices that capture data will be able to join a distributed network to process data, draw inferences, and take appropriate actions to provide intelligent behaviour. IoT devices will have their own digital wallets that will pay for the processing via clearly established smart contracts. People with smart homes, smart hospitals, smart vehicles, and wearable devices will be able to purchase distributed processing power based on their needs. DLT can provide IoT devices with a verifiable, secure and permanent method of recording data processed by these 'smart' machines.[8] DLT can verify the authenticity of IoT data, track the creation and movement of data from specific IoT devices, provide a trustful decentralized edge computing platform for IoT devices, monitoring and threat analytics, data privacy control, and trustless identity management.

As DLT is applied to more industries and use cases, it will enable organizations and application systems to collaborate in a decentralized manner, which will thereby create immense volumes of data in a decentralized environment. This problem is further exacerbated when combining IoT. 'Smart machines' using DLT will create large volumes of tamper-proof, real-time records, quickly making centralized analytics services bloated and unable to handle the large data volumes and number of connected devices. As advanced technologies in wireless communications like millimetre waves and 5G become more available, decentralized, distributed analytics services will become essential for analysing data and drawing insights, thereby improving actions and outcomes. DLT can provide a distributed analytics service that takes advantage of decentralized computing networks to provide users with distributed data analysis and analytics.

By 2020, our accumulated digital universe of data will grow from 4.4 zettabytes today to around 44 zettabytes, or 44 trillion gigabytes. We will have over 6.1 billion smartphone users globally, and there will be over 50 billion smart connected devices in the world, all developed to collect, analyse, and share data.[9] Big data analytics is becoming more important than ever, especially real-time stream processing required for drawing real-time inferences and reporting. Such analytics are

---

8 https://www.forbes.com/sites/bernardmarr/2018/01/28/blockchain-and-the-internet-of-things-4-important-benefits-of-combining-these-two-mega-trends/#349c98d619e7.
9 www.emc.com/leadership/digital-universe/2014iview/executive-summary.htm.

especially important for IoT applications which are producing immense amounts of data that need to be processed to drive actions and decisions. With exploding data volumes, a decentralized platform and associated marketplace for performing big data analytics will have a game changing impact.

Tying these concepts together, I propose a hypothetical platform called SecureChain, an Enterprise DLT Platform for AI and IoT. Secure-Chain takes the best of both permissionless and permissioned DLT networks to provide a fast and scalable enterprise platform.

SecureChain

As a decentralized platform-as-a-service (DPaaS), SecureChain takes a holistic approach towards solving issues of scalability and privacy while providing integration with advancing technologies to include AI and IoT. SecureChain provides a privacy-controlled, scalable platform with all the key components required for implementing fully functional, rich applications allowing enterprises to solve complex business use cases and handle large complex data sets. SecureChain is powered by a highly secure and privacy oriented multi-chain network allowing for the creation of infinite function-specific chains (FSCs) that are suited to different business scenarios and enterprises. The SecureChain platform uses multiple components including:

A decentralized processing network (DPN) to provide edge cloud computing to SecureChain applications.

A distributed artificial intelligence (AI) engine.

Distributed analytics.

A flexible smart contract policy engine.

Data contracts for governing how data is stored and managed to meet regulatory and privacy requirements.

A data adapter framework for complex intra/inter-enterprise integration.

A decentralized multimedia storage network and protocol with decentralized digital rights management.

A chain adapter framework for cross-chain/off-chain communication with other networks.

A radio frequency identification (RFID) and device adapter framework for supporting internet of things (IoT) applications.

An integrated application development kit for complex, sophisticated application systems on the platform.

SecureChain establishes a multi-tier heterogeneous node-based network including masternodes to maintain overall network health. This includes a decentralized storage network (DSN) where miners earn rewards by providing storage services, decentralized digital rights management (DDRM) and a decentralized processing network (DPN) where miners run nodes for AI processing, edge cloud computing, data processing and data analytics, with a framework in place for adding additional types of computing nodes.

SecureChain provides the ability to configure multiple blockchains, each of which an enterprise can customize to best suit their needs. As an example, SecureChain can implement a 'Smart Home Controls' FSC that is suited for tracking the life cycle of a home from the time of construction on a distributed, trust-free ledger. However, another home builder could use the 'Smart Home Controls' FSC as a template and define their own Blockchain and consensus algorithm for their specific needs.

The SecureChain Public Master Chain (PMC) provides the foundational chain and template for creating FSCs.

The Master Chain implements the base protocol for the platform, provides time synchronization for the platform, and configurable privacy parameters for FSCs. It contains both platform-level parameters and function-specific parameters, which can be modified. This structure maintains the immutability and large node network of a public Blockchain while preserving low latency and high transaction throughput of a private Blockchain. For example, an organization can use a highly efficient FSC for internal processes and auditing, but push data through a permissioned data contract to the Public Master Chain if the data requires immutability and enhanced decentralization.

SecureChain also provides a meta-language for creating additional privacy parameters that FSCs may require, but are not defined in the base platform. The PMC plays an important role in the operation of the multi-tier SecureChain network. It delivers the base framework for tracking associated masternodes and validators, while implementing a sandbox that makes sure that developers using the platform are working per the standards while not exploiting the platform. As described above, FSCs play a key role in achieving SecureChain's goal to provide a highly extensible platform. FSCs are customizable, permissioned Blockchains designed for a specific use case or service which can communicate with other FSCs, the PMC, or other Blockchain networks.

Developers can implement FSCs using various parameters and a meta-language to define optimized, function-specific behaviour and facilities. As an example, a Department of Defense (DoD) application may have special data storage requirements, requiring all data to be kept within the United States, and classification requirements to govern who has access to specific data.

Similarly, an Electronic Medical Record (EMR) oriented chain will have special requirements related to the types of users – physicians, patients, medical administrators, etc. – and the types of data and actions they can perform, including authorizing access to sensitive data. It will also have highly sensitive data, which needs special handling based on its category. SecureChain is designed to provide a Blockchain platform for supporting multiple industries and business use cases.

A key construct for supporting this is the SecureChain Multi-Chain. The Multi-Chain in SecureChain is unique in that it doesn't just allow the creation of multiple instances of the same blockchain such as TON;[10] rather, it allows for the creation of 'multiple types' of chains. Each of these FSCs can be configured to have its own consensus algorithm and have its own data structures so that it can be easily customized to handle the data required for its specific function or use case. This can be understood via the principles of object orientation, abstraction, and encapsulation. Blockchains in the SecureChain platforms have base templates. Each FSC is formed by extending a Blockchain template. In doing so, it inherits the functions and properties of the parent chain and can extend or override these functions and properties to implement its own features. The foundational template that is at the root of all FSCs is the PMC, which is an instance of the Master Chain template. Whenever an FSC is created by instantiating the Master Chain template or another chain template, it can also implement its

---

10   https://drive.google.com/file/d/1oaKoJDWvhtlvtQEuqxgfkUHcI5np1t5Q/view.

own consensus algorithm. This is possible as the consensus algorithm is abstracted from the Blockchain template. The consensus algorithm is an encapsulated implementation that implements a standard interface. Whenever an FSC is instantiated, you can specify the consensus algorithm that it should use, which the FSC will then call via the standard interface. This is done dynamically at runtime, and via configuration, without having to copy and modify the code (i.e. without having to fork the code). This is equivalent of dynamic polymorphism and provides an extremely powerful construct for rapidly customizing Blockchains without extensive coding.

APIs (application program interfaces) play an important role in distributed computing. APIs provide the specification or protocol for how to exchange information or request online services from an organization.[11] APIs are the way that modern computer systems make their services and data available to other computer programs and organizations in a secure and standardized manner. Salesforce.com generates 50% of its revenue through APIs, Expedia.com generates 90%, and eBay, 60%. Salesforce.com has an app marketplace with hundreds of apps created by its partners using the SalesForce API. APIs also play an important role for DLT. The SecureChain platform will implement a comprehensive set of APIs for all components in the platform and for accessing all features and functionality in the platform. The platform API also plays a key role in implementing a well-organized, flexible, extensible platform, which has discreet, well-defined functions that can interact with each other in a service-oriented manner.

The following are various types of APIs that SecureChain will provide:

The BlockChain API provides access to all Blockchain features allowing client applications to access the SecureChain PMC and FSCs. SecureChain provides access to functions, including wallet services, sending and receiving payments, querying for blocks and transactions, web socket-based notifications API, market data, and statistics. Similarly, the Blockchain API provides FNCs access to specific data. For example an FSC for Electronic Medical Records (EMR) will query

---

11   Harvard Business Review: The Strategic Value of APIs: https://hbr.org/2015/01/the-strategic-value-of-apis.

the Blockchain API for EMR specific functions and data, such as registering a physician, adding a patient's record, updating a patient's record, reading a patient's record, or authorizing a physician. The platform provides a base Blockchain API that provides essential services, which can be leveraged and extended for a FSC as required.

The Data API provides a data-oriented API for managing and accessing information stored on FSCs. While Blockchains are inherently decentralized and designed to form a global network, organizations using the Blockchain may have restrictions on their data (location, user, type). Additionally, certain data needs to be handled with different levels of sensitivity and confidentiality. For example, an EMR Blockchain will hold PHI (private health information) that must be kept private to the individual within the health record. As another example, government entities may need to classify some information and restrict how and where it is stored. Keeping this in mind, SecureChain provides a unique feature that is critical for widespread adoption and use of Blockchain by complex enterprises – the ability to configure and setup data contracts.

Data contracts allow for setting up how the data is stored and accessed for an FSC, including but not limited to, data storage policy governing in which geographical regions the data for a chain is stored, like a US-based healthcare organization, or the Department of Defense (DoD), which may require that the data be stored only within the USA or within specific organizations; or have data access policies, e.g. role-based access control, such as electronic medical records or sensitive DoD projects.

The SecureChain platform includes a Data Storage Network (DSN) for distributed, decentralized storage of files and multimedia assets. It also provides an entire digital rights management system for managing the publication and access to digital content. The SecureChain Blockchain stores information about a digital asset in an immutable way and provides this information in all transactions related to the digital asset. The Media & DRM API enables this functionality.

The Media & DRM API provides access to the publication, retrieval, and digital rights management of files and media on the Distributed Media Storage Network within SecureChain. The Media & DRM API allows media and content management platforms to interact with SecureChain to publish their content and protect it with a full featured rights management system, including setting the price of their content for customers.

For example, an independent producer can publish a music video, or an author can publish a book and set a price for these digital assets. The Blockchain will immutably store their rights and will apply them to every transaction related to their assets. SecureChain also allows the setting of intelligent rules related to digital rights, including the expiration of rights, transfer of rights, etc. For every transaction related to digital assets, the Blockchain stores an immutable record of buyer and seller transactions, allowing content producers and receivers to maintain and track their publications and access rights. The Media & DRM network also works seamlessly with the SecureChain PMC to tie value and payments to digital content, including tying payment transaction records to digital content access records.

One of the most impactful features of SecureChain is the Distributed Artificial Intelligence (AI) Engine included in the platform. It applies the principles of decentralized, large-scale, parallel processing provided by Blockchain technology to artificial intelligence. This is one of the SecureChain solutions that will encourage people to contribute computing power (for rewards) to solve complex problems and utilize energy for useful tasks as opposed to transaction confirmation. The Distributed AI Engine will solicit computing power across the world via AI nodes that will provide rewards for contributing computing power to solve complex learning, planning, and decision-making problems.[12,13] It is an embarrassingly parallel[14] platform, able to exploit large-scale computation and spatial distribution of computing resources.

The AI API provides the interface for accessing, interacting with, and using the Distributed AI engine. AI clients can structure and pass tasks requiring AI processing, and accessing results processed by distributed AI nodes. It supports various types of AI services, including machine learning, natural language processing, emotion recognition and processing, neural networks, image recognition, and more,

---

12   https://en.wikipedia.org/wiki/Distributed_artificial_intelligence.
13   Multi-Agent System: An Introduction to Distributed Artificial Intelligence, by Jacques Ferber, 1999 (ISBN 0-201-36048-9).
14   https://en.wikipedia.org/wiki/Embarrassingly_parallel.

providing the foundation for developing multiple types of AI applications leveraging distributed computing power.

The SecureChain platform provides an interface for creating and managing smart contracts. It goes beyond existing smart contract implementations on the Blockchain to provide functionality that is geared towards additional types of applications. As an example, it provides integration with a Smart Contract Policy Engine for processing complex rules with the Distributed AI Engine for intelligent processing where required. The smart contract API allows platform clients to use the SecureChain meta-language to define and configure various types of smart contracts. The API also allows customers to set parameters for the Smart Contract Policy Engine and for leveraging the Distributed AI Engine for supporting smart contract functionality.

The IoT provides always-online, data-gathering devices that are becoming increasingly prevalent in our work and personal lives. Blockchain can provide IoT devices with a verifiable, secure, and permanent method of recording data processed by 'smart' machines in the IoT[15].

The IoT API within SecureChain provides an API for IoT integration included within SecureChain. It allows platform clients to configure device endpoints, communicate with and aggregate device messages, and processed results. Platform clients can add, remove, update, and delete device endpoints. They can also set up security policies, authorization levels, and other access policies that may leverage the smart contracts functionality and even the AI engine. Today, no overall flexible, dynamic IoT security model exists that is capable of supporting mission-critical systems while simultaneously enabling the expected rapid advances and disruptors for tomorrow's IoT. SecureChain looks to solve this by allowing clients to verify the authenticity of IoT data, track the creation and movement of data from specific IoT devices, provide a trustful decentralized edge computing platform for IoT devices, IoT monitoring and threat analytics, data privacy control, and trustless identity management.

The SecureChain Management API provides the interface for managing all aspects of the SecureChain platform. For example, platform

---

15 https://www.forbes.com/sites/bernardmarr/2018/01/28/blockchain-and-the-internet-of-things-4-important-benefits-of-combining-these-two-mega-trends/#50e3328119e7.

clients can create and configure FSCs, set up data contracts and smart contracts, register masternodes, AI nodes, digital content hubs and nodes, and more. The Management API has been specifically designed to manage and interact with a multichain platform that has a variety of different FSCs. Client interaction with the SecureChain platform via the Management API is governed by various platform level, component level, and chain level policies and rules.

Given the overview of SecureChain, here are some use cases that could be possible when combining DLT, AI, and IoT technologies.

Use Case #1 Decentralized US Border Patrol

The US–Mexico border spans over 1900 miles. Estimated costs of building a physical wall are as high as $70bn while maintenance could exceed $250m per year.[16] Alternative options include building an invisible wall with advanced sensors and monitoring equipment but with roughly 16,000 border patrol agents, it is infeasible for the US government to man and maintain the equipment. Companies like Anduril Industries are using AI-based sensor fusion platforms and unmanned aerial systems to help solve the problem, but what if the US government decentralized aspects of border patrol and created incentives for ordinary people to solve the issue while harnessing the innovations of AI and DLT? Many companies in the autonomous vehicle space have developed sensors that 3D map the environment around them while using AI algorithms to provide object motion/detection/recognition in most weather conditions, day or night. 3D mapping and localization is paramount for autonomous vehicles to drive safely. This 3D mapping technology is becoming cheaper and more widely used in a plethora of applications. What if an ordinary person bought a small 3D mapping device and strapped it to a tripod or unmanned aerial system? The US government then partitions the border into 1-mile grids and creates smart contracts where people can be paid to continuously 3D map a section of the border for a financial reward. Each 3D mapping device uses an AI algorithm for object detection and objects that meet a specific threshold are sent to US Border Patrol. Each 3D mapping device is on a distributed network that enables secure device-to-device

---

16 https://www.foxnews.com/opinion/trumps-border-wall-how-much-it-will-actually-cost-according-to-a-statistician.

authentication and communication. Smart contracts are verified based on time, location, and map data from the 3D mapping device and once a 1-mile grid is effectively mapped over a given period of time, the smart contract executes. Further rewards could be given based on performance or high volume areas. Even if the US government paid $250 per mile for each day of 3D mapping in unfenced areas, it would cost an order of magnitude less than existing solutions. These incentive structures using DLT in combination with AI and IoT advancements could greatly reduce costs and provide a better product to the US Border Patrol.

Use Case #2 Proof of Provenance for Physical Assets to Combat Counterfeit

Counterfeiting is now the largest criminal enterprise in the world. The trade in counterfeit is currently $1.7 trillion per year – that's more than drugs and human trafficking – and is expected to grow to $2.8tn by 2020.[17] The Federal Aviation Administration (FAA) estimates that 520,000 counterfeit or unapproved parts are being installed in aircrafts each year.[18] The US government estimates that 15% of all spare or replacement parts for the US military are counterfeit.[19] Up to 40% of online prescription drugs were found to be counterfeit in specific regions while urine, bacteria, antifreeze, beryllium, cadmium, and lead have been found in counterfeit perfume sold to US shoppers, with labels such as Gucci, Chanel, and Prada.[20] Apple reported that 90% of all Apple products that they purchased directly from Amazon were counterfeit.[21] Counterfeiting is a huge problem but with the advancements of IoT and DLT, viable solutions can exist to dramatically combat this global problem. One company that is focused on a solution is Borsetta, based in Denver, Colorado. Borsetta uses nano-identifiers that can be embedded into products which

---

17 www.iacc.org/resources/about/statistics.
18 https://www.gdca.com/counterfeit-components-is-more-than-parts-it-is-about-people/.
19 https://www.scientificamerican.com/article/the-pentagon-rsquo-s-seek-and-destroy-mission-for-counterfeit-electronics.
20 www.cnbc.com/id/44759526.
21 https://www.digitaltrends.com/mobile/amazon-counterfeit-apple-product.

are scanned and tracked throughout the supply chain and uploaded to a DLT network that is tamper-proof and immutable. These identifiers range from nearly microscopic IoT microprocessors to ink-based nanotaggant solutions a hundred times smaller than the width of a human hair. These unique identifiers can be applied to a wide variety of substrates and products to include diamonds, currency, silicon, plastic, metal, and cotton. The result is a tamper-proof, verifiable, immutable 'digital title' of the product that shows chain of custody and ownership information for the life of the product. Warranty information, technical data, or other important information can be uploaded to the 'digital title' from the manufacturer as well. With this technology all your high-value assets including your home, car, computer, phone, jewellery, etc. could be stored as a digital title in your digital wallet. Let's say you want to buy an expensive Louis Vuitton handbag from a Louis Vuitton store, reseller, or an individual from a third party e-commerce site like eBay. Up to 40% of Louis Vuitton handbags are counterfeit in some regions.[22] How do you really know the handbag you are buying is authentic? For the most part you rely on trust. With Borsetta's nano-identifiers and DLT network, each handbag can be uniquely identified and uploaded to a tamper proof 'digital title' at fabrication. In this case, you simply scan the handbag in the store and verify the authenticity by looking at the digital title. If you want to buy online, you enter into a smart contract with the seller and shipping company. Once the product arrives and the shipping company verifies the product has shipped to your door, you scan the nano-identifier on the handbag and verify the authenticity via the digital title. Once you verify the handbag, the smart contract executes, and funds are released to the seller. This technology not only combats counterfeiting but creates trustful transactions. Additionally, Borsetta's technology can provide transparency within supply chains so that consumers can make informed decisions about their purchases.

---

22 https://euipo.europa.eu/ohimportal/en/web/observatory/ipr_infringement_handbags_and_luggage.

Use Case #3 Decentralized Ride Sharing with Autonomous Vehicles

Companies like Uber and Lyft have revolutionized ride sharing around the world. These companies created rapid growth due to one primary reason: incentive. These companies incentivize ordinary people to drive strangers around all over the world for a financial reward. This same model can be applied to autonomous vehicles using DLT, AI, and IoT technologies together. Right now, there are a handful of autonomous vehicle companies that are aiming to become the premiere autonomous taxi service. But what if I could buy an autonomous vehicle or retrofit my existing vehicle and get paid to have my autonomous vehicle drive strangers around while I eat breakfast with my family. The reliability, performance, and maintenance information of my autonomous vehicle can be stored on an FSC for potential customers to view to verify trust, prior to getting in the vehicle. Additionally, AI algorithms using object detection in these autonomous vehicles can provide accident information to insurance companies or local governments on a secure FSC when an autonomous vehicle witnesses an accident. Ride-sharing customers can enter into smart contracts with the autonomous vehicle and once a ride is complete and verified, funds are released.

The combination of DLT, AI, and IoT unlock new powerful opportunities in almost every industry. Over the next 5–10 years, it is imperative to analyse and build DLT as a complementary technology to other emerging fields to unlock its full potential.

13

Future of Blockchain

In my final chapter, I thought it would be quite strange to look at the future of Blockchain technology, when at the beginning I state that we are only at version 0.7 or 0.8. To talk about the future seems far away, but this is not the case. The speed at which Blockchain technology is growing will mean the future thoughts will be a reality much sooner than we think. Even the crazy ideas will have been tested and working, or parked in the learning pile for reference.

We are at an exciting time in the Blockchain revolution and here are a few thoughts on what the long-term future may look like.

What Will Blockchain Technology Look Like in 2025?

Focusing now on the future of Blockchain technology, I am going to share my views of the future, and then I am pleased to share the future thinking from a few of my colleagues from around the Blockchain world.

I have asked them to give me no more than 500 words on their view of the future of Blockchain technology, and their thoughts and opinions follow (a few of my contributors are not the best at sticking to word counts, but they have some great future thoughts for you to enjoy).

I summarize my thoughts on their views at the end of the chapter.

Let's start with my views and where we are today: #theyearofblockchain2019.

I truly believe that 2019 is the year of enterprise Blockchain technology. We are in the 'testing and trialling use case' phase of the adoption

Commercializing Blockchain: Strategic Applications in the Real World,
First Edition. Antony Welfare.
© 2019 John Wiley & Sons Ltd. Published 2019 by John Wiley & Sons Ltd.

of Blockchain technology and this will take time, especially for enterprise and complex organizations.

We have moved from 'What is Bitcoin?' to 'Ohhhh I thought Bitcoin was Blockchain' to 'What is this Blockchain technology and how can we use it?' This is an excellent change and very positive for the future of Blockchain technology. Once the leaders of organizations ask, 'What is this Blockchain technology and how can we use it?' you know they are serious about implementing Blockchain technology.

Use cases are becoming clearer and more defined. The use cases start small, but can scale once the benefits are seen. This is starting to happen across the ecosystem and we are seeing the big companies do multiple trials and tests, especially in supply chain and financial services.

The ecosystem is developing at speed with a great mix of organizations – large organizations, start-up, and end customers are all working together on use cases and driving the rapid development of Blockchain technology.

The important catalyst for any change is always the end customer, and they will drive transparency requirements and we will start to see trust as Blockchain technology.

> Once Blockchain technology becomes synonymous with trust, we will be able to change from our 'gut feel' trust we have today, to trust built on Blockchain technology.

By 2020 there will be large roll outs and wider areas of business utilizing Blockchain technology, as more commercial benefits will be found and more efficiencies achieved. This will lead to the customer demand increasing and roll outs will scale rapidly.

From 2025 onwards will see Blockchain technology become the norm – we will not even talk about Blockchain technology, it will just be there as all our technology today just happens.

Governments, institutions, enterprise will all be benefiting from this transformational technology and new problems will be occurring and new emerging technologies will appear to fix these.

> Adoption of Blockchain technology is a process and we are at the very beginning; we will progress quickly and benefits will drive the faster adoption.

If you can be 30% more efficient in your operations, if you can save 70% of your admin processes, if you can increase NPS by transparent track and trace, if you can sell your second-hand luxury products and track their history, if you can buy your next property with the peace of mind that it is correct – these will all be reality by 2025.

We must start to inspire people to develop Blockchain technology and maximize the benefits of this transformational new technology.

I would summarize my thoughts on the future into these areas:

- More information will be shared with many more people around the world. The days of control of data and misuse of data will diminish, and we will all be able to access our data in a more efficient and secure way. We will know more about ourselves and the world we live in.
- With access to more data and better quality data (due to the consensus mechanisms) we will be able to make better decisions. Often our data and information today is inaccurate, incomplete, incorrect, or completely false, and we have to make decisions using this. Take the Brexit vote in 2016, when the entire population of over 67 million people were asked to vote on a life-changing decision. Unfortunately, the information they were given was incorrect, incomplete, and some of the information was found to be false. In any functioning society, making life-changing decisions for a country must be based on accurate and shared information. With Blockchain technology, we will move much closer to sharing accurate, complete, and correct information for our citizens and organizations.
- New leaders will emerge, with a different understanding of the world and organizations. They will have access to much better quality data, they will share more data and they will be held accountable for their actions and decisions. The old styles of leadership will be challenged by the Blockchain revolution.
- Continued learning will become the norm. Once we have more access to more information, we are able to learn new hobbies, skills, and interests, easily and with the knowledge that the information is more than likely correct, accurate, and complete.
- New industries, new business models and new ideas we have not even thought of will emerge.

Importantly, there will be a number of new business models created using Blockchain technology and other emerging technology. Some of these I have covered in the book and here are a couple more examples which I like.

New Business Models Examples:

The Circular Economy Powered by Blockchain

I have asked Geri Cupi from MonoChain to discuss an exciting new business model around the circular economy. This is important for the entire world as populations grow, and waste becomes ever more problematic. Geri talks through what this is, and the technology solutions for this issue, including the implementation of Blockchain technology.

The world's population is growing fast and this is impacting the environment. As the earth has finite resources and we need to ensure there is enough food, water, and prosperity in the next few decades, switching from linear economy to a circular economy is not optional, it is inevitable. This is the reason why many governments, including the UK government, have started to implement their programmes to accelerate this shift.

In this section, we will explain what circular economy is, why it is important and examine how Blockchain can facilitate the circular economy.

A Primer on Circular Economy
By Geri Cupi

Traditionally we have been using a linear economy, which means raw materials are used to make a product, and then after the usage any waste is thrown away. This economic model is reaching its physical limits. A viable alternative which is already being explored by businesses is the circular economy.

The notion of the circular economy has gained popularity among scholars since the late 1970s. Despite this, there are no real definitions yet. According to Kirchherr, Reike & Hekkert (2017),[1] most scholars describe circular economy by referring to the 3Rs: Reducing materials need and waste, Reusing product, and Recycling materials. So, products and services are traded in closed loops or cycles. The purpose is to have an economy which is restorative or regenerative by intention and design, in order to maximize the value of products, part, and materials (Kraaijenhagen, Van Oppen & Bocken, 2016).[2]

Why is it Important?

In the last few decades, the life of product usage has decreased massively, which has led to more consumption. In other words consumers want new products faster, and use their 'old' products less. The issue is that there is a shortage of resources on the planet. The linear economy has led to the creation of waste. During the disposal stage, a large number of products and materials are not used but burned or left in landfills.

As the linear economy is no longer a tenable economic model, there is an urgency for an alternative model. The circular economy provides many benefits such as economic growth, environmental benefits, more employment, and innovation incentives (Ellen MacArthur Foundation, 2015a).[3]

McKinsey indicates the circular economy can boost Europe's resource productivity by 3% by 2030, generating cost savings of more than €600 billion a year and €1.8 trillion more in other economic benefits. Additionally, the same study found that another 100,000 jobs will be created by 2025. The circular economy is a new way of thinking that requires innovative solutions which reflect on circular rather than linear value chains. This will result in new insights, and interdisciplinary collaboration between designers, manufacturers, recyclers, and sustainable innovations (Kraajjenhagen, Van Oppen & Bocken, 2016).[4]

---

1 www.sciencedirect.com/science/article/pii/S0921344917302835.

2 https://circularcollaboration.com. See the diagram from Ellen MacArthur Foundation, which illustrates the continuous flow of materials through the value circle: www.ellenmacarthurfoundation.org/circular-economy/infographic.

3 www.ellenmacarthurfoundation.org/assets/downloads/TCE_Ellen-MacArthur-Foundation_9-Dec-2015.pdf.

4 www.researchgate.net/publication/305264796_Circular_Business_Collaborate_and_Circulate.

According to the Ellen MacArthur Foundation, applying the circular economy to the construction, food, and mobility sectors will reduce CO2 emissions by 48% in 2030 and even 83% by 2050. This is a result of minimization of the use of fossil fuels, optimal usage scenarios for transport and the complete elimination of fertilizer use, restoring the nutrient cycle. Due to this optimization the infrastructure can be replaced by green areas and housing, thus increasing the liveability of cities and improving air quality (Ellen MacArthur Foundation, 2015b, pp. 34–35).[5]

How Blockchain Can Help

To move a from a 'throw–away' society to one that looks at waste as a valuable resource, we need to reduce, reuse, and recycle.

Reduce

Some of the ways we can reduce the consumption is through sustainable production, by helping customers take more considered action which includes reducing the production of counterfeited items.

Transparency and traceability is becoming an important requirement and in many industries a legal requirement such as pharmaceutics, wines, and tobacco. Blockchain enables the provenance of an item. This can become beneficial in three ways. Firstly, counterfeiting is worth nearly 0.5 trillion dollars according to OECD.[6] A good proportion of it is deceptive counterfeiting where customers get tricked into buying a fake item or are not aware (that the item is counterfeit) at all. This causes thousands of deaths every year.[7] Through provenance of an item being shown, customers can make better informed decisions. Thus, this reduces the usage of counterfeited items. Secondly, it provides an assurance of human rights and fair work practices. For example, provenance assures buyers that the item being purchased is supplied and manufactured from sources that have been verified as being ethically sound. Thirdly, when it comes to product recalls all

---

5 https://www.ellenmacarthurfoundation.org/assets/downloads/publications/
EllenMacArthurFoundation_Growth-Within_July15.pdf.
6 https:// www.oecd.org/gov/risk/trade-in-counterfeit-and-pirated-goods-
9789264252653-en.htm.
7 https://uk.reuters.com/article/uk-pharmaceuticals-fakes/tens-of-thousands-dying-
from-30-billion-fake-drugs-trade-who-says-idUKKBN1DS1ZB.

impacted items quite often end up in a landfill. Once the origin of the issue is identified, it can recall only the minimum number of items, eliminating waste.

In almost every industry during the production there is wasted material; in construction for instance it is around 10%–15% according to McKinsey. In the fashion industry the term is 'dead stock' and its value is over $100bn per annum. All this waste goes to landfills. There are marketplace solutions using Blockchain for this excess material to be traded between producers.

Reuse

Blockchain can be used to facilitate reuse of items. Solutions like MonoChain by providing a certificate of ownership facilitate reselling of clothes. Using platforms to resell clothes you no longer want is definitely the way to go in prolonging the clothing life cycle and reaching a circular fashion industry (Accenture, 2017)[8]. For instance, increasing second hand sales by 10% would decrease the UK's carbon footprint by 3%, water footprint by 4%, and waste footprint by 1%, per tonne of clothing (WRAP, 2017).[9]

Another way is by incentivizing owners to use a product or service longer through financial incentives. The way this can work is the more they use a product or service the more they get rewarded though crypto tokens.

Recycle

Also, Blockchain can be used to improve recycling. Firstly, millions are spent every year by recycling companies to manually inspect item labels of materials being used, as some of them cannot be recycled. i.e. because of being toxic. By checking their provenance on Blockchain these costs can be reduced massively. Secondly, financial incentives might be used to motivate people and organizations to recycle more. The way it will work is that in exchange for recycling items such as cans or bottles they get rewarded through tokens. There are a few companies building these type of applications.

---

8 https://www.accenture.com/t20170410T044051Z__w__/us-en/_acnmedia/
Accenture/Conversion-Assets/DotCom/Documents/Global/PDF/Consulting/
Accenture-HM-Global-Change-Award-Report.pdf.
9 www.wrap.org.uk/sustainable-textiles/valuing-our-clothes%20.

Use Case: Auto Industry and Blockchain Technology

The future could include a world full of driverless vehicles; numerous Blockchain start-ups are helping make this future become a reality.
Possible applications for Blockchain technology include:

- Totally autonomous car system – using tokens to pay for its own electricity and road tolls.
- A solution to securely and wirelessly distribute data.
- A system to lock and unlock car doors using Blockchain based keys.
- Tracking ethically sourced supplies for electric vehicles.

Auto suppliers will need to invest money and resources into emerging technologies, as cars will depend increasingly on software. As vehicle software becomes the main differentiator, suppliers need to build up the necessary competencies to ensure future competitiveness.

According to Intel, autonomous driving technology will enable a new 'passenger economy' that will be worth $7 trillion (that's approximately twice as big as Germany's GDP) by 2050. Mobility as a service will outpace car ownership, and autonomous vehicles will spread into commercial spaces like package delivery and long-haul transportation.

Cryptocurrency and Blockchain companies are at the forefront of this new economy. They are already partnering with car companies all over the world.

Berlin-based start-up XAIN has been working with Porsche to develop Blockchain automotive apps since February 2018. Porsche said possible applications for the technology include locking and unlocking car doors via apps, as well as improving autonomous driving functions.

IOTA and Volkswagen have demonstrated a proof of concept for an autonomous car system. Volkswagen intends to use IOTA's Tangle Blockchain architecture to securely and wirelessly distribute data.

BMW is working with UK-based Circulor to track ethically sourced supplies. Circulor's CEO, Douglas Johnson-Poensgen, said Blockchain tech is BMW's ticket to guaranteeing a sustainable supply chain.

The Future of Blockchain – Contributors' Views

In this next section, I have asked my contributors to give me no more than 500 words on their view of the future of Blockchain technology, and here are their thoughts and opinions. You will notice that my 500-word limit has not been enforced to allow you to see the entire contribution.

A massive thanks to all my contributors – their opinions and expertise are extremely important as we grow the new world of Blockchain technology.

Future of Blockchain – Paolo Tasca

To the eyes of the most, Blockchain is simply Bitcoin and the speculative hangover and irrational bubbles in the cryptocurrency market. The few interpret Blockchain through the lens of information communication technologies, as a new technology that enables people to use a decentralized ledger to record ownership of on/off platform assets and rights/obligations arising from agreements.

But what is generally less comprehended is that Blockchain can also be understood through the lens of institutional economics; and as such, it is a tool that can be used to decentralize governance structures for coordinating people and making economic transactions. This is the most powerful innovative aspect of Blockchain that will change our business models in the years to come and will force our historical economic, political, and legal formal institutions to redesign their institutional settings and frameworks.

In a hyper-interconnected society populated by 8.5 billion peoples and up to 100 trillion sensors all connected to the internet, Blockchain will be indeed part of a toolbox composed of Artificial Intelligence, bigdata, IoT, additive manufacturing, and quantum computing, to cite a few.

It will be a world where your driverless car moves to the private filling station when their battery is low and directly pays peer-to-peer the host, where your fridge automatically buys your beers when some sensors detect they are below a certain predefined and personal threshold.

It will be a world where machine-to-machine communication is the norm and artificial intelligent agents exchange agreements between them without human intervention. Imagine entire business ventures entirely run by decentralized autonomous organizations that manage their assets and take decisions independently from human intervention. Where, for example, a decentralized autonomous organization manages a self-replicating cloud computing service which runs automated services on virtual private servers. Once the profits increase, the decentralized autonomous organization will be able to select the better type of server provider (e.g. QHoster vs. RockHoster). Moreover, with the use of AI, it will be able to upgrade its own software and eventually it will also be able to discover and enter new industries.

A world where governments use Blockchain technologies instead of polling booths to manage elections: every individual holds a completely verified identity on the ledger, from which all the relevant information (name, citizenship, residency, age, criminal charges) can be easily accessed. Imagine a future where hospitals share among each other verified data about patients, where medical records are immutably written in a distributed database: it is not visible but it is there in the air. Imagine farmers bringing directly slow food to your home using a smart contracts' platform, who control smart and automatized drones. Where the supply chain and logistic is automated, transparent, and the origin of the food is traceable. Imagine a trip to Paris with your partner: entering in the house booked via decentralized platform based on a smart contract that automatically opens the door.

A world populated by full autonomous agents, or full decentralized autonomous organizations is still somehow a dream; but such entities have already been tested and experimented with success. This is not a science fiction or a fancy narrative: it could be seen as such now but it is not pure fantasy on a 10+ years projection. We are living in an era affected by almost daily and constant changes, more often driven by technology improvements; and Blockchain is one of such technologies. It is not the only one but certainly one of the most promising ones.

Certainly the challenges toward such a data driven hyper-connected world are still high and new sources of risks and hindrances will emerge that we will be asked to face (Aste, Tasca, Di Matteo, 2017)[10].

---

10 Aste, T., Tasca, P., & Di Matteo, T. (2017) Blockchain technologies: The foreseeable impact on society and industry, *Computer*, 50(9), 18–28.

So, when we try to image the world by 2025, we could face three scenarios.

1. Blockchain as positive trigger: the technology will be generally accepted for the good outcomes, or it could take over brutally the traditional paradigm of our social and economic relations: public institutions will use Blockchain for specific registry-related activities, private institutions will become even leaner by relying on episodic aggregations of professionals and machines via smart contracts. In both cases, Blockchain will dominate our society as a common and essential infrastructure, in a way not too distant from the dreams of the first crypto-utopians. And it will definitely end up in changing our mindset and habits. However, this is not likely to be the case.

2. Blockchain as enabler of existing tendencies and not steering the society: the technology will be used to serve old dynamics, in government, economy, and society. This means that multinational companies will find a way to use it for their profit, by filing patents they will monopolize its development, and intermediaries will use it to make their intermediation more efficient and legitimize their role. A common standard will be used to cut down systems and its development will be managed by a non-profit organization of a handful of superpower individuals. All the dreams of the first digital punks and crypto-utopians will turn to paradoxical concentrations of power, discriminations, governance issues, and obscure procedures. States will completely lose every power or control over the technology. This scenario is also quite unlikely to happen.

3. Blockchain as slow-change-facilitator: the technology will be initially implemented by private parties and intermediaries but then, when the masses are aware of its true potential, Blockchain will be used for good. In such a scenario, we will experience in the short run a privately financed development which might bring it in the wrong direction; eventually when it has reached mass adoption, the power of the code will bring the crypto-revolution to its final stage. States, regulators, and forward-looking people will join forces to establish distributed control and avoid discrimination. Finally, the Blockchain code will win but some limitations will be imposed on its functioning.

If this is the case, I would be happy to let my fridge order a beer in my place.

Future of Blockchain – Chris Wing

To give my opinion on what I think Blockchain will look like in 2025, I first need to give my opinion on what I think of the technology now. In my eyes, Blockchain is a technology that provides new, efficient, and most importantly, trustworthy solutions for specific problems in all walks of life. Whether you work in the financial services, retail, or gambling, I believe there is a viable reason to be using Blockchain.

It's value has been proven within the retail space for its uses and applications in supply chain management; financial services has seen how important it can be for trustworthy payment mechanisms; and online gambling companies are saving a lot of money, as it can be used to prevent cheating.

Saying this, however, I do believe that Blockchain is only part of any given solution, not the entire solution itself. By this I mean that Blockchain itself does not in any way completely solve the issue of fraudulent suppliers within the supply chain model. Let's take olive oil producers for example; if I only want to buy specific olive oil – say from Tuscany – how can I make sure that the label on the bottle really does mean this oil is from Tuscany? In reality I can't, not without being at the orchard the olives are grown in, watching the oil getting pressed out of them and bottled before my eyes.

How does Blockchain help in this situation? Well, because Blockchain provides a high level of immutability between records, if a supplier commits themselves to saying all the olive oil they produce originated from Tuscany, and a quality control agent turns up at their door and finds out they are from Umbria instead, the entirety of the supply chain now knows this supplier is untrustworthy. Either the supplier will completely lose all business, or they will be forced to change the labelling on their bottle to reflect the oil's true origin.

This, however, is not labelling Blockchain as the whole solution, merely part of it. The rest of the solution involves customer feedback, quality control agents, etc.

Blockchain, in 2025, I believe will look very similar to what it is now, with some differences. The first difference I can see (which is already happening) is that networks will have a high level of interoperability between all other networks. As problems that require some form of Blockchain technology to solve get ever more complicated, I believe there is going to be a growing demand for inter-network communication (see Chapter 3).

I believe the POW (explained in Chapter 3) consensus mechanisms will slowly fade out and POS/POI consensus mechanisms will become the go-to when tackling consensus. This is largely down to the fact that POW is extremely environmentally unfriendly, amongst other reasons.

Lastly, I think we will see almost all major banks and financial institutions using enterprise Blockchain technologies in some form or another for themselves and their customers, whether it's offering Blockchain services, utilizing Blockchain for payment processing, or integrating it into loan systems.

Future of Blockchain – Nikhil Vadgama

We will come to see Blockchain technology as another tool that can be called on for use in any system. As the internet has become ubiquitous in our lives and is now taken for granted as the communication layer the world operates on, so too will Blockchain technology. It will become the ledger for value transfer – the economic layer underpinning the global economy. As the internet boosted the economy of the world, so too will incorporating DLT into our socio-economic systems.

It took 30 years to go from TCP/IP to the World Wide Web. In the case of DLT, 10 years on from the Satoshi Nakamoto paper that kicked off this revolution we are still only at the beginning. The promise of digitizing assets and placing them on a global ledger will enable economic value to grow in unprecedented ways through unlocking new business models and novel utilization of this new technology.

In countries where modern infrastructure is still being developed, DLT can be adopted from the outset as the transaction layer and its benefits realized immediately.

I am confident the issues we face regarding interoperability and scalability will be solved as Blockchain technology evolves in the future. Even the dreaded coopetition paradox will be resolved because the benefits are just too good to forgo.

The convergence of multiple technologies such as artificial intelligence and other emerging technologies with Blockchain technology will also bring new opportunities.

All of this coming to fruition is the exciting part I look forward to being involved with.

Future of Blockchain – Marta Piekarska

I hope for Blockchain to become a very prevailing technology that backs a lot of solutions. However, I believe that most customers will not hear about it as much anymore. It will be like artificial intelligence – everywhere, but hidden. I also think we will see a trend towards closer collaboration and having enterprises become more comfortable with creating more diverse networks, rather than personal Blockchain solutions with no participants.

The next trend will be around unification and clarifying of language. Today, there are as many definitions of Blockchain, nodes, or even consensus, as there are people out there using the technology. We come from different cultures and nationalities, and it is crucial to come to an agreement on what we are talking about. Finally, an explosion of the truly open-source nature of Blockchain and a growth in diversity are things I would like to see.

Future of Blockchain – Peter Bambridge

By 2025, Blockchain will be well established in what Gartner Hype Cycles like to call the 'Plateau of Productivity'. Having progressed from the hype around the 'Peak of Inflated Expectations' and the 'Trough of Disillusionment' phases, and finally climbed the 'Slope of Enlightenment', having gained general acceptance. Without the Gartner speak, this simply means that the technology will have reached adoption at scale in a wide spectrum of industry applications and the current levels of excitement will have died down.

Geoffrey A. Moore, the highly respected author of the *Crossing the Chasm* and related books on technology life cycle adoption, would describe this as when not only the conservative 'late majority', but also the sceptic 'laggards' actively adopt the technology.

By this time, Blockchain will be embedded into all types of enterprise applications and it will be an inherent part of enabling technology platforms, where it will become an alternative data store alongside options such as the database for appropriate types of data storage.

Some technology organizations have already started to embed application programming interfaces (APIs) into their enterprise solutions to simplify the integration of Blockchain into operational systems. This approach will accelerate the adoption of Blockchain across the retail value chain as the benefits of Blockchain will be realized quicker and easier.

As mentioned in Chapter 12 'Powering the Next Revolution', Blockchain is one of a growing list of emerging technologies that together will have a significant impact on the way businesses operate. These emerging technologies that can combine with Blockchain include: artificial intelligence/machine learning (AI/ML), the internet of things (IoT), robotic process automation (RPA), and quantum computing.

The interesting combination of these emerging technologies will result in smarter solutions that predict problems and recommend resolving actions, learn from previous experience, sense real-world status information and react accordingly, automate routine tasks, and in the future will use subatomic particles to deliver supercomputing power not achievable with traditional binary digital electronic computers.

Each of these emerging technologies are at their own stage of maturity on an adoption hype cycle. What will be interesting to see is how they will interact to combine strengths, accelerate the realization of business benefits, and drive wider adoption.

Future of Blockchain – Areiel Wolanow

Predicting what the future holds for enabling technology innovations is notoriously difficult. In the midst of the dot-com boom of the 1990s, we all knew that the internet would change everything, but we couldn't predict with any accuracy the kind of business models that would end up changing our day-to-day lives so significantly. The impact on less mature economies is even more profound; since the advent of the internet, the number of people living in extreme poverty has fallen by more than 70% according to the World Bank.

With this in mind, saying something meaningful about the future of DLT seems a daunting task. Yet even in its nascency, some developing patterns are clear. When I think about the applications of DLT, I see its evolution as a series of waves.

The first wave, which we are in the midst of now, involves the use of DLT as a transactional record. This was the purpose for which Blockchain was invented, and almost all of the current compelling use cases – trading networks, supply chain provenance, land registry, and indeed cryptocurrency itself – fall into this category.

The second wave will consist of use cases and business models that make full use of DLT's smart contract capabilities. We have seen some abortive forays into this realm already, but almost every major hack or breach in the DLT world to date has been due to poorly implemented smart contracts, and the main thing we have learned so far is that they are much harder to implement than they seem. Nevertheless, it seems likely that this is a problem that will be solved in short order, and that reliable smart contracts are going to yield business models in which humans will continue to be released from administrative and reconciliation tasks and be able to focus increasingly on higher value and more customer facing activities.

The third wave, and to my mind the one with the most transformational potential, will come when DLT can be reliably used not only as a method of sharing transactional data and contractual terms, but of executable code itself. This will have far-ranging implications. In the realm of security, the ability to perform a consensus check to validate a block of code will render ineffective almost all of the hacking exploits currently in use. With regards to interoperability, DLT applications will be able to seamlessly apply bug fixes or feature upgrades on their own ledgers, vastly reducing both cost and risk of deployment, as well as eliminating the support nightmare of users running lagged versions. With regard to piracy, it will virtually eliminate all current methods of counterfeiting. Within 10 years, I predict that DLT will underlie the deployment mechanism for at least 90% of all software applications, both business and consumer. And for many of the same reasons, it seems likely that DLT will underpin the distribution of most media products – music, movies, games – as well.

But all this being said, the reality is that the most significant, most world-changing applications of DLT are the ones none of us could currently predict. I look forward to learning how wrong I was. :-)

Future of Blockchain – Carlos Vivas Augier

I believe that, by 2025, Blockchain technology will be like a utility service or the internet. Today, we don't engage in long conversations and debates about TCP/IP, how we can use it and what it is best for. We no longer care about downloading, emailing, or storing large amounts of data. We expect to get internet access in every coffee shop, airport, or restaurant, not caring at all what Wi-Fi technology is, how it works, and what it is useful for. I envision a future where we use Blockchain technology without knowing we are using it.

I think of a Blockchain-enabled world, in which I am able to verify that my vote was really accounted for the party I voted for and politicians are both accountable and transparent; an anywhere banking system where I can get a loan from a bank in Japan to buy a house in Spain while I am living in Nicaragua; an integrated global registry to exchange value, property, assets, and ownership in a matter seconds between peers without information asymmetries.

Future of Blockchain – Vikram Kimyani

By 2025, you won't even think about Blockchain as it will be so pervasive and ubiquitous throughout your normal day. What do I mean by this? I mean it will be similar to using your smartphone today, the first phones let you make calls but nowadays we use it to consume entertainment, socially connect to others, guide us when we get lost, listen to music, and occasionally we might even call someone!

It will be similar with Blockchain, you will send payments to another person or business on the other side of the globe instantly; you won't think about foreign exchange, and the transaction fee will be negligible. You'll be able to auction your unwanted items or bid on things others no longer need and it will seem crazy people were paying eBay large amounts of fees, fees to list, fees to be paid, and fees to transfer money. You'll get into your taxi and not even think about how the driver no longer has prices set and fees deducted by a platform such as

Uber instead of the decentralized autonomous organization you're both using. Think it sounds fanciful? There are already services to replace social networks and Uber and we are still in the early days. Simple everyday things will become seamless, you will have far better control over your data, and you won't even think about the Blockchain behind it.

Future of Blockchain Summary

After reading through my contributors, views on the future of Blockchain technology, it is clear to see that we have only just started this journey. As I have said previously, Peter and Paolo also refer to the fact that we are still at the beginning of the journey – in the 'hype' phase, but moving rapidly towards real organizational benefits using Blockchain technology.

> The common theme for the future is the 'invisibility of Blockchain'; by this I mean that we will not know we are using Blockchain technology in our everyday life.

This is a critical message from all my contributors, who understand the technology adoption cycle, and we will not know we are using the technology when it is a successful technology.

I am excited to see the future of Blockchain technology, and the thoughts of these experts in this space I hope will give you confidence in the future of this technology.

The last chapter of the book is the use cases using Blockchain technology, where you can start to implement these in your organizations now. My advice is to 'get stuck in' and start to understand how the Blockchain revolution will change your organization, and your life, forever.

14

Use Cases in Real World – 2019 Highlights

The final section of *Commercializing Blockchain* will take you through a few live use cases which have been happening in late 2018 and early 2019. These will, of course, be out of date by the time you read this, but these are real use cases happening or that have happened. This is important to review, as this will show you where to look for the start of your journey on the Blockchain revolution.

I am not endorsing any of the use cases and I do not know any of them personally – this is just from my extensive research over the last few years.

Use Case	Antony Welfare Definition
Financial Transactions	Trusted and secured transactions using Blockchain technology to allow fast and secure transfer without intermediaries
Cryptocurrencies	Digital payment networks used to transfer payments in cryptocurrency
Tokenization	Digitalizing any asset as a token on a secure and trusted Blockchain ledger
Identity Management	Safe and secure identity using cryptography on the Blockchain to only share relevant data with relevant parties, whilst keeping the entire identity secure
Loyalty	Using Blockchain technology to reward, share, and redeem loyalty tokens in any entity and across entities
Gift Cards	Management of gift card data securely, and trusted on the Blockchain ledger ensuring accurate gift cards and real-time issuing and redemption

Commercializing Blockchain: Strategic Applications in the Real World,
First Edition. Antony Welfare.
© 2019 John Wiley & Sons Ltd. Published 2019 by John Wiley & Sons Ltd.

Use Case	Antony Welfare Definition
Warranty Management	Using Blockchain technology to record, distribute, and share warranty data across entities in a trusted manner
Refunds Management	Issuing refunds and returns using Blockchain technology to ensure accurate and secure tracking on purchase and subsequent actions
Supply Chain Transparency	An open and transparent Blockchain-based ledger of supply chain transactions
Global Shipping and Freight	Automate and speed up shipping and freight paperwork and data requirements, using secure and trusted Blockchain networks
Improved Sourcing	Shared and trusted supply chain data can be used to improve decisions made around sourcing and supplier partnerships
Certification and Authentication	An accurate and trusted record of achievement or certification
Inventory Management	Improved inventory management using shared and trusted data across the inventory network
Traceability	Enabling the tracing of products, make up and locations via a trusted and shared Blockchain ledger
Provenance	Allowing the clear and complete make up of a product to be seen across a trusted and secured Blockchain network
Counterfeit Products	Ensuring authentic products are recorded using Blockchain technology allowing non-authentic products to be easily tracked and managed

Financial Transactions

There is significant work happening in the financial transactions arena. This makes sense as all of the Blockchain work has been initiated by the Bitcoin paper after the financial crisis. There was a lot of work before this, but this was the catalyst to start the revolution we are now beginning with Blockchain technology.

I am not going to spend a lot of time on this here; Nikhil has covered this in great depth in the earlier chapter on financial services.

If you need any proof that Blockchain technology within the financial transaction area will be big, here is some recent research:

Blockchain could well usher in the next technological revolution in invoice financing. Estimates suggest that the global factoring industry has a value of about $3 trillion annually. Significantly, the factoring industry will continue to grow by approximately 10% each year. These numbers highlight that the businesses that succeed in realizing the complete potential of this technology will acquire a hard-to-beat competitive edge.[1]

Financial Transactions Benefits and Outcomes

There are many benefits for using Blockchain technology for financial transactions such as:

- Immutable transactions, smart contracts and transparent, shared data will transform financial transactions.
- As this technology evolves, the use of Blockchain technology will:
  - Speed up the processing of transactions
  - Reduce the occurrence of fraud
  - Eliminate intermediaries for holding money in a contract, while the funds flow from one party to another.

A great quote from Dataconomy of why Blockchain is important in Financial transactions:

> [Blockchain] has an opportunity for a serious takeover in finance and purchasing. As a means of reducing costs, improving efficiency, controlling fraud, and boosting transparency, blockchain has tangible, real-world benefits for procurement functions – whatever the market or business.
>
> Blockchain allows purchases to be representative as immutable items on the blockchain. When a supplier approves a purchase order, they are immediately committed to the cost listed. They could never issue an invoice that would be more or less money than the recorded purchase order.[2]

These financial use cases are very important areas to explore. Anybody who works with ERP systems (finance and back office systems), will understand the issues of reconciliation and matching discrepancies inside their business, and more importantly, outside their business with suppliers and other partners. I have covered this in depth earlier in the book.

---

1 https://gomedici.com/how-blockchain-will-revolutionize-invoice-backed-financing/.
2 http://dataconomy.com/2018/01/blockchain-will-kill-invoice/.

Dataconomy goes on to show how real-time sharing of transaction data would render invoices obsolete:

> And because the data in Blockchain transactions cannot be modified, invoices will effectively be rendered obsolete.
>
> Shared access databases mean that it's no longer necessary to manually scan invoices. This dramatically accelerates the reconciliation process, as all parties are allowed to view the same transaction.
>
> Blockchain effectively cuts out the middlemen. By removing all intermediaries, it makes the processing of payments and transactions much faster.

And the real world impacts on the issue with invoicing are also mentioned:

> Invoice processing, and invoice fraud by proxy, are the biggest threats to company money out there today. Just look at Facebook and Google, who were victims of a $100M payment scam.

Financial Transactions Examples

Let's have a look at a few more financial transaction use cases:

HSBC Bank – Testing Blockchain-Powered Trade Finance

HSBC has completed a test for trade finance opening the door to the $9tn market. There are many documents involved in trade finance transactions, making Blockchain technology a perfect fit for removing the paperwork and sharing the information across many parties.

HSBC completed the world's first commercially viable trade finance transaction using Blockchain technology. The scale of this test could allow the opening of the door to mass adoption of Blockchain technology in the $9tn market for trade finance.

HSBC said the Blockchain trade, which processed a letter of credit for the US food and agricultural group Cargill, had shown the platform was ready to be commercially adopted across the industry. The introduction of Blockchain, is expected to shake up the centuries-old trade-finance industry, reducing the numerous documents and several days of processing needed for a single transaction to a paperless task that can be completed in hours.[3]

Government Tax Reporting – Tencent and China Government Example
All governments are looking to move to a digital and transactional tax basis – the growth of ecommerce and online business has meant that governments need to track more and more transactions online. There are many solutions in progress, but the overall transparency and trust fundamentals of Blockchain technology mean that government tax reporting would significantly benefit from Blockchain solutions.

For example, in China there is a national test using Blockchain technology which has been developed by Tencent – the developer of the 1 billion-user social media platform WeChat – together with the Shenzhen Municipal Taxation Bureau.

The test looks at the traditional scenario, where processing an invoice entails multiple and complex steps: when a customer completes a given transaction, they must wait for the merchant to generate the invoice, file it away safely, complete a returns form in the finance department, wait for the return to be processed, and then receive their returns.

Using Blockchain technology to produce digital invoices means that the customer can manage all the steps using one click on the WeChat app after checkout and is then able to track their reimbursement status in real time, using Tencent's Blockchain technology.

This test of simplifying the invoice process for retail customers, makes complete sense to me. We all need the invoice (or receipt in Western economies) but we do not want to keep the paper-based records, or store emails with invoices or receipts. If we could have a Blockchain 'wallet' we could then keep all our invoices and receipts in one place, helping to securely manage our finances and also returns and warranty processes, which I discuss later.

Cryptocurrencies

There is an entire chapter on cryptocurrencies (Chapter 8), and there are many other books specifically on this area. My focus is on use cases for enterprise organizations for which cryptocurrencies are a very small use case, in terms of delivering strategic benefits.

---

3   Based on data from Ft.com.

Tokenization

Chapter 8 covers tokenization, and I will not repeat the details in there. I will instead focus on a few real use cases to help you understand some of the details we covered earlier.

Tokenization Benefits and Outcomes

The main benefit of tokenization is the ability to 'tokenize' any asset. This could be physical or intellectual property, and using tokenization you can in essence, split and share the 'asset' in many different ways. Using Blockchain technology to 'track' everything that happens to the tokenized asset:

- Gives an opportunity to monetize assets which were not possible before Blockchain technology.
- Allows the ability to trade fractional ownership on assets that are not possible now (real estate, art, diamonds, etc.).
- Opens markets to smaller players, through removing the need for transportation of physical assets.
- Increases global trade using tokens across borders.
- Develops the opportunity to develop new markets with direct and instant trade.

Tokenization Examples

Wells Fargo Patents Tokenization for IP

Wells Fargo & Company is an American multinational financial services company headquartered in San Francisco, California, with central offices throughout the US. It is the world's second-largest bank by market capitalization and the fourth largest bank in the US by total assets. Wells Fargo have begun investigating tokenizing data (e.g. finance documents, data, graphics, etc.), where access and security can both be controlled, to ensure control even when used in the public arena.

Wells Fargo has applied for a patent. The published patent application details a system in which any type of data element – whether a document, graphic, or database value – could be located, accessed, and protected by means of tokenization.

Tokenization, according to the patent filing, uses encryption methods to process an originally unrestricted data element into a corresponding restricted token that can subsequently only be retrieved

– or 'detokenized' – by a specified user. The system uses cryptography to ensure the data can be kept securely and accessed only using an authenticated digital signature.

Wells Fargo explains that tokenization can be used to protect data 'even when it is stored in a publicly accessible environment, such as the cloud, within a blockchain...in a flexible way that is file and data element neutral.'

This type of patent application, by a global banking institution, shows how the usage of tokenization across sectors, can become a large part of the Blockchain use case world.

I must also mention that the thought of patenting anything to do with Blockchain technology is a little against the entire sharing and ecosystem philosophy. That said, anything that helps to grow the Blockchain ecosystem with standard processes and rules will help grow wider adoption.

MasterCard has Applied for a Blockchain-Based Tokenization of Fiat Currency Patent

MasterCard has applied for a Blockchain-based tokenization of fiat currency patent. The application relates to management of fractional reserves of Blockchain currency, specifically the use of centralized accounts to manage fractional reserves of fiat and Blockchain currency updated via transaction messages corresponding to fiat- and blockchain-based payment transactions.

The company has applied for patent with the US Patent office and the details of the patent are as follows:

METHOD AND SYSTEM FOR LINKAGE OF BLOCKCHAIN-BASED ASSETS TO FIAT CURRENCY ACCOUNTS

Abstract

A method for managing fractional reserves of blockchain currency includes: storing, in a first central account, a fiat amount associated with a fiat currency; storing, in a second central account, a blockchain amount associated with a blockchain currency; storing a plurality of account profiles, each profile including a fiat currency amount, blockchain currency amount, account identifier, and address; receiving a transaction message associated with a payment transaction, the message being formatted based on one or more standards and including a plurality of data elements, including a data element reserved for private use including a specific address and a transaction amount; identifying a specific account profile that includes the specific address included in the data element in the received transaction message; and updating the blockchain currency amount included in the identified specific account profile based on the transaction amount included in the data element in the received transaction message.[4]

Identity Management

Identity management is a hot topic and there are many trials and tests on this use case. The concept of 'owning' our own ID has been discussed for many years, but the discussions accelerated over the last few years, as large social media companies, as well as other organizations, have used our 'data' and 'identity' to make money and influence decisions.

Blockchain technology has the potential to revolutionize the ownership of our data and our identity – often called digital identity, the promise here is that once we have our ID secured on Blockchain, we can allow access to parts of our data for uses that we agree with and we want to be used for.

Importantly, we will be able to track what happens with our ID and what data is used in relation to ID. We would be able to see where organizations are using our ID for marketing for example, or where social media companies are using our data for personalization.

Controlling our ID and data does not mean stopping people accessing our data; it means controlling who uses our ID and what they use that data for.

Digital identity (diD) can help by:

- Managing a person's identity securely and allowing them control over its usage.
- Tokenizing identity for trading online – making it easier and safer to shop with retailers.
- Making it easier to prove entitlements – i.e. with proof of age, proof of address, etc.
- Identity proofing based on mobile app – using your smartphone as your diD for everything you may need in your daily life.
- Linking, once verified, diD to proofing documents/attestations.

---

4 https://patents.justia.com/patent/10026082.

Identity Management Benefits and Outcomes

The use cases around diD are often to do with organizations and platforms using our data and information for their own purposes, where we often do not know what they are using this data for. Areas involved are:

- Common identity creation across applications, platforms, and organizations.
- Digital/Trusted credentials to access platforms, applications, and services.
- Trusted Identity Information.
  - Accurate, up-to-date identity information is made available to partners for authenticating users to access programs and services where identity is required.

Let's look at a few benefits of implementing diD using Blockchain technology:

- Users can leverage diD in the commercial sector for opening bank accounts, utility registration, etc.
- An institution (e.g. a bank or utility) can prompt the user for diD, to use the service or access funds.
- A user's mobile app is notified of the request, and upon user's permission will authorize the system to share information.
- User sign up to organizations is simplified and accelerated.
- Relevant personal reputation info can be tracked with diD.

Identity Management Examples

There are a few great examples of identity use cases using Blockchain technology, from Visa payments to the Estonian government.

Visa using Blockchain for diD on cross-border payments

Visa is one of the world's biggest payment networks and processes up to 30,000 simultaneous transactions and up to 100 billion computations every second. Every transaction is checked past 500 variables including 100 fraud-detection parameters – such as the location and spending habits of the customer and the merchant's location – before being accepted.[5]

Visa has applied for a US patent for 'METHODS AND SYSTEMS FOR USING DIGITAL SIGNATURES TO CREATE TRUSTED DIGITAL ASSET TRANSFERS.'

---

5 https://www.forbes.com/sites/danielfisher/2015/05/06/visa-moves-at-the-speed-of-money/#3291af0857c3.

A method and system are provided for transferring digital assets in a digital asset network. Network users can be centrally enrolled and screened for compliance. Standardized transfer processes and unique identifiers can provide a transparent and direct transfer process. Digital assets can include sufficient information for ensuring that a value will be provided, including one or more digital signatures, such that value can be made immediately available to recipients.

The patent looks to suggest that VISA will use Blockchain technology to provide its own payment transfers, to remove the current complex and lengthy payment process we currently use.

According to the patent application, a digital asset network can be the solution for the issue. The company plans to launch a platform using blockchain technology to allow the transfer of digital assets between clients. These transfers can be used to make payments, or provide access rights and login credentials and more. The firm emphasized that the participants of the platform will be 'legitimate organizations' who will be screened for compliance with the rules of the network.[6]

uPort Self-Sovereign Wallet – used for e-voting in Zug, Switzerland
uPort allows you to set up a diD to: Sign transactions and manage your keys and data in one simple, secure location.

This mobile wallet is your connection to the uPort platform, an interoperable identity network for a secure, private, decentralized web. uPort provides open protocols for decentralized identity and interoperable messaging that enable trusted source attribution for all web communication. By allowing message recipients to trust message senders without centralized servers, we can create an entirely new framework for building applications, and many developers are already building on this system.[7]

Global technology consultancy Luxoft have provided the entire system and talk about the benefits:

---

6   https://patents.google.com/patent/US20170237554A1/en.
7   https://www.uport.me/.

'Luxoft is proud to have an opportunity to work together with the city of Zug to explore various blockchain applications,' said Vasily Suvorov, Chief Technology Officer at Luxoft. 'As Europe's leading supporter of blockchain, Zug already accepts cryptocurrency for services, has digitized ID registrations built on the blockchain, and now we have helped them create and try the means to safely and securely move voting online'.

Luxoft built the permissioned Blockchain based solution e-Vote, including the platform itself, software and algorithms on Hyperledger Fabric. This was then integrated with Zug's Ethereum-based digital ID registration application, enabled by uPort, to allow residents to cast votes on the Blockchain. The solution uses an innovative encryption technology that on the one hand anonymizes the votes and on the other hand allows tamper-proof tally and secure audit.[8]

This is a powerful use case for the people to own their own identity using Blockchain technology, and a country like Switzerland using this technology, alongside global tech giants such as Luxoft, shows the serious potential of Blockchain for identity

Blockchain for Citizens – Estonia

Estonia has been leading the digital revolution since 2007, and has adopted Blockchain technology to help solve many of the 'e-government' opportunities, such as diD, health records, education, etc. Estonian e-residents can establish and run a company trusted internationally, sign documents, make bank transfers, file tax returns, and conduct other business – all using the internet and their smartphones.

- Health records can now be secured digitally, and Estonians have control over what records their doctors have produced.
- Grades and educational certifications are now on a digital ledger, allowing the possibility of sharing educational qualification information with employers.
- Estonians can vote digitally online using their unique ID cards. They simply log in to their smartphone and place their votes from anywhere in the world.
- Additionally, the government allows testing of level three autonomous cars (with a human behind the steering wheel 'watching' the car) on all roads in Estonia.

---

8 https://www.luxoft.com/pr/luxofts-evoting-platform-enables-first-consultative-vote-based-on-blockchain-in-switzerland/.

Loyalty

Customer loyalty is critical in today's competitive consumer society. There are well over one billion websites today, many of which sell goods and services to the end customer. With such global volumes of competition, retaining your customers – keeping them loyal to your brand – is of critical importance.

Blockchain technology enables trust and trust is a key part of loyalty. If a customer trusts the brand, they will become more loyal, spend more and refer more customers to your brand.

Let's look at a few use cases for loyalty using Blockchain technology:

- More flexible and valuable reward schemes for the customer.
- Cross-industry scheme – allowing customer to interchange rewards – retailer, brands, airlines, hotels, restaurants, etc.
- Real time rewards – using Blockchain technology to issue the benefits of the reward schemes in real time.

Loyalty Benefits and Outcomes

The loyalty systems in place need to work for the end customer. The scheme must be of benefit to the customer for them to use and interact with the brand and the scheme. Examples of benefits:

- Real-time rewards issue and tracking.
- Reduced system management costs via smart contracts, removing costs associated to error and fraud.
- Opportunity to create a 'wallet' for customers, a centralized, frictionless system for all of the customer's schemes, where points are universal and accumulated in one place.
- Relieve balance sheet liability, where revenue is attributable to value of loyalty points must be deferred until points are redeemed.

Travel miles became successful because they solved the problem of rewarding loyalty and selling vacant seats. They created a desirable currency that resulted in a new revenue system.

> Many companies are broadening their consumer loyalty programs to cover multiple brands. For instance, airlines offer passengers an opportunity to earn extra points for renting a car from a preferred vendor, or shoppers at a grocery chain get discounts on gasoline at affiliated stations.

The easy use of points at a variety of merchants reduces the liability of the originating retailer (which according to a 2013 study amounts to nearly $117 billion). It also generates considerable incremental business for retail partners and increases consumer satisfaction with the loyalty program.[9]

Loyalty Examples

Transforming Loyalty Programs Through Blockchain

Global technology consultancy Luxoft have been working on the problem on loyalty programmes for a few years. According to their research, there are over 3 billion loyalty programme memberships in the United States alone.

The important fact is the lack of participation in the scheme, with as many as 76% not using their rewards. As a result, unclaimed points can pile up and become a liability on an organization's balance sheet. In 2017, many major companies in the industry lost billions due to unredeemed points: Hilton at $1.4bn, American Airlines at $2.7bn, and Marriott at a whopping $4.9bn – just to name a few.[10]

The solution developed by Luxoft, using Blockchain technology, allows loyalty tokens on a Blockchain which makes them unique, traceable, and fraud-proof.

This allows the loyalty companies to gain full transparency into tokens and how they are used, as well as increase participant and partner satisfaction by connecting participants to numerous redemption options.

Luxoft found that '70% of consumers prefer programs that partner with other brands in order to offer more ways to earn loyalty tokens. This helps promote brand recognition, too'.

Remember that using Blockchain technology requires no middleman to manage the transactions and is extremely cost efficient when it comes to data analysis.

Gift Cards

Gift cards and gift vouchers have been used for years to help improve customer loyalty and give loved ones gifts that enable them to choose their own presents. The systems used for this are often old, complex, and lack real time tracking.

---

9   https://www.cognizant.com/whitepapers/how-blockchain-can-help-retailers-fight-fraud-boost-margins-and-build-brands-codex2361.pdf.
10   https://www.luxoft.com/blog/shodges/how-could-blockchain-solve-the-loyalty-program-conundrum/.

Using Blockchain solutions, the ecosystem of the gift card can be used in real time and cross partners to ensure a better experience for the customer and a more efficient process for the brand and retailer.

Gift cards need to be simplified and improved expiry, fraud, and usage controls need to be put in place.

According to Tokky.io there are two fundamental problems with gift cards around; fraud and unredeemed cards. With estimates of around 10% to 20% of gift cards unredeemed and fraud being a major issue, there is a strong need for Blockchain technology solutions for gift cards.[11]

The scale of this gift card redemption issue is seen, for example in the US, where $160bn worth of gift cards were sold last year, and 20% of these were unused.

The loyalty factor is critical to the use of gift cards, when customers shop using gift cards they spend an average of 30% to 40% more than the face value of the credit – this is important for the competitive world the retail market now faces.

Gift Cards Benefits and Outcomes

- There are many benefits for gift card issuers using Blockchain technology, and whilst the transition to e-gift cards has become widely accepted and makes it a much more streamlined experience (whilst also cutting costs) but does not fix the key issues around redemption and fraud.
- Using Blockchain technology eliminates the risk of fraud by offering a completely secured solution, with key data being stored using cryptography and blockchain technology.
- This will also create the opportunity for a liquid secondary market where gift cards can be sold/exchanged – something very difficult to do today due to the lack of trust in the gift card systems.
- Adding the gift card to a Blockchain also removes the risk of theft and fraud i.e. you will be giving an identity to the card which will make it traceable and only usable by the user with the correct private key.
- You will also remove barriers to entry for smaller firms and developing countries, i.e. the reduction in high costs to entry, fraud, and counterfeiting.

---

11 https://blog.tokky.io/why-blockchain-technology-makes-sense-for-the-gift-card-industry-28fa688d3ec7.

Gift Cards Examples

Coinbase Introduced e-Gifts after Gaining an e-Money Licence from the FCA in the UK

- Coinbase (a global cryptocurrency exchange and wallet) are now allowing cryptocurrency to be transferred to e-gift cards, which in the UK are classed as 'e-money' and the company needed to get regulatory approval.
- This e-money licence was granted in 2018, by the UK's Financial Conduct Authority. The licence enables the company the ability to provide payment services and issue digital cash alternatives, which can then be used to make card, internet, or phone payments.
- To provide the service, Coinbase partnered with WeGift, so their customers can now spend their cryptocurrency with many retailers, including Nike, Tesco, Uber, Google Play, Ticketmaster, and Zalando. This was a first for the Blockchain world and a great benefit for both Coinbase and the retailers.

Warranty Management

When you purchase a large electrical item or a large purchase such as a sofa or car, you often buy a warranty with it. This protects the product from damages over a set period of time and is a great way to look after your purchases. The problem with the warranty world is the lack of shared and transparent data on the ownership of the warranties and the associated products. This lack of transparency and shared data makes Blockchain technology a great solution for this industry.

Warranty Management Benefits and Outcomes

There are a few benefits for using Blockchain solutions within the warranty management world:

- The seller and buyer will have automatic access to purchase history, confirming entitlements for all.
- The ability to transfer the ownership of the warranty with the asset – something which has never been used before, but will be of great importance to customers who are stuck with a warranty for a product they no longer own.

- Open records across the ecosystem – with retailer, supplier, and the organizations who may need to fix or service the products.

Most customers do not think about the warranty on their products until something goes wrong. Then they start searching through the warranty to see whether or not they are covered, and they often then give up at this stage.

I have a classic example in my own house in 2018. I purchased a gaming PC, as my old PC had become too old and slow. I bought the gaming PC so that I could mine cryptocurrency and do my work. So I bought a hi-spec graphics card. Suffice to say, one of the fans on the graphics card stopped working just after the main 12-month warranty had expired (why does that always happen!).

I could not find the receipt, as I bought this online, but the name of the seller was on the PC. I emailed them and they eventually sent the invoice and when I asked for the warranty they just said it is not covered by them, but by the graphics card company. Twelve emails later, and after three weeks had passed, I could not find a contact for the graphics card online. The seller eventually gave me an email address. After another six weeks my replacement fan arrived. This wasted my time and their time and I am sure you all have similar experiences.

It should be a simple process to determine if your warranty will save you from paying for repairs. But the warranty industry's supply chain has a number of issues and inefficiencies that prevent a simple process for both companies and customers.

False claims, fake products, and confusion about eligibility are some of the most common issues companies face. These are passed on to consumers in the form of tedious processes and poor customer experiences, which I suffered.

Blockchain technology has the potential to help streamline the industry by securing supply chains and providing track-and-trace capabilities for products under warranty.

Warranty Management Examples

Bitmark – Assigning Digital Blockchain-Based IDs Which Can Be Used for Warranty Information

A company looking to fix the warranty world is Bitmark, a global warranty management company, implementing a world of 'Bitmarks'.

Bitmarks are digital property titles that prove the origin, authenticity, and history of ownership for digital property, and works well as a serial number or warranty code. One possible method to fight warranty fraud is to give each product a warranty code and then have customers "claim" the corresponding bitmark. Only one customer can hold a bitmark at a time. (The blockchain enforces this scarcity.) Once the manufacturer transfers ownership of the bitmark to their customer they can rest assured that it cannot be forged, swapped, or cloned.[12]

Using a warranty identifier, similar to any Blockchain-based ID, is a great way to allow the customer and the retailer access to the warranty data, when they need it and with complete trust and clarity.

Warranteer Moving Your Warranties from the Shoebox to the Cloud!
The old world of warranties lost in draws and in email boxes are gone, if we are to believe the word from Warranteer – a pioneer in the 'e-warranty' world, using Blockchain technology to secure our warranties.

Rather than relying on paper, which can easily be misplaced, Warranteer offers customers a digital warranty wallet. They can store all of their warranties in the Blockchain, keep them up-to-date in real-time and easily transfer them from one provider to another if desired. All parties are privy to the same information which helps reduce any disputes.

The ability to transfer warrantees securely and with transparency greatly benefits the secondary market.

False claims, fake products, and confusion about coverage are some of the most common issues companies face. And these are passed on to consumers in the form of tedious processes and poor customer experiences.[13]

---

12 https://blog.bitmark.com/hardware-companies-can-use-bitmark-to-solve-warranty-fraud-bec9730f68dc.
13 http://www.warranteer.com/blog.

Refunds Management

Refunds management using Blockchain technology will simplify an old and paper-based process, which we all use daily. Receipts are often issued on paper and there is often no connection made between the purchaser and the product (apart from high value items). This means that come refund time, there is often issue around eligibility for the refund and the proof of ownership of the person trying to receive a refund.

Refunds Management Benefits and Outcomes

I have been in the retail industry long enough to see (1) the vast cost of refunds, and (2) the fraud-related refunds.

Whilst this section is on refunds, it is worth noting that the implementation of Blockchain technology to track the returns process will be of great benefit to retailers, where online retailers see return rates of up to 40% – a massive cost to the business and a big issue to tackle in the future.

According to IBM research, 'Fraudulent transactions and returns cost retailers between $9.1 billion and $15.9 billion annually and with so many transactions and a complex supply chain, deciphering which returns are fraudulent is becoming increasingly more difficult.'

IBM also found that 'Returns equate to approximately $260.5 billion in lost sales for U.S. retailers, according to the National Retail Federation.'[14]

These figures are staggering and show the extent of refunds and returns management within the retail world. Looking to Blockchain technology for solutions makes sense, as the entire process is exceedingly complex and involves many parties.

According to Insider Trends,

> Blockchain will not only assist retailers move into accepting crypto-currency payments but the digital records created will also help streamline the returns and refunds process.
>
> In-store purchases could be assigned digital receipts, which will not only give customers and retailers a simpler way of dealing with returns and refunds, but could also help the industry become paperless. Customers can also get a better overview of their spending habits with all receipts in one place.

---

14   https://www.ibm.com/blogs/think/2018/01/blockchain-retail/.

Implementing a Blockchain solution into refund management will allow for complete transparency, which would ensure the eligibility of the refund. Paperless receipts mean you can collect email address and contacts.[15]

In the earlier parts of the book, there are large sections dedicated to the issues within supply chains. Most of those focus on the supply chain to a customer, but this is the supply chain from a customer back to the retailer and supplier.

The same rules apply both ways, hence why track and trace, provenance and lineage are all concepts equally applicable here as they are in the incoming supply chain.

Refunds Management Examples

WeChat uses Blockchain to Refund Corporate Expenses

WeChat, the Chinese messaging app owned by Tencent, believes that Blockchain technology can speed up the reimbursement of expenses for company employees, and it's trialling a feature on its WeChat app to do just that.

In 2018, Tencent piloted the application at a local restaurant in Shenzhen, China, where a user paid the bill through its existing payments service WeChat Pay.

By sending the payment data to its Blockchain platform, the user's employer, the restaurant, and Shenzhen's local taxation authority, were all able to see the transaction immediately.

Tencent said delays normally encountered via the standard manual claims process are eliminated. The company hopes its system will eventually find use in streamlining the expense reimbursement process.

China has a somewhat complex expenses system whereby merchants issue different payment receipts for individuals and firms. When staff need to be reimbursed for dining expenses, for instance, they must request a receipt for companies listing the exact taxpayer number of their employer.

In order to do that, employees need to have the merchant manually type in the taxpayer number on the receipt in every instance. Furthermore, that process is typically followed by additional manual tasks, such as collecting receipts and filing a claim before they can receive a refund.

---

15 https://www.insider-trends.com/blockchain-changing-future-retail/.

Using Blockchain technology and WeChat as the application:

- The employees can spend their expenses quickly and simply.
- The employer can account for the expense correctly.
- The government can claim their tax.
- The restaurant has less admin.

With Blockchain technology, in this case, everybody is happy!

Global Shipping and Freight

The global shipping market is a highly paper-based system, involving a significant number of parties within the vast ecosystem; from the container ship owners to the port owners, to the customs agencies, to the freight forwarders to the transportation companies and the retailers who may own the stock on board.

With any global container shipment, there are around 30 paper-based documents required each time they leave a dock and arrive in another dock. This means a massively inefficient system, with many delays and a massive lack of transparency and planning capabilities.

One of the first recognized global use cases for Blockchain technology, this complex use case has many organizations looking at solutions. Many of these are focusing on specific areas within the process, and this is allowing progress to be made at speed. The entire process will take years to develop, but the vast number of parties involved is ensuring that real progress is being made daily.

For example, CargoSmart and Oracle have estimated a 65% saving in managing the shipping documentation and paperwork. This is a significant efficiency saving, on top of the benefits of improved transparency to allow the whole ecosystem to react faster and smarter to the ship's arrival in port.

Global Shipping and Freight Benefits and Outcomes

The world of global shipping and freight is significant and there are many areas where Blockchain technology will help revolutionize this area. When you look at the fact that for every large container ship, there are around 30 manual documents, you will see the potential where Blockchain technology can eliminate this paperwork.

More than $4tn in goods are shipped each year, and more than 80% of the goods consumers use daily are carried by the ocean shipping industry.

The prize for the world of trade is a revolution in world trade on a scale not seen since the move to standard containers in the 1960s – a change that ushered in the age of globalization.

To make the Blockchain revolution work, dozens of shipping lines and thousands of related businesses around the world – including manufacturers, banks, insurers, brokers, and port authorities – will have to work out a protocol that can integrate all the new systems onto one vast platform.

This has started and there will be some great progress made – the benefits of this are too big to ignore:

- Enhanced predictability of the arrivals – this allows all the parties involved to prepare for the ship's arrival, with full knowledge of the contents and its location on the vessel.
- Global shipping paperwork significantly improved – e.g. bill of lading, invoicing, customs documents etc.
- Delivery transparency and accuracy is greatly enhanced – if you know that the ship will arrive at X hour, and be unloaded by Y hour, you can ensure your transportation is ready to collect the shipment as soon as it is ready. This can then be shipped straight to the warehouse or stores.

According to the World Economic Forum, the costs of processing trade documents are as much as a fifth of those of shifting goods. Removing administrative blockages in supply chains could do more to boost international trade than eliminating tariffs.

And the benefits wouldn't be confined to shipping. Improving communications and border administration using Blockchain could generate an additional $1 trillion in global trade, according to the World Economic Forum.[16]

> In 2014, Maersk followed a refrigerated container filled with roses and avocados from Kenya to the Netherlands. The company found that almost 30 people and organizations were involved in processing the box on its journey to Europe. The shipment took about 34 days to get from the farm to the retailers, including 10 days waiting for documents to be processed. One of the critical documents went missing, only to be found later amid a pile of paper.[17]

---

16 https://www.economist.com/finance-and-economics/2018/03/22/the-digitisation-of-trades-paper-trail-may-be-at-hand.

17 https://techcentral.co.za/blockchain-about-to-revolutionise-global-shipping/80781/.

Global Shipping and Freight Examples

IBM and Maersk Introduce Shipping Tracking

One of the first major Blockchain use cases has been the IBM and Maersk partnership, which is looking to tackle some of the issues with global shipping.

Whilst small, the work done by IBM and Maersk has shown the way forward for many other companies to work on Blockchain technology solutions in this area.

> Using blockchain smart contracts, TradeLens enables digital collaboration across the multiple parties involved in international trade. The trade document module, released under a beta program and called ClearWay, enables importers/exporters, customs brokers, trusted third parties such as Customs, other government agencies, and NGOs to collaborate in cross-organizational business processes and information exchanges, all backed by a secure, non-repudiable audit trail.

> During the 12-month trial, Maersk and IBM worked with dozens of ecosystem partners to identify opportunities to prevent delays caused by documentation errors, information delays, and other impediments.

> One example demonstrated how TradeLens can reduce the transit time of a shipment of packaging materials to a production line in the United States by 40 percent, avoiding thousands of dollars in cost. Through better visibility and more efficient means of communicating, some supply chain participants estimate they could reduce the steps taken to answer basic operational questions such as "where is my container" from 10 steps and five people to, with TradeLens, one step and one person.[18]

CargoSmart Partners with Oracle to Deliver Blockchain Simplified Shipping Documentation

CargoSmart, a shipping company in Hong Kong, has carried out an implementation with the tech giant Oracle to improve the shipping document process. This has reduced the time taken to process the shipping documents by 65% – a significant saving in a very large area.

---

18 https://postandparcel.info/97815/news/parcel/ibm-and-maersk-introduce-shipping-solution-tradelens/.

Shipping document handling processes are complex and include dated paper processes that involve many stakeholders across countries. In addition, companies in global shipping have very diverse technical capabilities and data standards, exchanging documents in many formats including email, online forms, and Electronic Data Interchange (EDI). On average, a single shipment can involve more than 30 documents exchanged by all parties, often with multiple revisions due to human errors, before it leaves port.

CargoSmart's blockchain solution aims to simplify the shipping documentation process, increase trust, and boost efficiency. Connected through a blockchain documentation platform, the entire shipping ecosystem can reduce disputes, avoid late penalties from customs agencies, expedite documentation turnaround times, and better manage detention and demurrage costs. CargoSmart projects a 65% reduction in the amount of time required to collect, consolidate, and confirm data from multiple parties and to handle shipping data that is repetitive in different documents by leveraging its blockchain shipment documentation solution.[19]

Improved Sourcing and Procurement

Improving the sourcing of products within all supply chains will help to improve the entire supply chain efficiency and trust. Blockchain technologies will help to:

- Improve supplier trust and openness – sharing data and analysis across the ecosystem.
- Show the history across the entire ecosystem.
- Enhance the supplier comparisons, ensuring better and more accurate sourcing decisions are made.

Sourcing is a complex business process with stakeholders from many different teams. The process normal begins when supplier bids are collected using online sourcing technologies, but currently, a large part of the sourcing evaluation and award process is still manual in nature.

Utilizing Blockchain through all steps of the process – proposals, quotes, and bids – or auction, can offer greater efficiency and transparency.

The ultimate goal is to ensure that Blockchain technology empowers the buyer with the means to ensure authenticity and traceability of

---

19 https://www.cargosmart.com/en/news/cargosmart-launches-blockchain-initiative-to-simplify-shipment-documentation-processes.htm.

all goods throughout the purchasing cycle. With verifiable audit trails of suppliers' goods being established, critical supplier credentials, certificates and qualification statuses will become immutable and shared with all parties within the ecosystem (who require this data).

Improved Sourcing and Procurement Benefits and Outcomes

Improving the procurement process with Blockchain technology offers some great benefits to non-supply chain organizations as well as supply chain organizations.

Despite advancements in digital technologies, procurement processes are still in the dark ages and suffer many challenges, such as transparency, data inconsistency, trust, and time sensitivity. Paper-based processes are still common, resulting in reduced transparency across networks, as well as inaccuracy and delays.

Organizations facing these challenges are using technology and big data to improve the supply chain visibility. Cloud technologies are replacing older EDI technologies currently used in the supply chain.

Blockchain is a great solution for procurement and organizations will benefit from the various features Blockchain technology offers, such as secure collaboration for contracts, distributed and synchronized information management, and digitization and standardization of the multiparty supply chain.

Certification and Authentication

I have written about certification and authentication a number of times in the book, and want to just remind you of the key areas where Blockchain technology will help these use cases:

- Individual identification (diD)
- Certification of achievements and qualifications
- Intellectual property across all intangible products and services
- Certifying a country or place of origin
- Identifying the owners of digital products and designs.

When discussing identity, it is important to remember that anything, any person, and any item can have an identity. This enables anything giving information to or from the Blockchain to be tracked and traced, and their transactions committed to Blockchain. The details or content of the transactions is still kept confidential, but the transaction is noted between ID 1 and ID 2.

Certification and Authentication Benefits and Outcomes

With the increased cases of identity theft and data leaks all across the globe, authentication and identity is a major concern. By authentication I mean the authentication as to whether the person or 'thing' accessing the data is actually who they claim to be.

For most identity, Blockchain technology uses the key pairing for the users to register their identity. The confidential information is stored in form of hashes which can be used for several identity-related attributes like name, unique identity number or social security number, finger-print, or other biometric information.

Once the identity is set up using Blockchain technology, the user can request a recognized party to verify the hashes by authenticating that the information provided on the blockchain is true. Therefore, whenever someone requires the identity for any kind of authentication or identification, they can use the hashes of the block pre-verified by the trusted recognized party.

Certification and Authentication Examples

'Smart' IP Rights – Intellectual Property Using Blockchain Technology

The potential to use blockchain technology for the management of IP rights is well documented. Recording IP rights in a distributed ledger rather than a traditional database could effectively turn them into 'smart IP rights'.[20]

If you could move to a world where you record the IP rights you can then move one step further and create IP registered using blockchain technology to create 'smart IP registries' in the form of a centralized solution run by the IP office as an accountable authority which would create an immutable record of events in the life of a registered IP right.

For example, this registry could include trademark management from when a trademark was first applied for, registered, or first used in trade; or when a design, trademark or patent was licensed, assigned, and so on.

The ability to track the entire life cycle of a right would have many benefits, especially around the owners' rights and uses of the IP. This would enable the originator of the IP to have the ability to monetize their IP and track the usage of the IP.

---

20 http://www.wipo.int/wipo_magazine/en/2018/01/article_0005.html.

KodakOne – Reinventing the Printed Photograph Using Blockchain Technology
KodakOne is the reinvention of Kodak as a Blockchain-based company looking to help the significant issue of IP rights and photography. Who owns my photograph? This is a hot topic and Kodak has partnered with Wenn Digital to develop a Blockchain-based solution.

In 2018, when this was announced, the price of Kodak's shares rocketed and the mainstream press said that this was Kodak just using the word Blockchain to inflate their share price. I do not agree, what KodakOne is trying to do, makes perfect sense using Blockchain technology and is a perfect use case for applying the benefits of transparent ownership of IP, and assigning the royalties and copyrights correctly and transparently.

How it works for KodakOne:

> We build innovative blockchain technology that protects, distributes and licenses your work allowing you to focus on creating great imagery.

> Blockchain holds tremendous potential and business leaders around the world increasingly seek ways to apply the technology to specific industries and niches.

> Given the immutable nature of a blockchain ledger or system, the KODAKOne platform is focused on providing practical applications for professional photographers.

> Other KODAKOne platform features will include:

> Image Registration – Provides immutable proof of ownership of your images and enables members to take advantage of the platform's wider services.

> Rights Management – Every license will be documented by a smart contract on the blockchain confirming copyrights, licensing terms and conditions to the associated image or images.

> Transparent Accounting – Royalty payments will be able to be received instantly via KODAKOne platform's smart accounting and reporting system; community members don't need a separate accounting system, as all payment and accounting related information is saved on the blockchain.

Community Marketplace – Our KODAKOne platform marketplace will enable KODAKCoin token holders to buy, sell and book products and services.[21]

Inventory Management

The management of inventory or stock through a supply chain is a complex task. Once the finished products arrive with the retailer, brand, or partner, there are many different journeys that the products will take. With the growth of online, the options for delivery to the end customer have grown and include; bricks and mortar stores, collection points, vending machines, collection kiosks, delivery to home, delivery to an office, drive thru collections and many more. All of these options mean that the transparency and accuracy of stock in the network must be extremely accurate.

Blockchain technology can help improve inventory management in a few ways, by:

- Improving the order tracking for every single order, wherever they are in the network.
- Reducing the operational costs of running a complex inventory network.
- Allowing accurate and real-time tracking through the entire network to shelf or customer home.
- Much better management of product returns.

Inventory Management Benefits and Outcomes

If you are under any illusion that inventory is not a global challenge let's look at some research from Accenture: There are about 5000 companies worldwide that have $1 billion in annual revenue that are transacting between $100,000 and $20,000,000 a minute.

The complexity is obvious and tracking all of this inventory, and all of those purchases, invoices, shipments, serial numbers, and receipts, which collectively are endlessly reflected between all of the companies in the system.

There are many benefits for the retailers and supply chain companies using blockchain technology as described by Multichannel Merchant:

---

21   https://kodakone.com/.

Notably, since the data flows seamlessly and in real time between every sector of the value chain, organizations can gain instant insight into what consumers are buying. They can thereby optimize manufacturing planning and forecasting based on demand, rather than simply react to inventory stock-outs. Companies can ensure that they always have the right types of SKUs and amount of stock in their warehouses.

No matter how much their marketplaces may fluctuate, they will always have product available to satisfy consumers with limited excess, thereby eliminating lost sales, minimizing carrying costs and increasing revenue and profitability.

Blockchain can help companies and brands shift their approach to inventory management, replenishment and forecasting from reactive to proactive. They can drive business growth with complete transparency and real-time data flow from end to end. They can thereby optimize manufacturing levels upstream in the supply chain to meet consumer demands downstream, and back.[22]

The benefits to the improvements in customer service are clear to see, and this is why retailers spend a vast quantity of their time managing inventory.

Traceability

The ability to accurately trace a product and its components is one of the main use cases for organizations. Using Blockchain technology, you are able to capitalize on the transparency and trust element of Blockchain technology, to accurately and easily track and trace a product.

Traceability covers the following example journey:

- A product is produced on a farm or a factory.
- The item is then transported to a distributor. The item is then organized and transported to retailers where they are sold to consumers.
- An accurate audit trail is created for each item/batch that can be stored on a Blockchain ledger.

---

22 https://multichannelmerchant.com/operations/reactive-to-proactive-blockchain-for-inventory-planning-replenishment/.

- Consumers can be confident in the accuracy of the detail provided due to the immutability of the Blockchain.
- Information moving between each phase is sped up as update transactions can occur in near real-time.

Traceability Benefits and Outcomes

There are a number of use case benefits of building Blockchain technology for traceability in some of the following areas:

- Increased traceability of material supply chain to ensure corporate standards are met.
- Lower losses from counterfeit/grey market trading.
- Improved visibility and compliance over outsourced contract manufacturing.
- Reduced paperwork and administrative costs.

There are many outcomes from a transparent and real-time supply chain such as:

- Visibility across the entire supply chain – from raw material to finished goods.
- The ability to prevent counterfeit goods, by having a greater view of the entire supply chain.
- Track and trace of products is simple and quick.
- Easy tracking ensures swift payments up and down the supply chain.
- Recall identification and management is simplified and sped up.
- Customs, certification, and compliance is made easier and quicker.
- Supplier trust is enhanced and developed.
- History visibility helps to make better decisions for future products.
- Deeper supplier comparisons allow a more efficient procurement process and better pricing.
- Enhanced predictability of the arrival of the exact products.
- Delivery progress is easier to monitor and react to.
- Improved order progress can be shared with customer and suppliers.
- Reduced operational costs to sharing data and multiple copies of incorrect data.

Tracing a product component is complex due to the scale of our global networks, but there has been a great deal of work in this area and a few of the examples are here.

Traceability Examples

Tuna Fish – Traceability Use Case

The first traceability application enabled by Ethereum, was developed from January 2016 to June 2016. This was with tuna, where both yellowfin and skipjack tuna were tracked throughout the entire supply chain, from fishermen to distributors and on to the end customer.

The customers could track the 'journey' of their tuna sandwiches via a smartphone and understand the information about the producers, suppliers, and procedures undergone by the product on its journey to the customer's table.

Every unit of measure (by fish or by catch) was associated with a digital 'token' to confirm the fish's origin and tracked throughout the supply chain, presenting a viable model for product certification to an end customer.

The first case example, when implemented fully, will be the first large-scale Blockchain initiative within the $42-billion tuna industry.

The eight nations united under the Parties to the Nauru Agreement (PNA) hold 25% of the world's tuna stocks and 50% of the world's skipjack stocks in their waters. Pacifical is the global marketing company jointly set up by PNA, launching the platform in cooperation with Atato, a Thailand-based Blockchain service provider. Powered by Ethereum's Blockchain smart contracts and IPFS decentralized storage, integrating with Pacifical's traceability solutions.

The new Blockchain platform will cover the entire supply chain and chain of custody of about 35 million tuna fish caught annually. More than 200 million consumer units of Pacifical tuna per year in over 23 countries can soon be traced and verified through the Ethereum Blockchain. Environmental groups, retailers, consumers, and certifications bodies all over the world will be able to verify live on Ethereum's public Blockchain exactly how their sustainable Pacifical tuna was caught, by which captain, vessel, area, and period, as well as where and when it was processed.

This complex Blockchain integration will be powered by Atato Blockchain services and will cover over 100 large fishing vessels and provide an unprecedented level of transparency and traceability, to build the highest level of trust on the sustainability of the catch. All products carrying the Pacifical and MSC logo will be able to be traced on the Blockchain through their unique tracking code. The information will be collected from linking all information sources within the global tuna supply chain from the fishing boat through the production process up to the final point of sale.[23]

Walmart Partners with IBM to Solve the Traceability Food Use Case – from 7 Days to 2.2 Seconds

Product recalls are a significant issue for all food retailers. When there is contamination found in the food chain, the retailer must act swiftly and decisively to remove the contaminated products from the supply chain and the customers. The current process takes significant amount of time and resources, meaning that vast volumes of food product are needlessly destroyed in a food recall, as the retailer must adopt a zero tolerance approach and remove anything that could be affected.

With the vast complex, global food supply chains we have today, any recall involves countless partners and organizations – taking time to investigate, analyse, and fix. Walmart were one of the first to look for a solution using Blockchain technology.

In 2016, Walmart, IBM, and Tsinghua University began collaboration on a Blockchain pilot that traced pork in China using the IoT sensors along the supply chain. Later, a second Blockchain pilot was launched, tracing Mexican mangoes in the US.

Developed using the Hyperledger, the pilots were designed to accurately record the following:

- Farm origin data
- Batch number
- Factory and processing data
- Expiration dates
- Storage temperatures
- Shipping details.

Though the scale of the projects were limited, there were positive results seen. Walmart demonstrated how food tracking that would usually take seven days could be done in 2.2 seconds with Blockchain.

Once the Blockchain projects scale to include 10 or more nodes, IBM believes it can save the industry 'billions of dollars.'[24]

---

23 http://www.pacifical.com; http://www.pnatuna.com; http://www.atato.com.
24 https://www.altoros.com/blog/blockchain-at-walmart-tracking-food-from-farm-to-fork/.

Beer Ingredients Verified by Blockchain

The global technology giant Oracle has built a number of Blockchain applications for tracking and tracing the ingredients in a customer product. Here is a great extract discussing the Alpha Acid Brewery where the ingredients in the beer are traced using Blockchain technology. The project is called Blockchain Beer.

> Oracle Blockchain Applications enable customers to track products through the supply chain on a distributed ledger to increase trust in business transactions, get better visibility across a multitier supply chain, accelerate product delivery and contract execution, and improve customer satisfaction. One early adopter of the Oracle Blockchain applications is Alpha Acid Brewery in the Bay area. Alpha Acid Brewery is using Oracle Blockchain to authenticate the ingredients in their unique beer blend.

> 'Consumers are better informed than ever before and are increasingly interested in what is in the products they consume,' said Kyle Bozicevic, owner and brewer at Alpha Acid Brewing in Belmont, California. 'We can now track materials and premium ingredients from our suppliers and analyze sensor data from the production process for each batch. Oracle Intelligent Track and Trace Blockchain application helps ensure that we are getting the highest quality hops, malt, and yeast, and enables us to create a strong narrative around our products for customers.'[25]

Provenance

Understanding the provenance of a product is of interest to many customers in today's societies. With the challenges around fake products and scandals such as horse meat in UK food, there is an ever-growing interest in the makeup of the products that we buy and use in our daily lives.

Blockchain technology is a great use case of provenance and there have been many trials happening over the last few years on this use case.

The main use cases for provenance using Blockchain technology focus in the areas of:

- Tracking the origin and movement of high value items in a supply chain e.g. food, fashion, and cotton – see the MonoChain case study for more details.

---

25 https://blogs.oracle.com/blockchain/oracle-launches-blockchain-apps-to-increase-supply-chain-trust-and-transparency.

- Tracking critical items of documentation such as bills of lading or letters of credit.

A usual provenance solution:

1) Tracking the journey of a product begins at the source and ends with the customer.
2) Data is gathered about the supplier and their locations as well as the environmental and social impact of each business.
3) The Blockchain technology links together data from the farm to factory to depots and retail branches.
4) The digital history can be accessed and reviewed by store colleagues, the food team, and the customer.

Provenance Benefits and Outcomes

There are many benefits to implementing Blockchain technology for provenance such as:

- Keeping track of goods in the supply chain throughout their life cycle which improves trust and transparency between supplier parties, retailer and end customer.
- Helping to remove the problems of counterfeiting and theft.
- Reducing supply chain risk – each point of the product transfer is recorded on the Blockchain. Every business in the chain gets a digital passport to prove the authenticity of their product.
- Growing customer trust – real time product data can be accessed by all customers, brands can convert marketing and product claims into data powered information to trust.
- Increased efficiency – all relevant data is stored using Blockchain technology, which was traditionally separated into different silos making it hard to see the full picture.

Provenance Examples

Provenance the Company
One of the leaders in this area is the company called Provenance, who started their journey in 2013, and now help many of the global retailers and brands we interact with daily. Here is an extract on their future business plans:

We envision a future where every physical product has a digital history, allowing you to trace and verify its origins, attributes and impact.

Accessible, trustworthy information

Our platform allows businesses to make themselves, their products and supply chains more transparent and traceable. We use two kinds of data systems for this, packaged in one elegant user interface. Our tools assemble images, self-evidenced claims and locations to create your transparency foundation. Our trust engine confirms and stores verified identities, claims and proofs and passports products tracking them through supply chains on the blockchain.

The blockchain

Provenance is building a system for materials and products to be traceable and transparent using a new kind of data system called a blockchain. It is for securely storing information – inherently auditable, unchangeable and open. We are working towards an open protocol – that anyone can use to make their business and products transparent and trustworthy.

Linking digital with physical

Provenance data can be linked to any physical product – through labelling, smart tags and through embeds for your website or app. Bring Provenance to wherever your products are – online and on product. We often work in partnership with hardware and smart tagging companies.

A secure, open registry

Until now centralized data systems were the only way to power a transparency and traceability system for materials to ensure data was trustworthy. Blockchain technology changes this fundamentally. We believe it can disrupt how we track the attributes and journey of every material thing - powering a system everyone in the supply chain can be part of.[26]

---

26   https://www.provenance.org/technology.

Counterfeit Products

Fake news is all the rage at the moment, and fake products have been around for much longer than our current run of fake news. Ever since brands existed, there has always been the problem of counterfeit and fake products. Over the years there have been many solutions tried and tested and some have had some success.

With the development of Blockchain technology, brands and retailers can now be more certain of counterfeit issues and will be able to react faster using this technology. It is important to remember that Blockchain technology will not stop counterfeit products – people will always do bad things – but it will help reduce this impact and help find where the counterfeit issues are.

The main use case is around the ability to track and trace product better – both of which were covered in the previous two areas of traceability and provenance. Where these use cases can help are related to:

- The ability to see entire history of transactions of a shared database makes it easy to ensure authenticity.
- Increased transparency across a global supply chain removes risk and protects consumers and business.
- Preventing counterfeit products entering the market in the first place.
- Grey market tracking and monitoring using sophisticated technologies.
- Giving the end customer trust through lifetime visibility of products.

Counterfeit Products Benefits and Outcomes

The counterfeit market is big and here are some statistics:

- ICC estimate that counterfeit products will drain $4.2tn from the global economy and put 5.4 million legitimate jobs at risk by 2022.
- Even the biggest retailers fall short of counterfeit goods, including Amazon. Can be very damaging to reputation, loss of trust.
- Huge potential in a number of markets, serving a purpose of retaining brand value, protecting legitimate suppliers (and staff) and in some cases saving lives:

- Roughly 50% of drugs sold in developing countries are counter-feit, costing pharmaceutical companies almost $18 billion p.a.
- These illegal processes have also resulted in 100,000 deaths worldwide.[27]

> Fighting the scourge of counterfeiting.
>
> The total value of imported counterfeit products is estimated to be as high as $461 billion across the globe, annually. This trans-lates into considerable lost sales for retailers. In just one recent example, the maker of UGG footwear discovered more than 3,660 pairs of fake UGG products worth more than an esti-mated $700,000. Since 2009, the company says, it has seized more than 2.2 million counterfeit products.
>
> Perhaps even more damaging is the erosion of brand trust, par-ticularly with luxury products. As such, proving and continuously reinforcing product authenticity exacts significant recurring costs on retailers, manufacturers, and law enforcement.[28]

Both of these articles show the global scale of counterfeiting and the scale of the problem to solve. Blockchain technology is an ideal solution to these issues, due to its fundamental trusted, immutable ecosystem, where you will be able to find the fakes in a world of genuine product – the genuine product will be verified using Blockchain technology and the fake will not.

Counterfeit Products Examples

Luxochain uses Blockchain Technology to Fight Counterfeiting of Luxury Goods

> Luxochain SA, a Swiss company based in Lugano that operates in the anti-counterfeiting of luxury goods market, has, over the last two years, developed a blockchain certification service that will allow luxury brands and individual users to verify the authenticity of goods before making a purchase.

---

27 https://www.supplychaindigital.com/procurement/breaking-counterfeit-validating-supply-chains-using-blockchain.
28 https://www.cognizant.com/whitepapers/how-blockchain-can-help-retailers-fight-fraud-boost-margins-and-build-brands-codex2361.pdf.

The market for fake goods leads not only to significant financial losses for leading brands, but also causes significant job losses, damages brand integrity, undermines consumer confidence and aids the black market in its exploitation of men, women and children in unacceptable working conditions.

Luxochain's mission is to tackle the counterfeit market and restore customer confidence by utilizing a combination of blockchain technology with Near Field Communication (NFC), Radio Frequency Identification (RFID), and the new unique technologies Fingerprint Authentication (FPA) and Block ID.

At the production level, all authentic luxury products will be fitted with an invisible and encrypted serial number (a Block ID) and associated with a token that is registered on the blockchain and uniquely identifiable. Luxury brands can register their products on the blockchain using their unique serial number. Once inputted, the information can never be altered from the outside.

When making a purchase, consumers will be able to scan the code and ascertain the authenticity of their product. Their product's unique certificate reveals information including, but not limited to, the make, model, origin and history across the supply chain, which consequently leads to a significant strengthening in consumer trust. Upon purchase, merchants can also use the blockchain to transfer the ownership rights from themselves to the new owner.[29]

FarmaTrust – Provenance and Anti-Counterfeiting for the Pharmaceutical Industry

FarmaTrust is a future-proof blockchain and AI based provenance system for the pharmaceutical and healthcare sector. FarmaTrust's digital services create efficiencies and transparency for the supply chain, ease the burden of the compliance requirements, reduce costs, and eliminate counterfeit or substandard drugs. The system creates immutable and incorruptible records to ensure data integrity as well as using 'smart contracts' to automate processes leading to significant cost savings for its customers.

---

29 https://www.forbes.com/sites/icoengine/2018/09/28/luxochain-taps-blockchain-to-combat-the-counterfeit-luxury-goods-market/#63afc8f5231d.

Current problems?

Substandard and counterfeit drugs are a massive problem around the world, resulting in the deaths of up to 1 million people every year and with an estimated market size of 200 Billion USD. World Customs Organization's Anti-Counterfeiting and Piracy Coordinator Christophe Zimmerman has even made the shocking claim that 'We have more fakes than real drugs in the market.' Within the pharmaceutical supply chain, accountability, authentication, and visibility are of the utmost importance. Due to the inflexibility of legacy systems and fragmented technological solutions, it has become increasingly difficult to track a single packet of drugs from the point of manufacture to the point of consumption, and even more difficult to hold parties accountable when problems do arise. Legal obligations such as track-and-trace and the upcoming Falsified Medicines Directive (scheduled to go into effect in February 2019) and Drug Supply Chain Security Act – scheduled to go into effect in 2018 – mean that it is important for all members of the supply chain to be responsible for not only their operations, but for the integrity of their partners as well. Given this, an interoperable and collaborative solution will be essential not only for adapting to a shifting regulatory environment, but for improving patient wellbeing and saving lives.

FarmaTrust has identified four main areas of concern within the pharmaceutical industry and has a built a solution to address each one. Each solution is meant to work together to create a safer and more efficient supply chain, with the ultimate goal of eliminating counterfeit drugs entirely.[30]

---

30 https://www.farmatrust.com.

Retail Blockchain Consortium

In this book, I have introduced to you the transformative properties of Blockchain technology (also known as distributed ledger technology or DLT) and the benefits that it will bring to the retail value chain.

During this time, I have met many retailers, brands, supply chain companies, and other partners all interested in driving Blockchain technology adoption within their business.

Blockchain is hailed as a great coordination technology that can foster improved information sharing and trust among multiple parties. For this technology to succeed at scale, common standards need to be adopted among all the different users of this technology.

In order to help develop a retail value chain focused on Blockchain transformation and to set standards for widespread adoption, I am pleased to introduce the Retail Blockchain Consortium (RBC), whose role is to advance the usage of DLT within the retail industry.

About the RBC

The RBC explores and advances the use of DLT within the retail value chain. It facilitates collaboration, the pooling of resources and platforms, knowledge transfer, and mitigation of risks in the adoption of DLT for its members.

The consortium is a global collaboration led by Oracle, University College London (UCL) Centre for Blockchain Technology (CBT), and MonoChain, and involves leading retailers, universities, technology companies, Blockchain companies, and service providers.

Commercializing Blockchain: Strategic Applications in the Real World,
First Edition. Antony Welfare.
© 2019 John Wiley & Sons Ltd. Published 2019 by John Wiley & Sons Ltd.

Mission and Vision

The aim of the RBC is to share knowledge of Blockchain technology to foster adoption in the retail value chain. This will enable key players to understand the practical challenges of the deployment of Blockchain technology at scale across the globe.

The consortium will provide resources for academic and commercial partners to leverage this innovative transformational technology for specific retail value chain use cases.

How Will You Benefit from Joining?

As a retailer, brand, supply chain provider, or partner you can become a member of the RBC and benefit from the following:

- Access to workshops run by industry thought leaders.
- Intensive educational and technical accredited courses run by experts.
- Participation in members-only events and committees on Blockchain applications within the retail value chain.
- Helping to drive corporate social responsibility and improve the environment through relevant use of Blockchain.
- Access to the latest academic retail-focused research on Blockchain from the world's leading universities.

Get Involved – Join the Executive forum

The biggest opportunity within the Retail Blockchain Consortium, is to work with like-minded Executives, who are working in and interested in how Blockchain Technology will revolutionize the Retail Value Chain.

If you are an Exec within the value chain, and you want to understand how Blockchain technology can improve your business, this is the place to be.

RBC will educate, support, advise and develop you knowledge and understanding of Enterprise Blockchain, so that you can be confident you make the right Blockchain technology decisions to drive your business forward.

Please see the website for how to get involved in this exciting consortium and be a part of shaping the future of Blockchain technology www.retailblockchainconsortium.org/.

Index

Commercializing Blockchain: Strategic Applications in the Real World,
First Edition. Antony Welfare.
© 2019 John Wiley & Sons Ltd. Published 2019 by John Wiley & Sons Ltd.